Love Letters to Pete
A Korean War Memoir

January 1, 1953 to October 10, 1953

Ron Freedman

Court Jester Publications
Lady Lake, Florida

ISBN-13: 978-1493777914 / ISBN-10: 1493777912

Court Jester Publications
7043 SE 173rd Arlington Loop
Lady Lake, FL 32162

Cover Design by Mary Lois Sanders
Cover Photos from the author's private collection

Dedication

Webster's Dictionary defines "descendents" with an "e" or an "a" in the last syllable. I don't care which way it's spelled, but this book was written for my descendants and dedicated to all of them, now and in the future.

Acknowledgements

I would like to thank my editor and publisher Mary Lois Sanders who has not only helped with my grammar, language, and phraseology, but instructed me in how one goes about producing a book like this one. I owe her a great debt of gratitude, and a large thank you for all of her heard work!

.

Table of Contents

TABLE OF FIGURES

Figure 1 - Nancy "Pete" Smith & Ron Freedman, 1954

Prologue

In my retirement I have found it very comfortable volunteering at the Military Heritage Museum Fishermen's Village, Punta Gorda, Florida. The museum began about twelve years ago, a project of a group of local veterans who wanted to do something with all the personal artifacts that they brought home from their military service. I joined the operation about five years ago, and have been elected as the Volunteers liaison to the Board of Directors.

Recently, I came across a newsletter from the Army's 78th Division. Inside was a letter addressed to men who had served under a Captain Joseph Stanley Kimmitt during World War II (WWII). The letter asked for some sort of an honorarium donated in Captain Kimmitt's name as apparently he was held in very high esteem by his troops.

The letter writer was Len Cravath and I decided to send him a note explaining who I was and that I was sure that my commanding officer in Korea, Lt. Col. J. Stanley Kimmitt, was the same man. I also told him that Kimmitt's men in Korea were as devoted to him as his WWII men were.

Within a few days I received a phone call from Cravath. He was pleased to have received my letter, and had contacted the Colonel's family, who were delighted to hear about their dad. In fact, the Colonel's son General Mark Kimmitt called me at home to thank me and to talk about his father.

We talked about *Pork Chop Hill*[1] by General S.L.A. Marshal, an official Army historian both during WWII in the South Pacific and the Korea War. The first chapter is about a friend of mine, Bill DeWitt, and his connection with Colonel Kimmitt. That book itself was all about the unit to which I was attached, and the action took place only a month before my arrival there. Kimmitt is mentioned frequently, and is shown to be very compassionate and a man with whom soldiers could relate.

I mention this conversation with Gen. Mark Kimmitt because it took place just about the time that I was asked by my family to write my thoughts about the letters I sent from Korea to my future wife Nancy "Pete" Smith back in 1953 … letters she has kept all these years.

The memories of those days in Korea flooded my mind, and what follows is the account of my service … memories of actions not all mentioned in my letters to "Pete".

---

[1] *Pork Chop Hill* was made into a classic movie starring Gregory Peck.

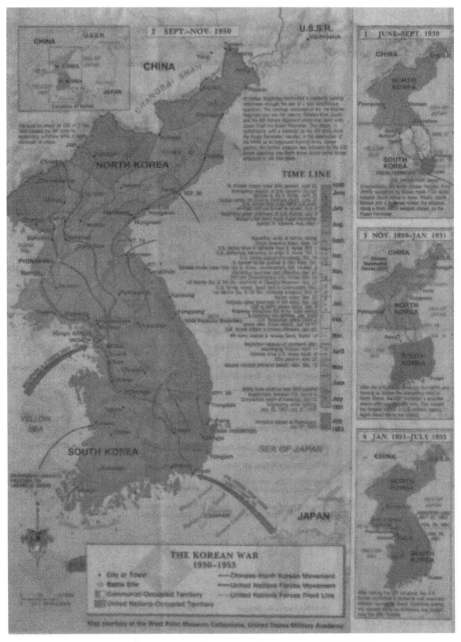

Figure 2 - Map of the Korean War, 1950-1953

Going to Korea - November 1952

In early November 1952, I, along with about 900 members of my battalion, boarded the Gen. Mark L. Hersey, a military transport ship docked at Pier 3 on Staten Island. Our destination ... South Korea. We knew we were going to Korea, but to leave from New York City? Didn't sound logical to us! But that's the Army and we did what we had to do.

Figure 3 - U.S.S. General Mark L. Hersey (A.P. 148)

We made a stop in San Juan Puerto Rico after about three days of sailing, and left immediately for our next destination, Cartagena, Columbia. We had loaded about 800 members of the Puerto Rican 65th Regiment, with no officers. In Columbia we boarded about the same number of men from the Columbian Regiment.

The next morning we entered the Panama Canal, which took us all day to traverse. It was a most interesting mini-cruise, and as an officer, I was allowed to view the trip from the ship's bridge. We spent the night in Colon, Panama, and left the next morning for our new destination. This turned out to be Hawaii. Viewing Diamond Head from the sea, with those beautiful green mountains and lightning storms and rainbows as a background, was a most enchanting sight. I was duty officer that afternoon and evening and stayed on board with nine enlisted men.

At midnight, the Hawaiian Armed Services Police (HASP) started dropping off all the drunken GIs they had picked up in Honolulu, and we had a devil of a time getting them on board. At 0300 (3 a.m.) the colonel came back and relieved me of my duties. I went below and showered, shaved and dressed in my cleanest khakis, then wandered the streets of Hawaii until just before 0900 when we departed for our next stop.

Somewhere west of Hawaii, two things happened. The first, a typhoon rocked and rolled the ship for eight days while we went nowhere but up and down. The second, we were given fifty Christmas cards with greetings from the ship, and I spent an afternoon trying to remember if I had fifty friends. I managed to get through forty-nine of them, and then remembered, Pete Smith, a girl I had once dated back in Boston. On a lark, I sent a card to her. I knew I wouldn't hear anything back from her as I had no return address at that time.

MILITARY SEA TRANSPORTATION SERVICE
ATLANTIC AREA

A Merry Christmas
A Prosperous New Year

Figure 4 - Actual Christmas Card I sent Nancy.

We docked in Inchon early in January 1953 and were posted to an Air Force Base in Osan, South Korea. What boredom! Our weapons had not arrived, and wouldn't for over two months, so we had nothing to do but sit and wait. Most of us didn't question why we were there. Our government said that we were involved in a war, and as younger brothers of the "Greatest Generation" we knew that we had to do as they did.

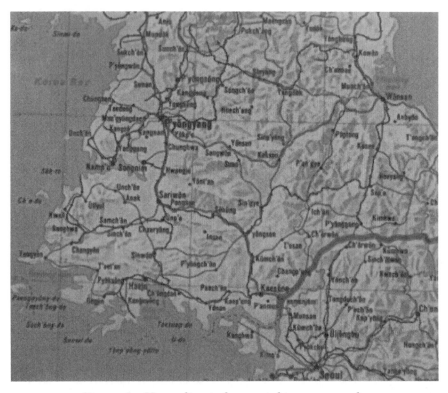

*Figure 5 - Heavy line in lower right corner marks
the DMZ (Demilitarized Zone)*

Letter #1

21 Mar. 53

Dear Pete,

Little surprised? Well, I am, too! I was just sitting here when I all of a sudden said to myself, "Pete Smith". So I leaned over, opened the stationary box, picked up my pen, and here I am.

I sent you a Christmas card while I was at sea, but like many of my friends, you never answered. Maybe it was you never received it. Mail service was bad from the ship. Half the letters we wrote were sent back for either more stamps or stamps from the country where they were mailed.

It seems so dammed long ago I saw you that day. I drove you to Boston. I left for Korea the following week. I've been here 3 months now, and only have the prospect of thirteen more facing me. I don't think I'll be able to take it. We do practically nothing, and the time goes by so slowly. We're stationed about forty miles south of Seoul. We're guarding the newest and biggest airstrip over here. We're just sitting and waiting for our first raid. Sometimes you get the feeling it will come very shortly, and then you're sure you'll never see an enemy plane.

Tonight I'm on duty as the Antiaircraft Operations Officer. I sit around a tent filled with maps, telephones, and radios. All we do is listen to everything, and inform the men on the guns when there is an alert. You can't imagine how unexciting it can be doing this for 24 hrs. every week or so. We have no cities to go to, nor do we have any entertainment to speak of. However, we're new over here, and aren't really set up. In a few months we'll have many of the things we are now lacking, and maybe things will pick up.

News and paper are running out, but not before I ask you to do two things. First, will you say hello to Polly Roberts and Franny Levine for me, and secondly, which is most important, will you answer me?

Love, Ronnie

Figure 6 - F86 Saber Jet, K55 (Osan AFB, S. Korea).
Photo by Ron Freedman

Figure 7 - Position 212 at K55, 40 mm gun. Photo by Ron Freedman

ಸಂ೦ಚ

Pete's letter was very happily received, and I felt like I had a new lease on life. Someone was thinking of me, and it was not just my family. The whole idea of the thing was almost as good as going home.

By the way, Pete was not my idea of a girl's nickname, especially as I knew where the thought came from. At that time in our lives, prior to the explosion of TV, we often went to the movies where we saw two feature length films plus News of The Day, and quite often, there would be a short subject as well. There was a big man who made a lot of 'Shorts'. His name was Pete Smith. Nancy went to Wheelock College in Boston at that time, and found out there was another girl in her class named Natalie Smith. Nancy's friends started calling her 'Pete' to separate their identities. I continued with the practice until I got home when I began calling her Nancy.

Life was not as boring now that I had a girl who wrote me, and maybe time would fly a little faster.

We held a lottery in our battalion amongst the officers to see who would be the first to go on R&R (Rest and Recuperation) leave. I won and opted for Kyoto as I had spent one night in Tokyo on the way over. Besides which, a C124, a very large transport plane, had crashed in the Tokyo area while bringing GI's back from R&R.

My stay in Kyoto was great. We went to a former Japanese naval seaplane base on the shores of Lake Biwa, and were assigned private rooms with baths. It was like heaven. The next night we were informed that we all had to move down to a dormitory in the basement as a general was coming down from Tokyo with his wife and four children, and our rooms were needed to make them comfortable. I had bumped into a fellow OCS candidate there by the name of John Christopher, and he and I decided that if we were being moved that we would continue our displacement by moving ourselves to downtown Kyoto. There we were brought by some very nice ladies to a *ryokan*, which is the equivalent to a bed and breakfast.

It was an illuminating stay. We slept on *tatamis* or thin pads on the floor. The rooms had sliding panels of rice paper for walls. I had a bath in a steaming wooden bucket, and we ate with the chefs. Almost every meal was spaghetti with peanuts. I am not a fish eater, and I think the cooks had been apprised of that fact which was why we had so much spaghetti.

The whole trip was made more special in a manner neither Nancy nor I will ever forget. As I ran to get the bus that would take me to the train to Osaka for the flight back to base, I decided to take a shortcut through a hotel and save a longer walk for myself. As I entered a side door there was a long narrow display window on my left decorated all in black velvet with only a small silver handbag spotlighted in the center. I don't know what made me ask a clerk the price of the handbag, and I think it was Y3000. At that time the exchange rate was 300Y (yen) to one American dollar. That meant it was only $10 American money, but not in scrip (GI money). The dollar was worth a lot more on the black market and when I showed her the $10 bill she said that they would pay the freight. What a good deal, I thought, and so I gave her Pete's address, and off I went. Nancy still has that little bag.

Back to the "Land of the Morning Calm" and boredom. I had sent a letter through requesting transfer to a front line unit. Like our soldiers in the Civil War, I wanted to "see the elephant", and peace talks were the talk of the area. If the war was going to end, I wanted to see what I could see in that supposed short time left.

Figure 8 - Near runway, Osan AFB

Letter #2

Sunday, 5 April

Dear Pete,

I don't think you can realize how happy you made me feel with your letter. I get very little mail as it is, and that which I do get is from my folks. They write about every other day, but there isn't too much to their mail as life with them is fairly unexciting. Mother gets tired of writing about the weather, and I get just as tired of reading about it. All my buddies wrote once, and now they've stopped. I guess they feel they've done all they have to!! I don't blame them in a way—there isn't too much doing with them.

I tell you, I only expected a short note saying it was very nice of me to write, and that you hoped that all was well. I was happily surprised to say the least, and I would appreciate it if you would keep writing.

The situation over here hasn't changed at all since I last wrote. We're still way behind the lines doing absolutely nothing. The men are getting stale, and I am thoroughly disgusted with the whole situation. I am trying to transfer to some forward area, but it looks doubtful. I went north to the front lines last weekend to bring a buddy up, and to visit some friends. It sure was an experience to remember. I got as close to Chinatown as I ever want to. I spent two days there, and never regretted a minute.

The people live differently up there. There wasn't one enlisted man I spoke to that wanted to come back off the lines. Someday when I get back I'll tell you all about it. I'm no glory-getter nor am I crazy in the head, but damn, you live like a human, and you know you're doing something while you're up there. I've got exactly one year from today more to do over here, and I don't plan on sitting back here on my little hill overlooking the rice paddies for all that time.

I never knew you went to China—that must have been quite an exciting trip! How long did you stay in the Far East, and where did you go?

I'm going on R&R (rest and recuperation) leave next Thursday to Japan. The Army flies you over, and gives you 5 days off starting from the day you arrive. I'm going to the Osaka area as I hear it is nicer than Tokyo, and I went to Tokyo when we docked in Yokohama. Osaka is the pearl center of Japan, I think, and a friend in Nagoya which is nearby, and I want to get over towards Kyoto. I understand the Air Force spared a few cities in Japan during the last war to leave as shrines, and Kyoto is one of them. There is a hotel for Officers and civilian government employees on the ocean near Kyoto, and I hope to stay there. It sure will be a treat to get away from here for a few days.

The peace talks will be resumed again tomorrow, and although hope is running high for a cease-fire, I don't think it will come too soon. If it does, I think we're making a mistake if we believe those jokers. I'm for an all-out offensive which will show Luke the Gook we're not to be trifled with. The average soldier over here doesn't pay too much interest in peace talks and politics. He just wants to go home, but, he would rather not go home if we don't get something worthwhile out of this war. It would be a big blow to our morale and prestige if we gave into those slant-eyes idiots. Enough speechmaking!

One of our Lieutenant is from Conn., and he'll be going home in July. I told him you'll be teaching there next year, and he said he'll come see you. I'm glad you got the job you did as you sound happy about it, and because it is near enough for me to drop down to see you when I get home.

Well, Pete—I've got to start polishing brass and boots for R&R. I don't leave till Thursday morning, but I'm so damned excited about it I've got to start to work now. My first job was to shave off my mustache. I grew one after I left the states, and tonight it came off. Yesterday I took some pictures while I still had it, and if you want a laugh I'll send one—make sure you write.

Love, Ron

****

Letter #3

[Postmarked April 7, 1953-Letter not dated]

Hey—

After I wrote the letter I reread yours, and found I did leave some questions unanswered. Therefore, this extra note.

You just ask Steve Fenn if I know him. Ever since 1945 or so—Great guy—

I do remember the night we went to Storyville. It was a cold, cold night, and I must have parked the car 15 blocks away. We sat way down in the corner, and all we could hear or see was the trombonist. I thought you might have forgotten that night.

My singing is coming along fine. Every time I start, someone turns on the radio.

What is your ex-roommate's husband's name? I'll keep watching the lists on incoming Officers, and maybe I'll bump into him.

Well, gotta run—Say hello to people I might know, and take care of yourself.

Love Always, Ron

ॐ

Steve was a high school fraternity brother, and one of the truly good guys. One afternoon while I was sitting at my observation window my phone rang, and it was Steve. He was calling from Hokkaido, Japan, way up in the northern part of that country. He was a Russian translator, which was a completely ludicrous job for him. He was an athlete not a student of foreign languages.

Pete's roommate was Connie, and she was married to a West Pointer by the name of Charlie Watkins. I never did meet him until after I got home

Life was still boring as I wrote in that letter. We were stationed on Hill 180 overlooking the largest air base in the Far Eastern Command. My platoon held the topmost part of that area. The Colonel decided that the first thing to do was build the Officers Club right there on the northern shoulder of that hill. One day he drove over to me, and told me I was to help a Korean man in his duties. Turned out the man was a stone mason, and my job was to hand him the stones while he built the chimney at the club. Not a very imposing position for an officer in the U.S. Army.

A few mornings later, the Colonel drove up again and informed me that the Inspector General was in the area, and that he did not want me to be seen doing that kind of job. Needless to say that I never left my position that day, and hopefully the Inspector General realized my rank when he drove by.

The terrain around that base was mostly rice paddies and garlic fields. It was either dusty or damp wherever you went. The GIs said that Korea was the only place one could stand waist deep in the mud and have dust blow in your eyes. I cleaned that description up a bit for the benefit of my future great grandchildren.

Things were so primitive over there that human excrement was used to fertilize the fields. When we arrived by boat we could smell the stench miles out to sea. We discovered that the farmers collected fertilizer in big buckets and transported them in wagons hitched to their *yaks*. We called them "Honey Wagons". As there were no mechanical vehicles for the Koreans to use, their *yaks* were put to every transportation use that could be found for them.

We called them "yaks" but we didn't know what breed of animal they were. They looked like small oxen, and appeared to be very docile. In the winter, they were kept in some portion of the farmer's home as their importance to the lives of these people was paramount.

The Koreans were ingenious in the way they heated their homes during the bitter months of winter. They built a firebox at one side of the house with flues that ran to the other side under the floor to a chimney. That way the heat was radiant and kept their homes quite warm.

Most houses I saw in the rural areas were made of mud bricks with thatched roofs. Usually a mud wall surrounded each home and the enclosed land was used for outside storage etc. The national dish called Kimchi was stored in earthenware jars in the yard. We were told never to eat any homegrown foods so I never tried Kimchi in 1953. However, when I revisited Korea in 2006 I did. By that time the government inspected all foods, so it would have been safe, but Kimchi never made it on my list.

There were very few roads other than yak trails, no telephones, no lighting, no electricity or running water, no transportation system, except for the KComZ Comet (Korean Communication Zone) a narrow gauge, one-track railroad that went from the northernmost point in South Korea to Pusan at the southeastern tip of the country, in our area of the country. If you wanted to go somewhere you just pointed your jeep in that direction and went. One problem did arise, however. The Koreans buried their people sitting up surveying their fields. This meant that each grave was a small hill. When driving we had to miss these bumps not only to keep the vehicle upright, but also as a matter of respect. It was a strange land to us all.

Figure 9 - Nearest tent on the right was our BOQ. Photo by Ron Freedman

Letter #4

Thursday, 14 April

Dear Pete,

Just a short note to let you know I mailed you a package. It may arrive before this letter, as I didn't enclose a note I thought I had better drop a line at the same time.

I've just completed my 5 day R&R (Rest and Recuperation) leave, and am heading back to Korea in about 10 minutes. This hotel is run by the Army and is a wonderful place. It's about 10 miles outside of Kyoto on Lake Biwa. I had me a real ball. Did everything but smoke opium and take a community bath!!

Well, I've got to run—Hope you like the gift, and will be able to use it.

Love,

Ron

Figure 10 - Hotel Biwako on Lake Biwa, near Kyoto, Japan.
Photo by Ron Freedman

Letter #5

Mon. 27 April

Dear Pete,

Just received your letter this afternoon, and decided to answer right away.

A few little things have happened while I've been awaiting your letter. Of course, you know I've been to Japan. I had one hell of a good time. I understand what you mean when you say those people are considerate and kind, but somehow I just can't get rid of that uneasy feeling when I walk down the street. It will be a long time I'm afraid, before I'd trust one with my life, believe me.

I spent my time in Kyoto, and was very much impressed with its beauty and culture. Very few G.I's go down that way, and the little kids are terribly impressed with an Army uniform. I didn't expect it to be that way at all. If I had known you were such a world- traveler, I never would have sent you that pocket book. You probably have plenty of stuff like that, that it's coming out your ears.

I returned on the 14th of April to find I was the only Officer in "B" Battery out on the hill in a little tent, and was on 24-hour duty until just yesterday. I actually did nothing but lie around and wait for something to happen. Nothing did happen until the night of the 19th of April, when Seoul got bombed.

We were on the guns for 3 hours that night waiting for the slant-eyes to come our way. Needless to say they still haven't shown up. Well, we've had alerts every night since then with the exception of last night. My duty involves getting rudely awakened at any hour of the night when we get the alert just to go over to the command post and see everything is running the way it should. I sure was exhausted there for a while.

Tonight I'm on duty as the anti-aircraft operations officer. I sleep in a tent with 5 radios and 8 phones going 24 hours a day. In case of an alert I am supposed to control the firings of the battalion, but our Colonel always comes up and takes over, and reduces the duty officer to a telephone operator.

This outfit is so fouled up it is a pity. The Colonel is an arrogant, a self-centered ____, and his exec is a little girl chaser—I mean 15 and 16 year olds. The staff is more interested in building the officers club than the troop quarters. The whole thing irritated all of us so much we all put in for transfers. The big brass up top is beginning to wonder what's going on, and our Colonel is heading for trouble. I think my transfer might go through as I had pretty good reason. None of them are 100% true. I told them I wanted to stay in the Army, but only to attend light plane school. I also said I wanted combat experience prior to attending school. So I asked to be a forward observer with the 2nd Division.

The exec called me in today and said he would approve the letter if I would sign up for 3 more years' right there on the spot. I finally got it through his thick skull one of the requisites for the light plane school was to sign for at least 2 or 3 more years, and I would sign when I went to the school. I can't apply for the school until I have less than 6 months to do over here. That won't be until next November or so. They can't hold my papers up–they have to forward them to 8th Army. It looks like I might get my transfer. If I like my new outfit, and can build some faith in the Army then I might stay in. This outfit would ruin any one's faith.

I expect to return to Tokyo or somewhere in Japan in a few more months, and I certainly will look up your friends and Uncle if I get near them.

Would you give Steve my address? I'll try and locate him, and maybe we can get a hold of him. Has Charlie Watkins arrived here as yet? I haven't seen his name or orders.

I can see why you might have a hard time teaching kids about democracy, but if you've seen kids grubbing around in a garbage barrel because their people were never united enough or strong enough to build themselves up so they would never grub around–then I'm sure you wouldn't find it so hard to teach democracy.

This country would collapse tomorrow if we really wanted to stop the black-market. These people were too afraid of the Japanese to form their own government. Right now they are staging demonstrations to prevent a truce-!! Pete, I could go on for pages about them, but someday when I get home I'll give you a real lecture about this place. I don't think you quite realize what your letters mean to me. I don't get too much mail. I think I mentioned it before to you, and especially—your letters are not curt and short. Maybe you find it a chore to write, but to me it seems you might enjoy it—or else I would get the usual 2 page letter—However, I've quite often been wrong.

Please continue writing. I promise someday to repay you for your time and effort.

I will send the mustache picture as soon as it returns from the photo shop. But I'll send it only on an even trade!!

Regards to all at school, and do say hello to your sister!!

Goodnight Pete—Love as always,

Ron

****

Letter #6

Tuesday 5 May

Hi, Pete,

Here I am congratulating you on your long letters, and then I get a tiny one—what happened? Nothing of interest doing around home? You will be forgiven if you make up for it with a long one next time.

I'm glad you liked the purse, but if I had known you had spent some time over here I would have tried to find something different. I saw it, and liked the colors so much I felt sure you would like it also.

My war over here is going along as usual. I say that possessively because I am waging a private conflict. I want out of this fouled up outfit so badly I'm almost ready to AWOL. My transfer was approved by the Colonel, and is on its way to Eighth Army headquarters. I hope to hear something around the 15th of the month. Normally, the Colonel disapproves any applications for transfer, but I worded mine so he couldn't refuse. It's all up to the 8th Army now, and I think they'll let me get what I want. I really pray they won't turn me down.

I got real clobbered last night at the club, and am paying dearly for it today. It's so hot one can hardly move around. There were only 4 of us at the club, and we tried to get the Chaplain drunk. He stayed sober—we didn't.

Tonight I'm on duty again, and plan to flake out real early. I've got absolutely no ambition left in me, and I honestly don't care if the gooks send down a 1000 planes tonight. It certainly would be one hell of a shot in the arm for all these rear area empire-builders. That's all the brass back of the lines care about. Building their own little empires. I am ashamed to say that the first building that will be completed in our new battalion area will be the officers club. We've been living in tents since Jan. 16, and it's time the troops got a different place to live. Our Colonel is a politician, and has ruined the outfit.

Tomorrow night I am defending two soldiers in a court martial. They are charged with armed robbery, and firing of weapons so as to endanger human life. They caused one Korean women to have a miscarriage, and scared the daylights out of a whole village. The whole incident took place in a brothel, and is very complicated. The G.I.'s are as guilty as can be, but I was appointed as defense counsel, and defend them I shall. If I had the patience I could sit down and write you a 20 page letter explaining and describing this war to you. I am sure it is unlike any other war that has ever been fought. I can't fathom it at all. The G.I.'s can't get it through their heads why they are here, and treat the whole affair like basic training. I'm speaking about rear—area troops. The front liners know the score. To them it's a shooting war; to these people back here it's all a joke.

Pete, don't let the papers fool you. Our government is spending millions supporting this war. I realize it must be done, but I feel it's an awful shame. The V.D. rate is terrific. Almost 90% of the prostitutes have it, and our government fights it only on paper. Prostitution is bad enough, but it runs hand in glove with the black market over here, and if we kill the black market the country of Korea will collapse. The people don't want a truce. They have it better than they ever did.

Here's an example. I saw an old man dressed in a complete
native costume brushing his teeth in front of his mud hut this
morning with chlorophyll toothpaste. I'll bet he never even
brushed his teeth before the G.I.'s ever came. These people have
robbed the G.I.'s blind. It really irritates me. Well, I won't go on
with a rear-area viewpoint. When I get up front I imagine I'll
have completely different ideas. Sorry if I bore you.

Love to you Pete,

Ron

Figure 11 - Village Elders. Photo by Ron Freedman

Figure 12 - Gathering on the hillside. Photo by Ron Freedman

Figure 13 - Papa San. Photo by Ron Freedman

Figure 14 - Little Sister

Figure 15 - "Pvt. Chang"

*Figure 16 - My folks sent me this
"Davy Crocket" Hat*

All photos by Ron Freedman

ಬೊC೮

At this time, the Colonel called me in to tell me that nobody leaves his command, and that included me. He said that he put a negative endorsement on my transfer request, and only if I would re-enlist then and there for an additional three years would he think of approving it.

I never talked back to a superior prior to this, but I stood up and said the "letter is not addressed to you only, sir, but to the Commanding General of the 8th United States Army, and as such I will wait for his reply."

Two days later, I was driven to the front by my closest friend (even to this day) Bud Gaynor, along with my battery clerk, Herbert Hester. In army parlance, a central unit of approximately 150 artillery men is called a Battery. In the Infantry it is called a Company, and other branches have their own designations, i.e., a troop of cavalry, or a squadron of tanks.

In the meanwhile, the Officers Club was coming along so that we were able to have an inauguration party very shortly. We invited people from all over the base, and I remember how crazy the Royal South African Air Force behaved. They did their famous (so they said) Zulu War Dance for us, and I never saw so much gin go down in all my life in such a short time. By the way, "short-timer" referred to anyone who got their papers sending them home in a few days.

I kept as busy as I could. I remember going for something our battery needed in Seoul by myself in a jeep. It was forty-two miles to the city on a dirt highway that was as bad as any road could be. On the way home, I got lost in Yung Dong Po, which is an area just southwest of Seoul on the Han River. I saw a church, and figured someone there could put me on the right road.

As I entered, I realized that the church had been moved out, and the building was now a MASH (Mobile Army Surgical Hospital) unit. There was an operating table with a black soldier on it and a group of people standing around him. Nobody recognized my appearance so I moved in closer to ask my question when I noticed the man on the table had a liquid dribbling from his mouth. I recognized the color of the stuff. It was Tincture of Merthiolate®. We had used it as a type of mercurochrome at the boy's camp I attended. I said the words under my breath. The man next to me heard and said I was right; the soldier had drunk a bottle of the stuff. He died before I got my driving instructions and went home.

The name Yung Dung Po reminds me of a little ditty I learned over there. It is to the tune of "On the Banks of the Wabash" It goes like this:

> "When the ice is on the rice beyond the Yalu,
> And the Chinese come a-creeping 'cross the snow.
> Don't you look for me GI to be there to help you;
> I'll be sitting on my ass in Yung Dong Po..."

At that time, I was also with the battalion Defense Counsel as the Defense Officer, and sat in on thirteen courts-martial while I was with that unit. I lost all thirteen. The only defense that seemed to work for these simple infractions was the old standard "Extenuating and Mitigating Circumstances".

What else was there to say about a GI who was ordered to leave a brothel, and in his drunken stupor managed to insult the arresting officer and his bodyguard. My biggest case was defending a former Flying Tiger by the name of DeBeau. I was called to Post Number 1 (the Main gate) one night to find De Beau lying on a stretcher. I was the only one he would talk to, and all I could get out of him was "four bottles of Lucky Strike".

The Koreans would very professionally use the labels from cigarette packs to glue on to their bottles of homemade booze, and DeBeau remembered drinking four bottles of "Lucky Strike". We do not know what ingredients went into making that stuff, but I am sure rice paddy water was one of them. De Beau died at that moment. Our trip to Korea took 38 days, and that poor man had been cooped up all alone in the brig the whole time. I used to walk him on deck every night to get him some fresh air.

Our courts-martial were held in a tent with the sides all rolled up so battalion personnel could see and hear everything that went on. Bob Huntley was the prosecutor, or Law Officer officially. He won all the cases I lost.

The troops enjoyed these little entertainments as it was the only thing going on every night. We didn't have any movies or USO groups. The only reading material was the "Stars and Stripes" or comic books the guys had brought with them. The black market flourished all around us at that time. We didn't have any mantles for our Coleman lamps, but the locals had them at 50 cents each as I recall. Also they sold us candles that were hollow and had a wick that ran down one side. Each lasted about twenty minutes, but like fools we bought them so we could read or write after dark.

I think that possibly the biggest item in their supplies were Army blankets. Everybody had a down sleeping bag, so that even in cold months the blankets were generally forgotten. The locals found them very useful. They made us tanker jackets and lined them with blanket material, but the main use was for making pants for the women to wear. They elasticized the waist and cuffs, and made them into sweat-pant-like items. All the women wore them in the cold months, and in the summer they wore little sleeveless vests on top. The older women would tuck their breasts into the waistband, and Huntley made a career of filming them all with his Brownie Movie camera.

Little Korean boys would slip into our tents at night and steal the wrist watches right off of our hands while we slept. We called those kids 'slicky-slicky boys'. It was a strange country.

Letter #7

Wed. 13 May—

Hi Pete—

Sort of in a gayish, saddish, letter writingish mood tonight, and though you owe me a line, I just felt like writing to you—

The weather has turned cold! We had 2 or 3 days of really glistening sun, but last night a fog rolled in and it brought low temperatures along with itself. I had my stove taken out of my tent, and tonight I'm realizing my error.

The lights just went out, and I'm now writing by flashlight. I may never finish this tonight as the flashlight is even flickering. The Koreans had a circus over on the next hill a few days ago, and they tapped into our lines for power. Ever since then the lights have acted real funny. These Koreans can foul anything up. You're right, my opinion of them isn't of the highest order.

The last few days have seen me do nothing. We've had no alerts, but an officer must be around the CP (command post) at all times. I just sit in my tent and read. I could sleep, but one never knows when the Colonel will be coming by. I don't know what he wants—"One officer will be present at the CP at all times. He will constantly make improvements in the area." One can make only so many improvements in a tent, and they've all been done. What's he want me to do—stand in the doorway at attention?

I'm sending these 2 pictures along only to impress you with my moustache. I've now shaved it off! However, I'll make a deal— Either you send me a picture right back or I will grow even a larger and uglier moustache, and will come home to haunt school teachers for the rest of my life. Think carefully now Pete, there's no sweat in sending me a picture, but think of what will become of our educational system if I carry out my threat? All our great advancements will crumble in one day when they (the school teachers) see a character straight out of L'il Abner come stalking into a classroom. The fate of the world rests in your hands!

NOW—how can you deny me—?   Love Always, Ron

Figure 17 - My mustache that lasted only a couple of weeks.

ഓയരു

After rereading this letter, I realize that I must have been in a strange mood when I wrote it. The remarks about the Korean people were valid for my thinking at that time. I truly didn't understand their thinking, and never spent much time regarding their position in life. Many of them were displaced persons. Some had fled their previous homes when the North Koreans invaded the south. A lot of them were from North Korea, and had run south from the Chinese when they moved in during November of 1950.

We couldn't tell who was who, and nobody higher up gave us any indication of how to find out the difference between them. Another problem was that their last names were either Kim or Lee for the most part, and they stated their names as 'Kim, Ping Pong'. Pong being what we would call their first name and Kim their last.

We had civilians all over our encampment—houseboys and cooks, trash men, carpenters, and this and that. One day I saw the local garbage men arriving on the base. There were about eight or ten sitting on a bed of garbage eating the stuff as they drove in, it was a sight to behold.

The carpenters were amazingly good. Their saws had teeth on both edges of the blade. One side was a ripsaw, and the other was a crosscut blade. They had only orangewood-like crates to use for building materials, but they could make almost anything we wanted, and for very low prices.

The barbers didn't have electric tools, but they could use their scissors almost as fast as a barber back home would use electric clippers. The price was $.25 in GI scrip, and it would have been less if the army printed any lower denominations.

The women did our laundry for as little as a bar of soap. How they got things clean I'll never figure out. The streams they used were mostly muddy, and their washing machines were a thick strip of wood with which they beat our uniforms to a 'bloody pulp', but because of the color they always looked clean.

After washing, they were required to dip everything in a barrel of miticide to kill all the mites. These mites lived on the backs and bodies of rats that lived in the hills where we were encamped, and would get into our clothing. They carried a disease known as hemorrhagic fever—nearly always fatal to us. We were told by our battalion surgeon that if we showed bleeding under our fingernails then we probably had the disease. I don't know of anyone who ever contracted it, however.

At the bottom of Hill 180 in Osan, Korea, was Osan Air Force Base, with the numerical designation of K-55. The personnel stationed there referred to it as 'Dogpatch' after the *Lil Abner* cartoon by Al Capp. The buildings there were all "Tropical Huts" made of a corrugated metal with sloping roofs and plywood floors. The main chow halls were quite big, also of a similar construction. The place in which I spent my free time was their Officers Club.

Almost every night we were off duty, we'd walk down after our evening meal for a few beers. When we walked in we were handed a booklet entitled "Songs My Mother Never Taught Me' which contained some of the most unheard of words to tunes we already knew. I still remember them but have been asked by Nancy not to sing them in public. My favorite is still "I Don't Want to Join the Navy" sung in a British accent.

I never ate in the officers' club as the food in our area did a number on my digestive system, and we were never hungry enough to eat any of another units cooking. Most of our meals were made of dehydrated vegetables and soups. Every army unit got the same food weekly, but each unit was allowed to cook it in its own way, and on its own schedule. We ate a lot of rice, but it was Louisiana grown, not local stuff.

The water we drank was trucked in, and heavily chlorinated, and after it was poured into Lister bags, (storage bags with 4 dispensers on the bottom), the taste was even worse. We would go down to the PX and buy Cokes® if they had them, but most of the time they only had a bottled drink called Yoo-Hoo. It was supposed to be a chocolate-milk-type drink in a glass bottle. To me the taste was sickening, and I couldn't swallow the stuff. All I could handle was the 3.2 beer. Even tried brushing my teeth with it, but that didn't taste right either. The milk we got was powdered, and we put ice in it to make it cold.

As officers, we were allowed to buy as much booze as we could afford. The Air Force flew it in from Japan and charged us $2.00 a bottle for any brand. I always had a bottle of Cherry Heering for my cough medicine, and once a month my Platoon Sergeant would come to me with $96.00 to buy 48 bottles of VO whiskey for the men in my platoon. They would take the gold and black ribbons from the bottle, and weave them through the ventilation holes in their fatigue hats as a decoration.

At that time, life in Korea was very simple. When our weapons finally arrived, they were placed all around the air base and each unit had to build its own Quonset Hut. These are made of corrugated metal and are rounded on the top. Each unit got a half a Quonset to house the men that formed that gun's crew. The big problem was how to close up the open half of the hut. The men were given planks of lumber and nails and each devised its own method of closure. I told my boys to overlap the boards so that rain couldn't come in. I don't know if it worked as I was transferred out of the unit before any group completed its work.

Figure 18 - Lived in this tent until transfer to 7ᵗʰ Division.
Photo by Ron Freedman

Figure 19 - Spring Day, Note the tire tracks. The thaw has begun!

Figure 20 - Putting up 1/2 Quonset Hut.
John Brosnan (facing camera) lives in Ireland now. Photo by Ron Freedman

Figure 21 - Looks like it's cold. I was AAA at Osan AFB K55

Letter #8

19 May 1953

Dearest Pete—

Just got your latest letter, and was very happy to find you are taking my apparent interest in griping—I thought for a while there I might be irritating or offensive to you, but now that you admit your interest, you're in for a licking because I'll never stop my griping now!

In answer to your question about my moustache picture, I have but one answer—you should have them by now, and should just about be over your shock—Maybe sometime soon I'll get a good one taken, and I'll send the thing along to prove I'm really not an ogre—Don't forget the deal I made!!

Today was a beautiful summery day—The sun was bright and hot. Just enough breeze to remind you that without it the day would have been a scorcher. If I were home on a day like this, and didn't have to work I think I'd play about 18 holes of golf in the morning, sit out on the lawn with a cold beer all afternoon, and then take a 2 hour nap from 4 to 6—Then I'd have me a cold lobster salad for supper—about 7:30 I'd put on a sport shirt, slacks, and jacket; put the top down on my car, and take some pretty girl like you for a nice long ride down the Cape along the beaches—Boy, what a dreamer!

To get back to reality, let me tell you what I did today— Chow at 7 A.M.—helped put the finishing touches on the fireplace at the new officers club—sat around the orderly room till noon waiting for something to happen. Noontime—chow—from 1 to 3 I sat around the orderly room waiting for mail—Your letter came—From 3 to 5 I rode around the air base informing my gun crews the Major would be around to inspect at 9 tomorrow morning—at 6 P.M. I went down to the Air Force and had a shower—now here it is 7 P.M., and I'm writing to you—

Believe me, honey—this is the most boring existence possible. Doubly so for me, because I'm awaiting news on my transfer and am completely disinterested in the whole situation. I'm quite confident of being transferred in the immediate future. As our Executive Officer says, "This outfit just like everyone else 20 miles south of the lines is more interested in building an empire than it is in fighting a war."

You say you're using my letters as a basis for your views on the war. Please don't get me wrong!! I am no military expert—I'm just a little raggedy old 2nd Lt. in an obscure little position. I see very, very little of the war, but what I see I don't like—

I want to get up there where something is being done about the whole mess—

This war must be won no matter what the cost, and if the commies ever really decided to break through (if they're capable of doing it) I think we'd be pushed way back to hell and gone—

Being in an air AAA outfit is bad for morale—You do nothing but sit and wait for the airplane that never comes—In between times you think of how you can get out of the outfit. Oh, we have our laughs, but they're few and far between—Like the one the other night—I was at the club drinking from 8:30 or so to about 11:30 when the Major came in and said he would chug-a-lug his double bourbon if we would do the same—Well, he had the bartender set up 14 glasses, but before they could be filled somebody ran in yelling. The Colonel said to knock it off as there was a lot of shooting going on near guard post 4 on the hill.

Well, I ran out of the club to see what I could see—I was drunker'n skunk. The shooting had died down, but there were a lot of flashlights shining on the hill. I ran into a tent, grabbed a sub-machine gun with 2 clips, and ran up the hill. I almost knocked the Colonel down when I reached the top. He, not realizing how drunk I was, told me to get 5 men and patrol the area directly to the front, and report back in 15 minutes—What a sight I must have been! I crawled under the barbed wire, and got my uniform caught—The Sgt. had to unhook me—we took off through the rice paddies, and I made more noise telling them to keep quiet than a regiment of tin soldiers would make—We came to some gullies, and in one was a cave—I crept up on it like I've seen them do in the movies.

See, we didn't know who had done the firing. We thought it must have been a guerilla attack! So we were really trying to be quiet and careful—I got to one side of the cave entrance, stuck my gun nuzzle inside, and yelling "*Eedeewah*" which is Korean for "come here". Nothing happened, so I had one of the guys get behind a rock and shine a flashlight in the entrance. Quick like a bunny I jumped out in front of the cave. Oh, I was a daring young Doug Fairbanks that night—the cave only went back 2 feet. There was nothing in it, but some ants—I came back to report to the Colonel, and then went to bed—My first patrol, and I was drunk—It wasn't funny then, but now it's uproarious—If you could have seen me confronting the colony of ants—what a hero— whatta life—

Well Pete—I guess that's about all from this end of the line—Your mail has been a real godsend, and now that I have you to write to I won't let you go—Please make sure you send me your address this summer—If you don't I'll be forced to get detectives on your trail—

Please write soon, and take care of yourself!! I may be late or I may be early, but anyway I want to congratulate you upon graduation day! I know just how relieved you must feel now that it's all over—

G'night now—
Love to you always, Ron

৪৩০৫৪

Waiting for the transfer notification was debilitating. There was absolutely nothing to do. I would get in my jeep and drive around to the different gun positions, but that got to be old hat as nothing ever changed there. The gun crews cleaned, polished and oiled their weapons every morning and constantly policed their areas. I was the Platoon Leader of the Second Platoon of Baker Battery of the 398th Anti-Aircraft Battalion Automatic Weapons (Semi-Mobile). The semi mobile part tells the story of this unit. It means exactly that. We were semi-mobile.

We had 64 weapons in the battalion, but only about thirty-five vehicles to transport them. If we had to cross a road from one side to the other it could take us all day and maybe all night. Each platoon in a battery, and there were two platoons in a firing battery, had 4 Quad 50 machine guns mounted on a self-contained traversing mechanism that had a gunner who sat in between all 4 machine guns. The weapon was capable of firing 2,400 .50 caliber rounds per minute if you used all 4 guns.

Because the Chinese did not use air against our troops this weapon was employed primarily as a direct fire weapon and proved to be one of the most potent weapons our army used. The Chinese called it "Whispering Death" because the tracer elements burned out, and they couldn't hear the sound of the bullets approaching. It cut them down like a scythe would in a wheat field. The other 4 guns in each platoon were of a Swedish design. They were made by the Bofors Company, and if you remember your WWII movies they were the guns that took turns at shooting at the enemy. The big difference was that our guns were single, not double like in those movies. We had two methods of aiming at a target, but we had employed only one. I'll explain why in a minute.

Figure 22 - Commo Section, Baker Battery, 2nd Platoon at K55, Osan AFB. On the lower extreme right: Pak Y Bong, our 'house boy'.

One method was electronic, which was quite advanced for that era. We used what was called a director that sat away from the gun with a good view of the target area. When airplanes flew at 200 or 300 miles-per-hour it was possible to track them and shoot them down using a director with two scopes attached. One scope corrected visually for line (elevation), and the other for lead (horizontal movement). That information was sent to the gun electrically through a cable that connected to the gun.

Before we left Cape Cod to go to Korea we'd spent weeks packing everything in Cosmolene (a substance we painted on everything to protect it from the weather). We then made these enormous crates in which to put everything, including our Quad 50's, 40mm Bofors and directors. When we got to Staten Island to board the ship we saw the longshoremen tipping our directors end over end down the dock to board them on another ship. When we uncrated them months later we found them to be smashed to pieces. So, we had to use an alternative method to aim the 40mm cannons.

This was the second method, what were called "Speed Rings". They were circular sights comprised of four decreasing sized rings mounted on a metal ring which were placed in front of the gunner's eyes on the weapon. There were two seats on the cannon, one on each side. The left seat controlled the line and the right controlled the lead (I think). This weapon had a 40mm warhead, and had a range of about 12,000 feet. It would have been effective if the enemy had a slow moving air force, but they didn't. They did send the occasional bi-winged open cockpit plane down towards Seoul to drop hand grenades, but they amounted to nothing, and I think the 398th only had one alert the whole time they were there in Korea

In the meantime, I was still hanging around the orderly room waiting for mail either from Nancy or from the man in Seoul. Our orderly room was a "Squad Tent" and could sleep up to fourteen men or be used for other purposes. Each Squad Tent had two diesel fuel heaters. These each had a rubber hose line attached to a 55-gallon drum that sat on a double-X-shaped frame placed outside of the tent. The flow into the heater was controlled by a mechanism that could be adjusted for more or less heat. Because the ground was frozen most of the heaters sank in almost out of sight until we learned how to prepare the ground.

Between the heaters and our down filled sleeping bags we were comfortable enough. We each had a folding cot, and a rubber air mattress. Our major thought it was great fun to pull the plugs on our mattresses while we slept, and every morning I got sick to my stomach blowing it up by mouth. That major was a jerk!

The orderly room (or our battery's office) was also in that tent and was populated by the CO, Capt. Owen Doherty, and Executive Officer, 1st Lt. Sid Archer, our First Sgt. Richard Harry Smith, and our Battery Clerk, Herbert Hester. They were there the majority of the time, but other people were in and out every day.

Bud Gaynor, who to this day is still my oldest and closest friend, was in Charlie battery, but we got together most evenings, and maintained our friendship that way. Bud, being a good, solid Irish Catholic, didn't like to go down to the Air Force Club and sing dirty songs with me. It's now almost sixty years later, and I am glad to report that he has changed his ways somewhat and doesn't blush when he hears those words. The Army made a man of him. I've maintained contact with other good friends: Bob Huntley, Ray Kalil, and John Brosnan. John lives in Ireland, where he grew up even though he is an American citizen. He retired a full bird Colonel. You've heard of the Ring of Kerry. I think he is known as the King of Kerry and Nancy and I have visited with him over there.

Back to the orderly room where I still waited for any kind of news. "Sgt. Smith, will you turn up the heat a little bit? Thanks!"

Figure 23 - Guns #1 & 2, Charlie Battery,
48th Field Artillery Battalion, North Korea, 1953

Letter #9

Sunday 31 May

Dear Pete,

I don't know whether or not you answered my last letter because I haven't been around to get my mail since last Tuesday. I'm no longer with the 398th—My transfer finally came through, and I got just what I wanted.

I'm with the top field artillery battalion over here. It's a part of the 7th Infantry Division which is situated just west of Chorwon. At the present time I'm living about 5000 yards behind the main line. The guns are situated all around us, the nearest being about 100 yards away, and when they go off everything including young Lt. Freedman trembles.

I'll stay around here for a few days sort of learning the ropes, and then I'll go up to the front as a forward observer. An observer lives in a little sandbag hut upon some high ground, and his job is to direct artillery fire for the infantry. My battalion has these sandbag bunkers (they are called observation posts or O.P.'s in artillery talk) spread out all along the front lines that is controlled by the 32nd Infantry Regiment, and the Ethiopian battalion. Some of the hills that are in our sector you have undoubtedly read about and heard about—Old Baldy—Yoke, Pork Chop, T-Bone, Alligator Jaws, Arsenal, 3 Sisters, etc.—All are pretty famous, but at the present are pretty quiet.

Out of the 5 officers in my tent including myself, 2 have won Bronze Stars and Purple Hearts. One guy got caught on Arsenal when the Chinks over ran it. His OP was blown up, and he called fire outside. He called for fire upon himself, and drove the Chinks off. I know it sounds tough, but those are rare examples, and though the life of an F.O. is tough—it isn't as bad as people usually make it out to be—The only thing that sort of worries me is that I'll have to go out on patrols with the Infantry, but what the hell—the Infantry boys do it—so can I—Anyway, I'll be drawing $45 a month more and 4 points a month—

Tonight is the last night they expect the Chinks to do much of anything so they've called a 100% alert—In other words—

everyone on the front line will be up for the whole night—Lucky I'm not up "on the hill" tonight—

Pete, honey—I'll write very shortly, but I've got to write my folks, and tell them where I am—Bye now—

Love as always,

Ron

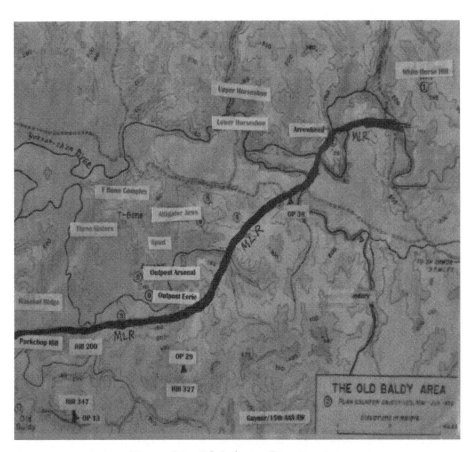

Figure 24 - 7th Infantry Division Area

ᘓᴑᘓ

Finally the transfer came through. I got the information late in the day as I was getting ready for the inaugural party at the Officers Club. As far as I was concerned, it was a going away party for me. Most of the other Officers Clubs, if not all, were invited, and I think they all came. The most outlandish of all were the Royal South African Air Force pilots. They spun a man around on a makeshift gadget that was mounted on roller skate wheels, while the poor guy was chug-a-lugging from a bottle of gin.

I was amazed that the building wasn't obliterated the next morning. We were supposed to occupy a Tropical Hut the next day and someone put a card with my name on it to signify that I was to live there. Instead I wrote under my name "Gone to Glory" and left the card in place. I had pre-arranged with my friend Bud Gaynor to drive me up to the 7th Division Headquarters where I was told to report. Hester, my battery clerk, also wanted to go so the three of us left early the next morning for the 80-mile trip to the front.

Figure 25 - Lt. Bud Gaynor & Lt. Ron Freedman, Photo by John Brosnan.

It was an uneventful ride, but a slow one as there was a lot of traffic on the main road called the Korea Highway No.1 by the troops. We arrived at around

1700 (5 pm), and I was told to occupy a squad tent off to the side of all the other tents. I had no idea where I was, but thought it was around five miles south of the Main Line of Resistance (The MLR). After a while I heard someone yell "chow!" so I followed a group of people down the slope and came across a tent with the sign "Transient Officers Mess". I sat down at a common table with around five other people. Not one said hello or even recognized me being there. I remember a Lt. Diana as the non-official leader of that group. I drifted over to the Officers Club after our meal, and was told that I couldn't use cash there, but that I could buy "chits" at the end of the bar. Beer was a nickel, and they told me that three out of the seven nights a week that beer was free. Wow! I wish I could have stayed there for the whole war.

I went back to my sleeping quarters to find that I was the sole occupant of the tent. It was only around 2100 (9 pm), and I knew I wouldn't fall asleep that early. The only reading material in the tent was an old comic book that took me about an hour to decide that I would at least look at the pictures. Even as a kid I was never interested in them.

I eventually fell asleep for some time when I awoke to hear what I thought was machine gun bullets ricocheting off of a boulder nearby. I rolled out of the cot and huddled under it, like it was going to protect me, but I didn't hear anyone else yelling "Attack" or anything at all, and after a while I figured that I would live through the night. I climbed back on my cot where I slept until I heard people outside getting ready for breakfast. I went back down to the chow hall from the night before to find the same 5 people sitting at the table. Again, no recognition from any of them, but I did hear someone say, "Those damned birds were at it again. They sound just like ricocheting rounds." Wow, and to think I almost got shot by birds. I'll be prepared the next time I hear them.

I was called into the Colonel's van to meet him and learn of my assignment. The van was his office and sleeping quarters. It was nicely paneled with wood trim, and he had some maps of the local area pinned on the wall. His name was Lt. Col. J. Stanley Kimmitt and he informed me that he was a Montanan. He turned out to be the opposite of my other Colonel, and was highly regarded by all the rest of the officers and men of the 48th Field Artillery Battalion.

I was assigned to Charlie battery, and I would be taken there shortly to meet the officers and men of that group. I arrived to find them all involved in softball and volleyball games. It was "Founders Day" in the battalion, and all the men had the day off. We drank pink champagne and filled ourselves with barbecued chicken the whole day.

I was taken to another squad tent where I was bunked next to a young Lt. who sat there cleaning blood out of a Chinese helmet. His name was Bill DeWitt of Vinita, Oklahoma and many years later I saw Bill at a Field Artillery reunion at Fort Sill, Oklahoma. He was a retired bird Colonel, and he told me that he'd only been cleaning the helmet that night to impress me.

Figure 26 - From an OP (Observation Post) looking at Arsenal Hill (1000 yards in front of our line). Bill Dewitt injured here.

Bill's story is the first chapter of the book *Pork Chop Hill* by Gen. S.L.A. Marshall, which was made into the movie of the same name starring Gregory Peck. That battle took place in April of 1953, and featured a number of people from my new battalion as they were protagonists of that affair. Bill had performed a heroic feat (it was his first taste of combat) for which he received a number of medals. His request to fly as an aerial observer was granted, and that took him away from us most of the time.

The next morning I was driven up to Observation Post 29, or OP29 in common parlance. This was called the "General's OP" as it had a rattan rug on the floor and Jeep windshields on the windows. It was also the main viewing spot for the big brass when they came to see the sights in the area. This OP had an Army radio unit attached to it, but I was told it was top secret, and so I never had anything to do with it.

From the windows one could see the T-Bone complex with Outposts Erie and Arsenal, the Alligator Jaws with Outposts Yoke and Uncle nearby. Just off to the left was Old Baldy, Chink Baldy, Hill 347, and the infamous Pork Chop Hill. Most of these prominent landmarks were named as they were because they looked like a specific object on a map. Pork Chop looked like a pork chop on a map, Old Baldy was bald on the top, and nearby there were four little ridgelines named Ace, King, Queen and Jack, collectively called Poker Flats.

I don't know why our bunker was call OP 29 as it sat on top of Hill 327, but I didn't argue or question the fact. My mentor was Allen Goode from Kansas City, and he was sitting behind a blanket hung from a roof beam that protected any light from a candle being seen by anyone near or far. Allan was writing home around 2200 (10pm) when I, taking my first turn at a window, spotted a myriad of fireflies in the valley below. I watched for a few moments before I realized that these fireflies only flew in straight lines, and therefore must be something other than good old New England fireflies that I always loved to watch when I was younger. I called Allen's attention to the sight below, whereby he immediately grabbed a telephone and yelled "OP 29er Fire Mission!"

Almost at once the Chinks fired on us, and I was under shelling for the first time in my life. Allen said that if I was nervous to duck down under the window sill, until I was ready to come up and watch the firefight down in the valley. By the time I came up the fight was over and Allen said that I had spent a couple of hours ducked down. I thought it was only twenty minutes or so, but when I saw the sun rising to the east I realized that what he said was true.

I couldn't quite believe what had happened. I wasn't frightened or afraid, but I didn't have anyone to tell about it as I didn't want my folks or Pete to worry, but it sure was a change from the life I had been living, and I felt ready for anything to happen.

The Korean War was originally a war between the South and North Koreans. In 1950 the North Koreans pushed their way south almost to the southern tip of the peninsula. However, by then our army had gained some strength, and we were able to hold the North Koreans off so that MacArthur could arrange his end run invasion at Inchon on the west coast of the peninsula. This not only attacked the North Korean forces half way up their supply lines, it also cut off their troops in the south. In essence, that was the end of the North Korean army, and the war would have ended right then and there except for the invasion of Korea by Chinese communist forces in October of 1950. After that time, the North Korean Forces were of little or no significance, and we primarily fought the Chinese.

Figure 27 - Dark hill center, is lower jaw of Alligator Jaws

Figure 28 - Back side of Out Post Yoke

Figure 29 - Trench leading to OP Arsenal

Figure 30 - Lt. Freedman, entrance to Out Post (OP) 38.
Grenades for effect only!

Letter #10

Thurs. 11 June

Dear Pete,

    May 27th I left my outfit, and since then I haven't had any mail. For some reason it hasn't been forwarded. I haven't the slightest idea what my folks have to say about my transfer. I'm sure they won't like it, but I do want to get something from home so I won't worry. Of course, I haven't heard from you or anyone else, and I'm getting a little impatient.

    I was assigned to my new outfit about 2 weeks ago, and

spent 3 days in the battery area. I believe I wrote you a letter at that time telling you my address, and asking you to write. Next I was told to pack a small bag, and move up "on the hill". We have a lot of slang terms in Artillery, and "on the hill" is one which means to be on the front line. My job is to sit in a "hoochie" (G.I. term for sandbag bunker) and direct fire upon the enemy.

This hoochie where we work is called an O.P. It means an observation post. We are F.O.'s or forward observers. Most O.P.'s are right on or forward of the MLR. That's an Army term for main line of resistance. Our MLR is an actual line of trenches and "hoochies" right along the crest of the hills from one coast of Korea to the other.

The Chinks have no actual line, but hide in caves and ditches in front of us. Some are only 500 yds. away, and some maybe 3000 yds. away. Our MLR is only about 50 yds wide, but all along the front we have various positions that jut out in front of the MLR. Some are quite a way in front, and some close in. It depends on the terrain—Their purpose is to keep the Chinks from hitting the MLR. I'm sure you've heard of Pork Chop, Yoke, Luke's Castle, etc. Some F.O.'s have their observation posts in front of the MLR, and some right on it. Being an F.O. can be dangerous because the Chinks try to knock out the O.P.'s to prevent our watching them.

The O.P. I was sent to was just in front of the MLR—20 yds or so—not much. It is known as the VIP O.P. That's where all the Generals and big wheels come to watch the proceedings. It commands one of the finest views along the whole front, and is beautifully built. It sits on top of a 1200 ft. hill, and has a helicopter landing spot built into the hillside for the VIP's. While I was there we had Gen. Taylor, Gen. Trudeau, Gen. Mark Clark, Sen. Dirksen and some other minor people up there.

Each F.O is assigned to an Infantry outfit, and luckily I was put with the 4th Company of the Ethiopian Kagnew Battalion. They are even more ferocious than the Turks, and are really respected more than anyone else over here. Some are real gory. One for example, has the habit of cutting off the ears and noses of the Chinks he kills.

Each F.O. is required to make patrols with their Inf. Company, and everyone wants to go with the "Epes" (Ethiopians).

They assign 2 men to act as the bodyguards for the accompanying FO, and so far the "Epes" haven't lost one on patrol. They gave me their battalion pin to wear to show that I work with them, and believe me I'm really proud of it.

Last week I had my first taste of real action. I was quite frightened, but strangely enough I didn't realize it until it was all over. All day I sat at the OP aperture with my field glasses trying to find something for our artillery to shoot at. No luck. About 4:30 P.M., the Chinks started shelling Outpost Yoke. Yoke was held by 57 Ethiopians. The shelling stopped after I called for a few rounds where I thought the Chinks were firing from. All was quiet until 9:30 P.M. when all hell broke loose. My first inkling was the tracers heading toward Yoke from all directions.

While I was on the phone contacting the "Epe" Captain, my hoochie was shaken by a terrific blast. It was like being hit by a car. The Chinks were trying to make me keep away from my window so I couldn't see where I wanted to place my artillery fire to protect Yoke.

However, they were lousy shots, and did nothing more than scare the living daylights out of me and my crew.

I got the incoming fire calmed down, and after an hour or so the Chinks—what was left of them, went crawling home. I stayed up the rest of the night just in case, but nothing happened. It was really a very, very small attack, but it gave me a real glimpse into the one thing I've wanted to know. How people could stand the scare of being shelled, and shot at. I find no one, or at least very few, realize their fear until it's all over. About 30 minutes after it was all over I found my throat hurt, and I was dying for a drink of water. My knees were shaking, and what a headache I had—That's how I felt. Imagine how those boys on Yoke felt?

You probably took very little interest in my description of what happened, but I wrote it just to let you have an idea of what is happening. It's going on all along the front all day and night, and little affairs like that don't ever make the papers. It's one headline I'll carry with me, however, for a long time.

At present, I'm in school learning how to be an executive officer, and boy is it rough! It's a refresher course for all the other boys, but for me it's all something brand new. I leave here next Sunday, and am going back up "on the hill." I have hopes of an Armistice by then. That's the main topic, of course all along the front, and is on our lips all day long.

There isn't a man who doesn't want a truce except Mr. Rhee, and are the G.I.'s ever tired of him. I'd shoot him tomorrow if I had the chance.

All night we hear the guns booming over near the ROK sector, while near the US sector all is fairly quiet. The boys are more interested in keeping their heads down than in anything else. We probably won't come home too much earlier, but at least the shooting will stop. I think the U.S. will squeeze the ROKs out of fighting back by cutting off their supplies. They can't win without us, of course, and I don't think Rhee will have any choice but to lay down arms until our troops can leave.

Where my division will go if we leave is anybody's guess. The gamblers say we'll go to Hawaii, Japan, Formosa, Okinawa, Philippines, or the states. Rumors really fly around here, and every guess is a good one—

To me it's been a war of principle, and very few of the G.I.'s understand that. They fought but didn't really know why. The only thing they knew was getting home, and the feeling they were forgotten. Nobody expected to be rotated home during World War II, but here everybody lives only to rotate home. It lowered morale greatly, and in my eyes lost us a lot of respect.

Enough preaching O.K.? Please write, Pete,

All my love as always,

Ron

Figure 31 - Sandbag "Hoochie" on Pork Chop

ഏൕഌ

When Pete's mail and something from my folks did not arrive made me quite impatient. I fretted day and night to hear from them. Being alone with my thoughts, and involved in a life and death situation at the same time, can be a nerve-racking thing. It, at least, was for me. My hoochie was only about 7x11 feet in size, and it had only one aperture, which looked out to White Horse Hill way off to the northeast, and as far west as the top row of hills on Alligator Jaws to my west.

To get to the OP I had to climb the smaller of two hills which were occupied by George Company of the 32nd Infantry Regiment. Once I crested the hill, I entered an east/west trench about seven feet deep and approximately six feet wide. I turned right and walked somewhat down to a tunnel of fifteen feet, which led into my bunker. In the bunker I had a cot with my equipment on it and nothing else but two telephones (line Able and line Baker) both connecting to the FDC (Fire Direction Center) via different routes.

I also had my radio, which was, as I recall, and ANGR9 or a PRC 25. ANGR9, Army Navy Ground Radio also called Angry9. The PRC was smaller and I assume the "P" stood for personal, as it was quite a bit smaller. Didn't matter too much as the batteries for both units were old and weak, and due to the hilly conditions didn't transmit as well as they should have. I also had what I consider to be the best piece of equipment that an FO could possibly have. Because we were in a permanent position we had installed a BC Scope bolted to our window sill. This was one half of the twin periscope that we used to see in the movies. It was much better than the binoculars the Army gave me, and of course it was much steadier. I even used it in the nighttime darkness after I had it fixed on a target during daylight hours.

Just a word about the darkness we encountered. I swear you couldn't see a person if they were standing right next to you. In some areas we had searchlights on the ground illuminating known areas that the Chinese would use when attempting to hit us. I went by one of these units in the morning and the men were using snow shovels to load up a 2½ truck with all the bugs that were attracted and then burned by the heat of the light. One other thing about the darkness, the Chinks would yell up to us in English from down in the no-man's land between us.

"George Company 32nd Infantry, *eedewah*." That word translates to "come here" in Korean, and to hear it at night was like scratching on a blackboard. Truly an irritating sound.

Something I forgot to mention in an earlier letter was a circumstance that occurred during my training on Hill 329. One nice day, right out in front of us, I noticed that the Chinese had draped a very long but narrow piece of white cloth across the rear hills of the T-Bone complex. On that cloth in bright red letters was a sign that read "Peace by noon 21 June" underneath it said "GI's number 1 soldiers. Now we all go home."

That was the best piece of news in a long time. After they put the sign away we saw men carrying scrub brush, which they placed on the ground and hid behind. They were showing us how they could deceive us even in broad daylight, which they quite often did. They were very good soldiers and tough as nails.

That mention of June 21 sure brightened my attitude. We never heard anything but pessimism from our leaders, and this gave us something to cheer about. We really never discussed the war and its causes as we were living for the moment. We didn't care about what might happen as we were too involved with what had already occurred, and what tomorrow might bring.

Figure 32 - Corp. Tom Trainor & PFC. Jim Holt, my wireman.

My FO crew consisted of my Jeep driver, Corporal Tom Trainor, my wireman PFC. Jim Holt, and an assistant FO who was a sergeant. I had originally been assigned a man by the name of Pensavalle, but our Battalion area had been shelled and he was accused of robbing the food store we had there during the shelling. They then assigned me a sergeant named Marino. He was a paratrooper who was a war lover. He did not speak. He snarled. I was more comfortable when he wasn't around.

Those three men had their own sleeping hoochie on the reverse slope of our hill, and could be in the OP within 30 seconds if there was a flap going on. That was what we called any action between us and the Chinks. Sounds English to me, but we adopted the term. In addition, we weren't involved "at the front" It was always referred to as being "on the hill". I always took the 1600 to 0100 watch in the bunker as almost all the action took place in the darker hours.

After that, while I slept one of the people would stand watch until he was relieved at about 0800. Then either I or one of the guys was always in the OP every day. Because it was so quiet in the daytime hours it was then that we drove down to a shower point where we stripped all our brass from our uniforms and were given all new clothing as a replacement including socks and underwear. When you live underground your clothing gets dirty very quickly.

At night I often slept wearing my flak jacket, and with my boots on and laced up. Those Chinks could be around and on top of your bunker before you even knew they were coming. They never attacked my OP, but an infantry sergeant in my area told me that you can smell them (garlic, etc.) before you see them. The Chinese told him that the UN soldiers smelled like rancid butter to them. Don't see how that could be true. I don't remember seeing any butter anywhere.

Speaking of food, I had had heartburn after almost every meal because of the Ethiopian love of Louisiana Hot Sauce. Their cooks used it in every way possible. I opted to stay in the OP, and eat the Tootsie Rolls that came in our C Rations. Also, very different eating situation than most people. As I lived in and among the Ethiopians called EEFKs (Ethiopian Expeditionary Forces, Korea), I also ate in their chow bunker.

Officers ate under cover in a sandbag hoochie attached to the kitchen. The EM (Enlisted Men) ate outside in all the elements. The U.S. Army supplied all the food and the unit chefs cooked it in their own style. The EEFKs had one bottle of hot sauce (Louisiana Hot Sauce brand) for two men every other day.

The hill I was on was quite steep, and my heartburn showed up when I climbed that hill. Included in a C-ration package was a round bar of compressed cocoa powder, dehydrated milk and sugar. I didn't have the means to start a fire, so I ate the thing right out of its cellophane wrapper. It was meant to be mixed with hot water to make a hot chocolate drink. No wonder I came home weighing only 118 pounds.

Figure 33 - On the road to my OP. The sign says,
"Keep the dust down! Joe can see you..."

Letter #11

Monday, June 15, 1953

Dearest Pete—

Well, I have a lot to say, and I really don't know where to start. As I told you in my last letter my mail was all fouled up, and I hadn't had any since 27 May. Finally, some of it caught up with me today, and I understand I still have quite a bit more in transit between here and school. Luckily, yours was one of those that didn't get lost, and honey, you have no idea how happy I was to find you had written me.

School ended today, and although I didn't set the world on fire, I certainly learned quite a bit. Being a battery executive officer entails one hell of a lot more work than I imagined. I certainly hope I am not being boring, but your letters do show me more interest in what is going on than any other person's. Therefore, I've tried to give you a little picture of what is going on, and I find you will understand me a lot more if I try to explain some of the more technical details. So please bear with me, honey, and if it gets on your nerves just let me know, and you shall hear no more of the life of a lost artillery man.

To explain the set-up of an artillery unit would take quite a few volumes, but in a nutshell here it is. This way when I tell you we had to call in the corps artillery you will get an idea of the volume of fire that was needed.

Each army division is a separate unit in itself composed of about 15,500 men. It has every type of unit necessary attached to it to make it self-sufficient. One of these units is the Division Artillery or Divarty as it is called. Each Divarty is composed of 4 artillery Battalions, and each battalion has 3 batteries of 6 guns each. Also each battalion has a Headquarters Battery whose main concern is control of the other batteries in the Battalion, and it has a Service Battery whose main job is supply. Now, each of the Batteries that have guns is called a firing battery. A, B, & C batteries. I am in C battery. To get back to the Divarty for a minute—remember I said there were 4 Batteries in all. Well, 3 are called "light" battalions. Those are battalions with guns of the smallest size. The fourth battalion is a medium artillery battalion. Those are middle sized guns.

Now—behind the Divarty we have Corps artillery. In the present situation we have about 7 battalions to a corps, and these are all either medium or heavy battalions. Those guns can really reach out, and get the enemy way in the back. Sometimes, when we find a target we only fire a gun at it, and sometimes a battery, or maybe a battalion. That little excitement I wrote about in my last letter required 6 battalions. Four from our Divarty, and 2 from Corps. It really wasn't a very big affair, but we have so very few targets to shoot at, that when we get one, we really let go. Right now, the battle going on over to the right of us about 30 miles is requiring almost all the corps battalions they can get. Our sector is very quiet, and some of our corps units have gone over to help the 3rd Div, and the 2nd ROKs.

I guess I've sort of confused you, and maybe I've bored you, but I hope it gives you an idea of the amount of fire we put out. That's important because it will give you an insight into this crazy war.

I've talked to some pilots back where I was, and they have told me when they fly over the U.N. area all they see are buildings, trucks, junk, and people, but when they reach Chinatown they see absolutely nothing but hills. One rarely ever sees a Chinaman during daylight. If we ever see 5 or six of them in the open we shoot all kinds of guns at them. Today an airplane spotted one stinking little chink mortar, and our battalion fired 18 rounds of shells at it. Each shell cost $120—Our boys sit in their bunkers all day cleaning their weapons, and getting ready for the night. Sometimes nothing happens for weeks or then it may get to be a little exiting like it is to our right now.

Our men wander around the trenches, making perfect targets of themselves all day, and nobody makes them get down. It's a crazy war. We know the Chinks are watching our every move, and can see us moving around, but yet they do nothing. The average G. I. doesn't care too much about what or how the war is coming along. He lives only for the "big R" or rotation home. There is no esprit de corps, no color, and almost very little pride in some outfits. People at home, with the exception of a few relatives, don't care what happens over here. I know I didn't until

I came here. I know my folks didn't think too much about it. I flatter myself to think I have brought you a little closer to what is happening.

The only people over here doing their jobs are the foreigners, the Ethiopians, Turks, Greeks, Siamese, etc. Those people are soldiers. They really give their jobs their all—We Americans are only interested in going home.

Please don't get me wrong Pete. The G. I. is one of the finest soldiers in the world, but this war has ruined his reputation. Nobody ever took the time to tell him in plain and simple words why he is here.

I've got my own reasons for being here—Maybe that's why I feel so strongly about the whole situation. Someday, when I get home I'll tell you all about it.

Korea is a funny place—There's no movie theaters, no neon lights—only Seoul and Pusan have paved roads. The people are poor, and the land is fertile and completely void of any large stands of timber—The people have chopped it all down for firewood. About 20 miles north of Seoul is the "no farm line." From there on up there isn't a house, a Korean, or a rice paddy to be seen. Of course we have the ROKs, and our indigenous personnel, but there are no elderly people, no kids, no girls—except those who are brought here by the soldiers.

The boys have nothing much to do, a movie at night, a couple of cans of beer after chow—Mail call, fire missions, and letter writing. Of course R&R leave in Japan is a goal to look forward to, but the "Big R" is even bigger.

Korea shows these boys nothing—They can't see why we are fighting for it. They just don't realize the fact our cause is a principle—not to gain ground.

About believing what you read in the papers. Why not believe it. Maybe we're losing a few more planes or men than they say, but we're doing alright. The papers give you the straight scoop. The only thing they don't do is tell you how the kid in the trench or bunker feels. The war is too big for that—I guess we need another Ernie Pyle—Even the movies aren't realistic enough about it. They make everything look so rosy. The American public needs to be shocked. I can get you mad when I tell you about the Lt. Ford in the 57th F.A, Battalion who volunteered to go on an infantry patrol through no-man's land. He got killed—By one of our men—when his group encountered another G.I. patrol, and both groups fired at each other thinking the others were Chinks. Nobody's fault of course, but the movies never show anything like that. The American people couldn't swallow it.

You'll be able to teach those kids all those principles because even though it seems like a worthless struggle—those principles have never lost their value.

Sure honey, I plan ahead—who doesn't? I'm probably one of the world's greatest daydreamers. I've got many plans—but I can't work them alone. I'm going to need someone to help me—but right now I've got to do my planning in the form of wishes only. I've got nothing solid to base them on as yet. I don't know whether I'll stay in the army or not. It will all depend on somebody else—What she says will probably be the final word. So, without a somebody I really don't know.

Sweetheart, if you can keep that lobster salad fresh, and that beer cold—I'll be over on a scooter if I can't find me a convertible, and we'll have us a ball. If you can wait until February, or March at the most, then it will be one of the best deals I've ever made—

Pete—I've seen you about twice, and that was in 3 years, but something is funny. I never write 7 or 8 pages to anyone—I never thought I could. I'm writing this by flashlight—it's late, and I'm tired, but I just don't want to put the pen down. There's so much I want to say and so much I want to know about you—How about obliging? Just the story of your life. What you're doing—What are you thinking about. What you want in life. Are you happy—sad—in between or what—just a nice long letter that will make me good and homesick—but happy—Got strange ideas, haven't I?

Here it is 10 minutes of eleven at night, and I just heard the battalion mail clerks call out to our battery mail clerks that he has a lot of air mail that just came in. Sort of explains what I meant about getting mail.

I'm waiting quite impatiently, to be frank with you, for your picture. I will get a better one of me to send as soon as I can get my camera fixed.

I didn't know you were going to California. Whatcha gonna do there? Whatever it is, have a good trip and a good time.

Don't worry about me taking care of myself—I'm just a little bit luckier than the next guy—Is there a G.I. that never said that to himself? I'll be alright as long as you have me in your thoughts. It makes the days go by a lot faster.

Tomorrow I'll have been in Korea—6 months. It certainly doesn't seem it.

Please keep writing as often as you find time, and keep in mind I think of you often, and though we've hardly ever spent any time together—I'm learning to miss you, and I send you

My love, as always

Ronnie

Figure 34 - Artillery Valley

ಹೊರಜ

Writing about things that occurred almost sixty years ago would normally present a problem, but having the original letters to Pete combined with my memory for many details, I find that I remember much more than I forgot. As an example, my mind starts thinking about one particular morning back at K55 when I took my jeep and rode out across the hills and valleys to inspect something or other.

I remember stopping on top of a rise looking out over a valley below, and thinking about a phrase that I read in some Army instructional booklet about Korea. It said that Koreans speak of their land as the "Land of the Morning Calm" It struck me then and there that that was a perfect description. There was a fairly heavy haze in the valley below, and some few trees managed to top the haze. The birds were chirping, and the world sure seemed right. That is until I was stuck in the mud a few minutes later. Thank God for four-wheeled drive! That memory is still with me, and I often think of it and how comfortable I felt at that moment.

However, in rereading Letter #11 brings me back to "the hill", and what things were like there. As a Forward Observer my job was to do just what those words say. I was supposed to keep my eyes open for anything and everything that might take place in and around my OP. Under normal circumstances an FO's life expectancy is quite short. When everybody else is down looking for cover the artillery observer should be up and searching for targets of opportunity.

During the first two thirds of the Korean War that was the way most FOs did their work, and the casualty lists show that they suffered badly in their positions. They did not have secure underground bunkers in which they were protected from most shrapnel, and their living accommodations were quite difficult to say the least. They did not get three square meals a day, and they had to brave the elements under all circumstances.

My life as an observer was far different as I lived in an underground bunker, slept on a cot with a down sleeping bag, had the opportunity to get three good meals a day, and could almost get a shower every day. After breakfast, I would check out my crew, clean the bunker (what was there to clean? It was all red clay dirt.). I would clean my carbine and .45 pistol, and the go to the window to see what I could see. However, there was not much to be seen since the enemy moved around at night, not during the day. Therefore, I had plenty of letter writing time on my hands.

Usually, I allowed my crew to take care of themselves, and only report to me for either duty or when I needed someone for something. We got along well, but Sgt. Marino was the only fly in the ointment. He was upset that we were not slugging it out with the enemy every day or fighting hand to hand. Thankfully, the rest of us were able to ignore him, and eventually he disappeared just as the war was ending.

The Army was a stickler for following all the rules. As an example, we were told to police all our brass (shell casings, etc.) every day, and in my outfit, we had to wear red neck scarves, as that was the artillery color. We had to shave every day, and our helmets were shellacked with the unit insignia decaled on the side. Proper military decorum, I suppose. If I did spot a target, I had to use the only acceptable method of calling in fire. Here's an example: on the phone, or over the radio:

FO: "This is OP 38. Fire Mission."
FDC: "Send your mission."
FO: "Coordinates 825 575."
FO: "Azimuth 5400, request Willie Peter, Fuse Victor Tare."
FO: "Active mortar crew. Will adjust, over."

We called all our missions into the FDC (Fire Direction Center at battalion HQ). The coordinates we determined by reading our maps, and putting a mark in place. The azimuth was a line of sight based on a total reckoning of a circle divided into 6400 mils or lines of sight, and a line drawn between our known position and a supposed enemy position

We then requested what type of shell we would like used which was primarily HE or High Explosive or Willie Peter, which is a phonetic way of saying White Phosphorous. WP was a highly used shell as it not only marked a target brightly, but its ability to burn through everything was of great import to us. I understand that it is now against the law to use this shell in a combat situation.

We also requested the type of fuse that would be employed. Victor Tare stood for VT fuse or Variable Time fuse. Developed in WWII, this fuse had a radio in its nose and when the radio beam was broken by the land below the fuse would cause the round to explode. It was usually set for 17 yards or about 50 feet above ground. The bursting range of the shell would cover around 50 yards, and the shrapnel would get everyone below in its umbrella. The "will adjust" was the FO saying that he will make corrections as to where the rounds land related to the target.

The FDC would wait until the round was supposed to land and they would say "Splash!". Our answer was "Splash Wait", and then we would give our correction or else say "Target" "Cease Fire. End of Mission".

We had to use those commands or they would not answer. Later on when involved in the Pork Chop Hill flap the call signals changed in the middle of the day, and all of a sudden I kept hearing "Unknown Station, Unknown station please say again." My call signal went from "Quinine Oboe Uncle 559 to Gallivant Charlie 5 Niner 5, but I was never given a sheet of information that would have told me that. I recognized the voice at the other end and gambled that I was now Gallivant Charlie 5 Niner 5. We said "niner" for the number nine so as not to confuse it with the number 5, its sound alike. As an aside, we never said "repeat" as it sounds like "retreat". Instead, we said "say again".

I volunteer at our local Military Museum, and many times young people have asked me "how many enemy did you kill?" I never knew the answer to that as I could not always see the results of my fire missions. I remember, one afternoon, seeing three Chinamen nonchalantly walking down a hillside footpath with towels around their necks. I didn't understand their motive other than they were going to bathe in the Yokkok-ch'on River which flowed at the bottom of their hill. I called the 4.2 Mortar unit attached to our company, and told them what I saw. They were anxious for something to do, and within a few minutes after I gave them the azimuth, etc., they fired, and there were three Chinese lying on the ground all the rest of the day. They were gone the next morning.

A few days later I saw four men wearing Red Cross brassards on their arms but carrying weapons over their shoulders, and figured them to be fair game because they didn't have a stretcher with them, and those weapons looked awfully lethal. I figured that our FDC probably wouldn't want to waste ammo on them, and instead called my pal Bud Gaynor, who had one of his half-tracks positioned on a hill just behind me. He was itching for some action, and he set to work immediately. His weapons had an azimuth scale painted on its turret and he figured out the elevation. Again, we left four Chinamen lying on a hill top the rest of the day.

Figure 35 - Lt. Bud Gaynor

That's what happened on a typical day in an OP in the northwest sector of the Korean MLR just west of Chorwon in west central North Korea.

When I first went up to OP 38, Colonel Kimmitt told me that my primary job was to keep watch on the Chorwon Valley to my east as it was the main way to Seoul for the enemy to use. I wasn't about to sit all day and look up a very quiet valley. Instead, I fired missions in support of the ROK (Republic of Korea) held outpost called Arrowhead to my immediate front. Just west of that area were two horseshoe shaped hills. The immediate one to my front was called the Lower Horseshoe and the one behind it was named the Upper Horseshoe. I found that the enemy was using those hills to cover up some mortars, and almost every night I fired missions into those areas. Those hill masses must be composed of mostly metal after everything I sent their way.

Figure 36 - The Horseshoes as seen from my left.
Yokkok-ch'on River in center of No-Man's Land. My favorite target!

I noticed that in my letter I mentioned that the GIs didn't seem very involved with what was happening over there. I realize now, that my reasoning was based on the fact that we all spoke the same language, and so I understood all their remarks. Also, most of the other UN units were all volunteers. They wanted to be there and most of us didn't. After sixty years I now understand the South Koreans a lot better than I did then, and I think they have done marvelous things with their country. Back in the fifties they seemed so backward and so far behind the rest of the civilized world that it looked like they could never catch up. I went back to Korea in 2006, and it is just as modern and up-to-date as any major U.S. city. One can apply almost any good adjective to their way of living, and one wouldn't be wrong.

I also noticed that my words of affection were cropping up all over my letters. I was falling for my "Pen Pal", and I didn't seem to be embarrassed to use those words. She was the prettiest girl I ever dated (and still is), and was I ever proud of her.

Letter #12

Tues. 23, June

Dear Pete—

I received your long-awaited letter today, and am answering it as soon as possible. This won't be a very long letter as I have many, many things to do tonight.

Last Tuesday I was sent up as a forward observer once again. My observation post is on the very right flank of the division. I overlook White Horse Mtn., Arrowhead, Dagmar, and off to the east I have been able to see the big battle going on between the Chinks and the 3rd Div. My O.P. is a cave, and at night is as cold as a winter's day. We're expecting the Chinks to pull an attack tonight on either us or Arrowhead, henceforth, the Chinks want to get White Horse Mtn. back, and are going to hit us as a diversionary attack. This O.P. is called a "sweat O.P. It's not the healthiest place in the world but [I] imagine there's worse.

I'm a pretty tired kid, Pete—Maybe this letter won't sound too coherent probably, and that's the reason. Tonight, makes only my 7th day on this O.P. and I haven't even taken off my shoes to sleep. I sack out at night with my flak-jacket, boots, pistol belt, and last night I even fell asleep with my helmet on. Boy, I hope I can last this week or two out.

The G.I.'s here are really disgusted with Synghman Rhee and are split in their opinions as to whether we should pull out of Korea. I think it would be an injustice to the parents of all those kids who have died over here if we did leave. However, I don't like being caught in a sandwich, and I think it's about time the U.S. really put their foot down, and squelched little snakes like Rhee—

Please, honey, don't worry a bit about me. I'm going to be alright—You know that—I'm sorry if this letter may be a little frightening or melodramatic, but I did want to answer you as soon as possible, and I can't think of anything else but the things I have to do tonight. Every time we hear of an impending attack it's usually fake anyway, but we still have to get prepared—Please

send me your Calif. address—

Love to you always, Pete

Ron

Figure 37 - ROK 105 mm artillery piece

୫୦ଔଓ

At this time, I felt that my life depended on my relationship with Pete. I was getting more and more nervous about the exposed position I was in, and I needed a rock or something to cling to, and she was it. I thought about her every waking minute, and even if she didn't realize it I knew that if she ever stopped writing me I would cease to exist. I spilled out my deepest thoughts to her, but she never answered me in the same vein. That didn't matter. As long as I felt the way I did, then I would continue to tell her all even if she didn't care or understand where I was coming from.

Being told by higher-ups that I might expect an attack that night was frightening. I knew that Joe Chink could crawl all around us before we even knew he was in the area. We had chicken wire strung on our window face in case he got on the roof of our bunker and threw satchel charges in on us. Normally, they would throw up red colored flares just prior to their shelling us, and then they would fire off green flares for their infantry attack. Some nights the flares would be other colors like purple and yellow. I guess that was supposed to confuse us, but I just figured it would be shelling and then infantry no matter the color of their flares. If we called for illumination, the Air Force would send big planes, which would circle our area. The star shells they dropped would open with "boi-i-i-ng" which reminded me of that cartoon that was popular around that time—Gerald McBoing-Boing. Our mortar companies would also light up the valley below with their illumination shells.

White Horse Hill was to my right front and was too far away for me to observe anything closely. Instead, I would concentrate on helping Arrowhead, which was to my immediate right front. That hill was occupied by ROK forces, and firing directly on it would be impossible as I didn't speak any Korean, and besides that, it was their battle and was out of our Division's area of responsibility

I kept my eyes on the Horseshoes in case they were also attacking the west side of Arrowhead. On those occasions the whole crew would crowd into my OP, and I would let them give me the corrections to send to the FDC. It was amazing. We'd spend the night trying to kill each other, and then the next day the sun would shine, and we could almost think about spending the day at a beach somewhere.

The first day on the hill at OP 38, as I climbed up a short trench leading to the MLR trench, I heard two rounds go over my head. L never thought anything was out of the ordinary, and so I waited for an hour or two before I climbed down the hill to the two craters those rounds had left. We were taught to send in what were called shell reports by digging out the fuse plug from the crater and measuring the back azimuth and elevation using two twigs as measuring devices.

I kept the back azimuths in my head, until I realized I might be able to plot them on my map and see where they came from. Those Chinks were greeting me with those rounds, and I ought to answer them. The plots led to a very steep side hill, and I thought I could see a cave facing us up near the top. That night I put my BC scope[2] on the cave, and am quite sure that I saw a weapon firing from up there. I knew that it must be a portable gun of 76mm up there, but also realized that my howitzers could not come close to hitting such a small target. Our 105mm cannons were designed to fire in arcs rather than in a straight line. I took a walk over to a tank that was dug in on the saddle between our company hill position, and got permission to bore-sight their 90mm cannon on the cave. The next night when they saw cannon fire from that cave the tankers fired back, and that was the end of those people. I was a young kid at that time, and enjoyed

---

[2] BC Scope refers to Battery Commander's Telescope, mounted on the wooded aperture framework. This scope with its crosshairs made viewing the target very stable.

doing young kid things like that.

Figure 38 - Tank used in this action.

****

Letter #13

24 June 1953

Dear Pete,

    I'm sorry about the letter I wrote last night. I guess I was a bit nervous, and I really couldn't concentrate on writing.

    As I said probably nothing would happen, and I was right. Joe Chink never came across the valley. The reason for the expected attack last night is that yesterday was the anniversary of one of Jacob Malik's biggest speeches, and the higher-ups thought Joe might want to try something.

    Tomorrow is June 25th, and it will be the start of the 4th year of this police action. We have on our side Chinese Nationals who infiltrate through the Chink lines to gather information. They say the Chinks are planning to hit White Horse, and that was supposed to have come off last night. The last few days have seen much more enemy activity than usual. We've had flares, artillery barrages, smoke screens, etc. thrown at us, but no actual contacts as yet. It's sure strange.

Just after darkness really settled down last night, 3 or 4 Chinks across the valley started yelling indistinguishable words at us. It sounded like they were yelling through megaphones, as it was quite distorted. I did, however, catch the words "G.I.— George Company, and 32nd Infantry Regiment." (I'm attached to George Company). Boy, after we reported that in, my phones wouldn't stop ringing. Everybody and his brother wanted to know what was going on. About an hour later one of the Chinese Nationalists sneaked across the lines, and told us 3 Chink units were moving across the valley. I was really sweating. Every infantryman was awakened, and went to their positions—but it was all called off about midnight. So tonight we sweat all over again.

It's quite difficult to figure out what Joe Chink is thinking of doing. We know he's building supplies up across the valley, but now that we're in the midst of the rainy season it's hard to believe he'll do anything. Today is foggy and rainy, and our planes can't go out and bomb. I can't see over the valley, so it's a perfect day for Joe to move around.

Another buddy of mine from my old outfit transferred up here with me, and is with the 15th AAA. He's sitting on a hill right behind me, and as soon as I can borrow his camera I will send you a better Picture. My camera broke and I haven't been able to get it fixed.

I've got to return to Battalion Headquarters this noon for class, and it will be a pleasure. My boots are falling apart, and the mud and water have soaked me through. Maybe I'll be able to get a shower at the same time. I sure could use one.

I haven't heard the news today, but I don't expect there'll be much of anything new. I heard last night Rhee said he also wants an armistice, but under 3 conditions. I don't know what those conditions are as the G.I. who told me had forgotten, but I do know the 4th condition, and that is to have Rhee commit suicide or let me do it for him.

That man is just a bum and petty thief who climbed up the ladder by crooked means, and he doesn't deserve a thing. He's looking out for his own interests, and seems to have forgotten how much help we have given him. He should be tried as a war criminal—most everybody feels the same as I do, but not all of them want to back out of Korea. I'm not sure just what I want to do about it all. I'm selfish enough to want to save my own skin, but we all have something we owe to the people back home. Yet, how can you want to fight when the Chinks are staring you in the face. 25,0000 more have a knife at your back, the Korean people in arms against you, ROK soldiers fighting on both sides, Korean laborers who signal across the lines, spy on you and cross over the lines, etc., working for you, and then for the enemy .

The soldier over here has a lot to put up with, and his actions should be recognized by all of the people, not just his relatives and friends. I think this is the biggest disgrace of the whole thing. Tell me honey—how many people do you know that really care? Boy, I get mad when I think of that! Well, maybe I'm all wrong. Maybe the people do care—

Have you heard from Steve lately? I wrote him at the address you sent, but haven't heard a word from him. Zeke Levin wrote and said Steve is somewhere in Japan—

Well—Pete—time to run along—Please write often, and don't forget to send me those pictures or that picture—

I miss you and send you all

My love—

Ron

Figure 39 - George Co. 32nd Inf. Reg't positions summer of 1953.
My OP was on the front of the small hill on the right

ஐௐ

In reviewing this letter, I realize that some of my thinking was misguided by my narrow view of what was really going on over there. Syngman Rhee, or as the locals called him Rhee Shing-man, was not a petty crook or anti-American as many of us believed. He was an ardent Nationalist, and really wanted us to attack northwards and retake all of Korea to satisfy his political dreams.

Later on in late June or early July, he released 25,000 enemy POW's behind our lines to force us to do his bidding against North Korea. It sure as hell made us mad, and the comments from our troops were unprintable. We closed our lines, and nothing more was heard of that maneuver, but its memory rankled us all. Remember, we did not have radio or television to bring us the news on a daily basis, and all we really knew was what was happening to us, and nobody else. We heard rumors, of course, but it took days for the true facts to filter on down. Frankly speaking, nobody discussed things except that which pertained to us.

The rains started coming down as it was the beginning of monsoon season, and living underground was not a waterproof world. Fortunately, I had bought a raincoat (military style) while I was on R&R, and I wore it much of the time. At night, raindrops or little pebbles fell from the tunnel roof that led in to the bunker, and being all alone hearing those sounds was frightening. I was sure they were enemy footsteps in the dark. I had a .45 Colt pistol with a round in the chamber and my carbine, also with a round in the chamber, and fifty-nine backup rounds for it both sitting on my windowsill in front of me. I wonder what would have happened if my thoughts all came to fruition.

I asked Pete if she had heard anything from or about my friend Steve, but she never responded to the question that I recall. However, one nice afternoon, between the rainstorms, my phone rang, and of all people, it was Steve himself calling from Japan. I do not know how he found me, but we had a nice long talk. He was in Hokkaido (Northern Japan) listening into Russian broadcasts. To me that was an amazing fact. Steve, because of a slight stuttering habit, sometimes had trouble getting out English words. I imagine that Russian must have caused him some problems.

Steve originally had thoughts of playing baseball for an Army team, but in practice the pitcher struck him out with three consecutive fastballs. Steve said that the glasses the Army gave him didn't work too well, but I think that the pitcher, former big leaguer Harvey Haddix, was just too much for Steve that day. Steve played for Brown University, and had a league leading average as a senior. We all loved Steve in growing up together, and his early passing after the war was a big blow to all his friends.

I can remember writing to Pete after my night watch at the window had ended, and one of the crew came in to relieve me. I was usually too wound up to just sack out, instead I would wrap myself with a blanket over my head and sit in the tunnel while I wrote. I would balance a flashlight on my shoulder, and made sure that no light leaked out to give our position away. Often this would take place after the evening shelling, but at times, I can remember steadying myself when a round fell nearby.

I mentioned in my letter that we had Nationalist Chinese people that would cross our lines at night, and bring us information in what was being planned over there. They were very brave fellows, but we didn't know who might be a double agent or not. One afternoon, I heard over my radio two GI's down below me in the brush talking to each other over their walkie-talkies. They had the call signs of Pigsty 1 and Pigsty 2, and apparently had come across a line crosser hiding in the bushes.

One soldier wanted to bring the agent in right away, and the other thought they should take him along while they finished their reconnaissance. It became quite a debate between them, and in the interim, the line crosser bolted away and ran towards our lines. I do not know which one did it, but someone shot and killed the man, and then that became a problem for the infantry commander to straighten out. I was just an observer, but I often wondered what information the man was bringing to us.

****

Letter #14

Thurs. 2, July

Dear Pete,

No mail from you in quite a while, but maybe it's because you are in transit. I'm writing you, however, in hopes you might appreciate a short note.

Things haven't changed too much since I last wrote. Our sector is still fairly quiet. We had the attack we were expecting when I last wrote, but it was on a very small scale. Joe Chink slammed into Arrowhead Ridge about 800 yards away from me, and clobbered the ROKs. He only threw some artillery at us—no troops. It started about 11 at night, and continued for almost 24 hours.

The outposts changed hands about 5 times, and I was an eyewitness to the whole damned thing. It was the most horrible, and yet exciting, experience of my life. I could see them fighting in the trenches through my field glasses. A lot of ROK soldiers died, but many more Chinks got it. It's quiet over there now, but you can never trust Joe. He still pops artillery at them every so often, and very occasionally a round or two over at us.

It seems the Chinks want peace as much as we do because they are hitting the ROKs only so far. Knock wood, I guess they're trying to impress Rhee with the fact that if the UN pulls out he will never be able to support his army. That's for sure. The ROKs wouldn't last one month if they stood alone against a concerted Chink drive.

Before I used to feel the U.S. was here for a very important reason. I still believe that, but I'm being swayed against that by many factors. Last night, as an example, my company sent out a 25 man patrol to capture a Chink. They no sooner had reached the spot where they were going to wait for the Chinks, when Joe hit them. I'm less than 4 minutes from where one man was killed, and nine others wounded—all seriously.

What in the hell did the patrol accomplish, nothing as far as I can see. I didn't see the boys when they came in, but I did see their clothing. I also saw some Chink stuff they brought in. At least one consoling factor is they got at least 4 Chinks. This Lt. that led the patrol is the luckiest man I've ever met. Two men, one on either side of him were badly wounded. His carbine was shot out of his hands, and a dead Chink hand grenade bounced off his chest. I'll tell you it isn't worth all the hardship some of these people are going through when the enemy is in front and behind you at the same time.

I just wish they'd set up the Peace Conference tent in this little valley in front of me some night. I'd guarantee a truce in less than 15 minutes.

I have a Korean F.O. with me, and he brought 3 men along with him. That makes 7 in this little place, and it's almost impossible to write. I'll write again soon, and will tell you more.

So long till then, Pete,
All my love, always, Ron

P.S. An Infantry Officer that I know, named HULLEY, is a friend of Charlie Watkins!!

ဆာငဢ

This letter was written on July 2, 1953, and I'm sitting here at my desk in May of 2011. I feel like I've just written to Pete, and I can almost see myself at my window in OP38 looking out across the valley and the river beyond. The river is the Yokkok-ch'on, and I think the whole valley is also called the Yokkok-ch'on Valley. It really is not much more than a creek, and I think in a few spots it has gone underground.

One day I saw three enemy soldiers walking down the hill towards the river with towels around their neck like beachgoers on a Sunday afternoon. I wondered what they were saying to each other as it looked like they were having a pretty animated conversation. Either they were crazy to walk out in the open like that, or perhaps they did not realize what they were doing.

I thought that maybe I would give our mortar people something to do that afternoon. They were not as restricted on ammo as much as we were, and they would fire almost any mission you gave them in order to keep their people busy. The mortars I called on were what was known as 4.2 chemical mortars. That is probably an outdated name as of now as we were not using chemicals even then. The 4.2 stands for the size of the shell, which made it almost as large as our 105mm howitzer ammunition. They are very accurate weapons and one can adjust them down to a 12.5' bursting range. It didn't take too long before all three were lying there—dead, I presumed, as they lay there all the rest of the day. The bodies were gone by next morning.

It didn't bother me then, and it doesn't bother me now that I killed them. They would have done the same to me if I had been as stupid as they were. It wasn't too often that we could see the results of our efforts. Most days we did not see anything moving on their side of the line. Only birds, and even then they were not too plentiful. We had heard that they lived mostly underground and hollowed out a number of large caverns on their side of the hills.

We had ammo that used a delayed fuse that allowed the round to burrow into the ground before it detonated, but I don't remember ever calling for that in any of my fire missions. I almost always called for white phosphorous rounds. We used the designation "Willy Peter" as that was the army's phonetic way of using the alphabet. It bursts with a large cloud of white smoke and the material it throws out is like a burning metal. It caused severe burns, and was quite deadly. I understand it is forbidden now to use it against civilians, and the military uses it supposedly for smoke screen types of missions only. I liked it as I could see where my rounds were landing, and if I hit something flammable, like an ammo dump, it usually caused secondary fires, and I knew that I was on target.

The days of summer were long, hot, and quite humid. Not the Korea that most people remember as being snow covered with temperatures way below zero. We wore long sleeved fatigue jackets usually over a t-shirt, and a flak-jacket over that. The flak-jackets were of different materials. Gaynor had one of the newer ones—soft and flexible, but mine was an older type, with plates of a hard material (plastic probably as I don't think Kevlar had been invented at that time). Whatever it was, I hoped it would work if and when it was necessary.

We also wore our helmets all day, and by evening I could hardly hold my head up as I had a stiff neck from wearing that thing. It came in handy, unlike today's one-piece helmet, as ours had a liner we could pull out and use the steel pot for carrying water, or cooking in it. Our pants were of herringbone twill woven cotton and we bloused our pant legs into our boots. Some people did not know how to blouse a boot correctly, and Gaynor said they looked like they were screwed into their boots.

Sanitary conditions on the hill were non-existent. If you had to go, you found a wooden ammo box, and cut a hole in the bottom. You used your entrenching tool, and dug a small hole on the reverse side of the hill. We got toilet paper in our C rations, but often had to supplement that with newsprint from home or the Stars and Stripes. There were no urinals that I recall in the country, but the army implanted 3 or 4-inch plastic pipes into the ground, and scattered them all over the countryside. I recall when I was back near the air base that some of the GI's complained that the Korean people walking by would often stare at the men using these tubes, and so the army put up 3 sided screens of fabric around some of the tubes. That was an answer, except that many of the screens did not even cover you up to your knees. What an army!!!

I described our chow in some letters, but I never mentioned that we also fed a lot of Koreans who worked for us. They ate mostly rice, but our cooks prepared it for them. They appeared to be healthy, and I'm sure most of them gained weight.

One of my favorite memories is of being back at the airbase, and seeing our houseboy, Pak Y Bong running down the hill to the chow tent dressed in his cut down fatigues with his mess kit attached to his belt and all the parts flying around as he banged his way for dinner. After he got to speak a few English words he told us that his parents had been killed accidentally by an American airplane earlier in the war. The first night he lived in our tent we did not have a cot for him, so one of the people suggested he sleep on a stretcher. He cried and cried, and finally made us understand why all the tears. He sobbed "Dead man, Sayonara!" Sayonara in Japanese is "goodbye". We understood and he swapped places with one of the men until we got him a cot.

****

Letter #15

Fri. 10, July

My Dearest Pete,

I'm sorry if my letter frightened you, but you are the only one I can open my thoughts to. I don't dare tell my friends where I am, and especially what I'm doing as I'm afraid my folks might find out the truth.

I have to tell someone about it, however, as it weighs too heavily on my mind.

Last time, honey, when we were waiting for an attack, it never came off. They hit the ROKs just to the right. Tonight, Pete, I'm waiting to move to attack. I'm sure you've read about the battle of Pork Chop in the papers. The 3rd Battalion of my regiment had to go over there, and help out the 17th Regiment. They were practically decimated. We got so badly clobbered they relieved the 17th Regiment, and are replacing it with my regiment. I got a call this morning, and was told to be ready to move.by 5 o'clock tonight. I arrived back in the battery area where I am writing this from. There are 6 F.O. party's [sic] in the tent, and we can't leave the area.

We're all packed, and ready to pull out within 15 minutes. All I'm taking is my rifle, binoculars, map, and radio. I'm not even taking a raincoat. Naturally, we have no blankets or shaving equipment. I don't think we'll attack tonight, as I understand we have to rehearse. There is also a chance we may never have to go, as things seem to be getting better on the "Chop." You can imagine how I'm praying. I'm frightened badly, but can reason why. I have two hunches. The first is, I won't get hit (what G.I. doesn't think that), and second, I don't think they'll need us.

I spent the last 4 days watching hand-to-hand battles through my glasses over on Arrowhead. I've seen all I want.

It is a horrible, horrible thing. You, and everyone else must be forced to realize how awful war is, and then maybe there will be a stronger peace effort.

Darling, you know I would swim from here to California just to see you for a minute if I could. However, when I get home you and I will take one of those summer night drives. We'll put the top down, and the radio on low, and we'll ride, and ride, until we see the sun come up. When you write like that, you make me feel so homesick, lonesome, and blue. But it's the kind of a feeling that warms me through and through. Please keep writing like that.

Nancy, (it's strange why I used that name) I've got to sign off now. Please, darling, pray for me, and the rest, and wish us all luck. Don't worry too much, please—I'll be writing you again in a very few short days. We both know that.

Till then—all my love

Always, Ron

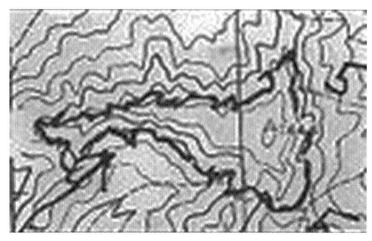

Figure 40 - Topographical map of Pork Chop Hill,
"Rat's Nest" upper right hand side of "pork chop".

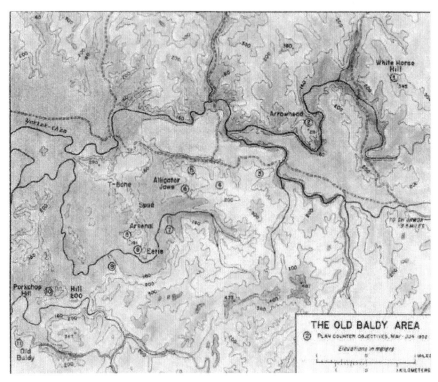

Figure 41 - 7th Infantry Division Area

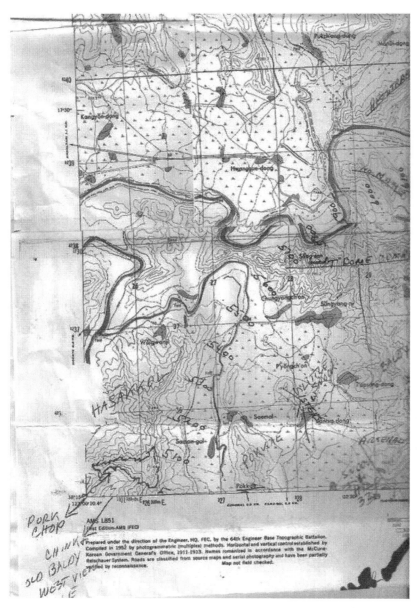

Figure 42 - Our map of battle area

෨Ს

This was a frightening time for me as we all knew about the flap that was going on at Pork Chop and that it was a pretty big to-do. Our sister regiment, the 17th, had been pretty badly mauled, and we were being called to either relieve or support them.

There were five or six FO teams called in and we all met in an empty squad tent in a big field. The only accoutrement was a telephone strapped to one of the main poles. Gough Thompson and I shared some jelly in a squeeze tube on some crackers, and a can of Lobster Bisque, items his family had sent him. He said he was only interested in the lobster, and would I mind if he drained the liquid it was in. Well, neither of us dopes knew that bisque is a liquid not a solid, and so we only had the crackers and jelly.

Soon, the phone rang and one of the FOs was told that he was assigned to a particular infantry company, and that he was to report with his team at once. It was close to sundown when these calls came in so we knew we weren't going over until morning. I was the last one called, and was told that I was to be the forward observer for our regiment. Was I ever thrilled that I didn't get assigned to an infantry unit.

I was told to meet Lt. Ray Barry at 0900 the next morning in an open field behind Hill 347 which was three or four miles down the road towards Pork Chop. Ray and I were to be a team as he was the Liaison Officer for the regiment. The plan was to make our regiment a "Regimental Combat Team" which meant that we were to be comprised of our own infantry, armor, artillery, engineers, etc. It was Ray's job to handle all the messages, etc., between the various units, and coordinate all the action. I, as the FO, was to coordinate all the artillery in that area, and to assign targets to various units.

Ray was a handsome man with blond curly hair, and he was very highly regarded by all the higher brass in the battalion. He was only a first lieutenant, but was the commander of Baker Battery. He was a West Point graduate

Figure 43 - Lt. Ray Barry

of the class of 1951, and carried himself with a real military bearing. Although I had never met the man I had heard about him, and felt that if I were to be in his company that I had received a somewhat signal honor. This was to be my first real combat attack, and I don't think I slept that well as I was quite excited about the whole prospect of the thing. I was really going to see the "elephant" now.

I think that my letter to Pete that night showed my nervousness, and even today it can send shivers up my spine thinking about it. If I was getting "jingly" about the next day, I wonder how those other teams felt about being assigned to assault companies.

Trying to remember who they all were taxes my mind to a degree. There were Thompson, Willy Dixon, Mac Grath, but Dave Hudnut had been sent back to run our ammo truck setup.

Dave was an FO on a hill to my west called The Ice Cream Cone due to its sharp point on top. He was told to set his BC scope up one afternoon to a certain latitude and longitude and be prepared to observe what we called a TOT. That was the acronym for "Time on Target" mission.

That particular setup was quite the exciting thing to watch as it meant that almost every artillery unit in the area was organized to have their rounds land on a target at the same time. There were many artillery units besides our division units in the area, and they were all to participate in the action. As FOs we were all on a "hot loop" telephone line where we could all talk to one another. We were told that the high brass would also be listening on our hot loop, and that meant General Trudeau, our division commander, was on the line.

Finally, we heard all the commands to fire the mission. It was Hudnut's job to be the observer, and we all waited to hear what he had to say. We heard the "splash" telling us all that the rounds would land in about 5 seconds. We then heard Dave say "Splash, wait". That was his way of saying "I'm ready to observe". Well, we all waited and waited but he did not say a thing. Finally a gruff voice said, "Well Lieutenant, what do you have to tell us?" All Hudnut said was "Lost".

We all were dumbfounded. How does one lose a couple of hundred artillery shells exploding out in front of him all at the same moment? The comments I heard on that telephone line are probably still ringing through the Yokkok-chon valley to this day. Hudnut was relieved the next morning and sent to the rear on a miserable detail trucking ammo around. I never saw him or heard from him again.

Letter #16

12 July 1953

Hiya, Honey—

Thank God this letter will reach before the one I wrote last night. I was a pretty frightened person, and I may have injected some of that fright into my letter. When you receive the letter you will understand just what the situation was, but I will try to explain it a little better in this one.

As you know, Joe has grabbed off part of Pork Chop, and the outfits that were there were so badly clobbered that they relieved them, and replaced them with my regiment. We were all pulled off the hill last night, and sent back to the battery area. About 7 or so, just after I finished my letter to you, 3 of the forward observers were called out, and sent to their infantry companies. I was left behind with one other guy.

I got a good night's rest, and at 10 A.M. this morning was notified I was one of the lucky ones. I was to be on an O.P. where the whole counterattack was to be coordinated. I got up there at 12:30 and by 5 o'clock I was on my way down. We were hit by four direct rounds. A major was killed. My buddy was badly wounded, and I got some real tiny shell splinters in my left shoulder. I had a log fall on my left knee, and can hardly move around. I still don't know if anyone knows where I am. I went to the aid station, and then hitchhiked back to the battery area. My knee hurts, I'm still deaf in my right ear, and my head aches like all hell, but I'm lucky—lucky—lucky.

I don't know yet if it's all over or not. They may even call for me to go back up. I'll go I guess, but not willingly. Those kids up there are suffering badly. It isn't worth it. Not for that stinking little piece of ground. It's just not worth the price honey—it's just not worth it. I could cry right now I feel so bad. Not because I hurt, but because of what I've seen this past week. I just want to lie down, and forget it all. I'll never sleep tonight, I'm sure, but I can't let it all bother me. Please Pete—pray it ends—make them end it. They've got to ...

I've seen what I wanted to see. I know now I'll never be

unappreciative of anything anyone does for me. My God—we have
to do something about wars. I don't want my kids to ever see
anything like this at all.

Darling—I'm sorry—I think I'm a bit nervous right now. It'll
be over by tomorrow, and I promise to try and write you, and
square away myself.

Please have yourself a wonderful time, and write me as
often as possible. Your letters mean so much to me I can never
be thankful enough. I hope to be home soon, Pete and we'll make
up for all this time we've lost. Is that a deal?

So—till then, and till tomorrow

Goodnight, and may God bless you always.

My love to you, Ronnie

੪੦੪੪

Although I had spent many an hour under Chinese shelling, I was not
prepared for what I was to face in the next day or two. The morning dawned
bright and clear, as I recall, and I figured the day to be a carbon copy of the day
before. All went as planned until around 1400 (2:00 pm) when I got the call to
pack up my equipment, and be ready to move back to the battery area. All of
the FOs gathered in the large tent got their orders and finally I received mine.

I met Lt. Ray Barry at 0900 the next morning in an open field behind Hill
347 which was three or four miles down the road towards Pork Chop. Ray and
I were to be a team as he was the Liaison Officer for the "Regimental Combat
Team" and handle all the messages, while I was to coordinate all the artillery
in that area, and to assign targets to various units.

Ray and I spread our maps out on a Jeep hood, like in the movies, and that
was the last and only time I saw a map of the area. Around 1030 we were driven
up to the top of that big hill, which I learned was called Hill 347, and Ray
suggested I pick the bunker with the best view of Pork Chop. Most of the
bunkers were filled with men, but I found one with good views of the
surrounding hills, and suggested we use that one. It was OP 13, and I've been
superstitious of that number ever since.

Upon entering we found the bunker had two apertures separated by a 4x4
upright timber. The right side looked somewhat northeast, and the left side was
more or less northerly oriented. Two majors from the 17th Regiment occupied
the right window—a Major Balthes (sp), and the other was Major Billy Fritts

(right) who was an Armor Officer with the 17th Regiment. Ray and I brought three men with us, Fritts had the other major and himself plus a radio operator with him, and there seemed to be a few extraneous soldiers standing by.

It was a large bunker, but handled all these people quite well. My wireman Jim Holt set us up with two telephone lines. Ray had one and I had the other. We were connected directly with the Addickes twins, Clark and Allan, who were stationed at the bottom of the hill and would relay all our commands to the Fire Direction Center. That was where all the information we sent down was collated and converted into information for the gunners back at battery to use in directing their weapons. In our case, eighteen 105 mm howitzers. They were given the azimuth, the elevation, the type of round and fuse to be fired. There were two officers there who ran the operation, Major Hawthorne, and Lt. Jack Arnold. I do not know how they did it, but they fired an awful lot of different units, and were able to keep things all sorted out.

I checked my radio at that time, and found it to work properly, but it had a very limited range possibly because the batteries were old and weak. We were not given maps or told anything about what targets to look for, so I remembered that the Chinese were using a valley on the northeast corner of Pork Chop as a rallying or jump off point. The area was called the "Rats Nest", and I had been told that I did not need to use any command other than "Fire in the Rat's Nest", and that's all that would be necessary.

Figure 44 - Major Billy Fritts

I started firing around 1100, and Ray waited for someone to call him as his job was to liaison with all the mother units that might need our help. It soon became apparent that this was a typical army SNAFU (Situation Normal, All Fouled Up). There we were with no maps, no radio info, such as code names and frequencies, nor did we have any rations with us. We expected however, that there would be a counter attack soon, and we should be ready to do whatever was asked of us.

Up to around 1430 (2:30 pm) the Chinese had only shelled us off and on, and we stayed right at the window as nothing was coming near. At 1430, I noticed an increase in the shelling in our area, and by 1600 (4:00 pm) it was raining incoming. Our wires were blasted out so we had to resort to the radio. I stuck the antenna out of the aperture, but it was to no avail. I could not hear a thing above the din of the bombardment, and so I knelt down below the sill of the window thinking that might give me an opportunity to hear something. I remember starting to rise up, and the next thing I knew I was lying on my face ten or fifteen feet from the window.

I recall getting up on my elbows and saying to myself "Geez! I don't think I'm dead". It was then I found that I could not move my legs, and thought that perhaps they had been blown off. I heard a funny gurgling sound near where my right leg should be and twisted my body around to find that Ray was lying across my legs, and he was why I could not move. His face was near mine to the right, and all I could see what a mass of blood where his head should be. I thought he was slashed across his neck, and that maybe an artery of his jugular vein was cut. I remembered my first aid training–stop the bleeding, cover the wound, and prevent shock. How was I to stop the bleeding? Put a tourniquet around the man's neck. I did not know what to do except call for help. I was deep inside a bunker, and all the noise outside would have drowned me out, and so I wriggled my way out from under Ray, and told him that I was going for help.

I stumbled to the entranceway and screamed at the top of my lungs "Medics! OP 13!" a number of times. The incoming had let up somewhat, but nobody moved in the area to my left where most people should be, and so I ran down the trench to the right until I had made a square circle following the trench line. I kept getting knocked down by nearby incoming, but soon I arrived back at our doorway where I found two medics working on Ray. Major Fritts had been decapitated and lay just off to our right.

One medic bandaged Ray while the other asked me what hurt. I told him my left leg, left shoulder and back was stinging. He cut my left sleeve and pants leg wide open so that he could see where to work. I had only shell splinters, and one gash on my left arm, but I found that I had done something to my left leg and now could not walk on it. Stretcher-bearers came in and Ray was taken outside. I was helped out by the medic, and placed on the ground near him. Soon an APC (armored personnel carrier) arrived, and I was picked up and put into the Assistant Drivers seat, and Ray was on his stretcher across the back of the carrier. We went on a crazy downhill ride to what was the Battalion Aid Station.

Ray was put on a table with what looked like a pool table light above him. The doctors surgically cut off his flak-jacket while I received both a tetanus and some other shot. I heard them say things like "too much blood loss" and "never make it", but very quickly they took us out and Ray was put on a chopper and was flown away. I was taken by ambulance to the Regimental Clearing Station where I was put on a stretcher and I never saw Ray again.

When a corporal came by with a clipboard I asked him where they got the info to send home the telegram, he said that that was his job, and he would be right back to me. I knew I was not that badly hurt, and so when he wasn't looking I rolled off of the stretcher, and using my carbine as sort of a crutch I hobbled out the door to the roadway and stuck out my thumb. I did not want my folks to know I had been hurt, and figured that this was the easiest way to keep them in the dark.

A GI driving by in a jeep picked me up and drove me back to my battery area. Gaynor had heard what had a happened and he was waiting for me to come back. I was filthy. I had been blown into a pile of old charcoal in the bunker, and was covered in soot. He took me to a shower point where a sergeant did not want to give me clean fatigues as the ones I was turning in were all torn up. But we prevailed and I went back to my bed and took a nap until chow time. It was quite a day to remember. We weren't told that the counterattack was called off at 1100 that morning, and that the army was abandoning Pork Chop. Over 340 men were killed and around 1,500 wounded in five days and six nights only to give the hill away. This has always rankled me, although I understand the military aspect of the decision.

Two Medals of Honor were awarded in that flap. Major Fritts received the Distinguished Service Medal, and Ray the Silver Star.

For years, I thought Ray had died of his wounds. Forty-five years later I went on an internet search, and found him … a retired full Bird Colonel living in Colorado. We talked and wrote and relived memories together.

My VA officer suggested that Ray write a letter to the War Department regarding my role, and on Veterans Day, with my mother in attendance, in Punta Gorda, Florida, I also, was awarded the Silver Star.

Figure 45 - Ray Barry's retirement photo.
Note wound scars on right side of his face.

Figure 46 - Article from the Boston Globe about the Silver Star

Figure 47 - (L to R) Ray Kalil, Ron Freedman, Bud Gaynor.

Figure 48 - With Mother at the ceremony.

The President of the United States of America, authorized by Act of Congress, July 9, 1918, has awarded the

SILVER STAR

RONALD K. FREEDMAN
(THEN SECOND LIEUTENANT, UNITED STATES ARMY)

For gallantry in action on 11 July 1953, while assigned as an Artillery Forward Observer on Outpost 13 on Hill 347, while dug in with front-line troops of the 7th Infantry Division at the main line of resistance. Second Lieutenant Freedman's unit, the 48th Field Artillery Battalion, was inflicting massive firepower on the Chinese forces. At the same time the enemy's incoming barrages on his position was devastating. Amid the shellfire, obscuring smoke, flying shrapnel, confusion, chaos and disorder, Lieutenant Freedman, at grave danger to himself, remained steadfast in an exposed position as he skillfully adjusted the crucial barrages from division artillery -- barrages that proved to be vital in turning back the enemy forces. Numerous times Lieutenant Freedman was knocked down by concussions from the incoming shells but was able to get back up and continue directing fire. Finally, Lieutenant Freedman's position received a direct hit that killed everyone in his outpost except himself and the Artillery Liaison Officer who was severely wounded. After examining and encouraging his severely wounded comrade, Lieutenant Freedman, although wounded himself, left the protection of the partially destroyed bunker, and with disregard for his own safety, ran out into the open trenches under an incoming artillery barrage to find medical aid for his severely wounded comrade. The gallant and courageous actions displayed by Lieutenant Freedman reflect the highest traditions of military service, and reflect great credit on himself, the 7th Infantry Regiment, and the United States Army.

Figure 49 - Silver Star Citation (transcription below)

****

The President of the United States of America, authorized by Act of Congress, July 8, 1918, has awarded the

SILVER STAR

RONALD K. FREEDMAN
(THEN SECOND LIEUTENANT, UNITED STATES ARMY)

For gallantry in action on 11 July 1953, while assigned as an Artillery Forward Observer on Outpost 13 on Hill 347, while dug in with front-line troops of the 7th Infantry Division at the main line of resistance. Second Lieutenant Freedman's unit, the 48th Field Artillery Battalion, was inflicting massive firepower on the Chinese forces. At the same time the enemy's incoming barrages on his position was devastating. Amid the shellfire, obscuring smoke, flying shrapnel, confusion, chaos, and disorder, Lieutenant Freedman, at grave danger to himself, remained steadfast in an exposed position as he skillfully adjusted the crucial barrages from division artillery – barrages that proved to be vital in turning back the enemy forces. Numerous times Lieutenant Freedman was knocked down by concussions from the incoming shells but was able to get back up and continue directing fire. Finally, Lieutenant Freedman's position received a direct hit that killed everyone in his outpost except himself and the Artillery Liaison Officer who was severely wounded. After examining and encouraging his severely wounded comrade, Lieutenant Freedman, although wounded himself, left the protection of the partially destroyed bunker, and with disregard for his own safety, ran out into the open trenches under an incoming artillery barrage to find medical aid for his severely wounded comrade. The gallant and courageous actions displayed by Lieutenant Freedman reflect the highest traditions of military service, and reflect great credit on himself, the 7th Infantry Regiment, and the United States Army.

Presented to Ronald K. Freedman on Veteran's Day 2000 at Punta Gorda, FL

****

Figure 50 - Rich Owens (R) VA Officer, Charlotte County, FL; Russell Holland (L) Iwo Jima Veteran and friend in Punta Gorda, Florida.

Figure 51 - Silver Star: Medal & Ribbon

Figure 52 - Purple Heart: Medal & Ribbon

Letter #17

12 July 1953

Hi Treasure,

No letter from you today, but I'm feeling a little blue and lonely, and wanted to write you. I'm still back in the battery area, and pretty thankful for it all—believe me.

Pete, something I've wanted to do of late, and just never had the right words to tell you. I love to write letters to people that warm me. That "warm" is a funny word to use, but I can't think of anything that better describes my feeling when I think of you.

It's strange—we really have never been together for any long periods of time, and most of our phone conversations were always one-sided. "No Ron, I'm sorry, I already have a date." I was never mad at you. I felt disappointed and a little foolish thinking you should ever even think of me. I thought of me. I thought of you often after that time we went out, but so many people told me you were tied up so I just gave up. Why or who told me last November or December you were back at school I can't possibly remember, but I'd like to thank them very much. We got fouled up on that last weekend, but even then I wasn't mad. Just disappointed and feeling foolish once again. To show you I hadn't forgotten you, however, I sent you the Xmas card from the ship. When your answer never came, I naturally figured you just didn't care enough. Still I never forgot you—I wrote you once more, and finally you answered me. You'll never know what that one letter did for my morale!! Now, honey, mail call is the biggest event of the day for it might bring a letter from you.

As I reread what I've said in these last paragraphs, it appears I am making a hero out of myself by my continual use of the word "I" and attached phrases.

Please believe I don't mean it that way. I just want you to know you have been on my mind, and that this isn't something I just dreamed up.

Of all the people I know, you are the only one I can tell the truth to. I feel ashamed of myself for I have no right to subject you to any of the rotten details, but your letters and thoughts of you bolster me so much I can't stop my pen when I sit down to write you.

I pray you really do feel the interest your letters show, and will continue to do so until I come home. Not that I do doubt your sincerity at all, Pete, but I can't help but think you feel sorry for me because I'm over here and how my letters might make you feel, but I honestly don't try to—believe me, honey—!! I want you to know just how I feel because I think you are one of the few people outside of my family that has a real interest in me and what I am doing.

Your job as a teacher is such a vital thing as young children you will instruct can be so easily swayed. You must for God's sake teach them the truth. Those kids could very well be yours or mine in a few years, and I know you feel like I do—only with the truth can we hope to save these kids from what I've seen and done. I've had it real easy compared to a hundred and thirty-seven thousand casualties we have suffered. If those guys could have opened there hearts to people like you I'd feel a lot better in the next few years. Devotion to our country, our jobs, our friends, and to our ideals must be drilled into these kids so they will never falter as they grow. It's like seasoning the wood before you build the house. Do you feel what I'm trying to say? Or do I sound like a fool?

I am so depressed, darling, I don't know which way to turn. I've needed someone to back me, to understand me and you've been so wonderful about it all, words almost fail me. I just can't thank you enough, and tell you how much I appreciate your thoughtfulness. As I said early in the letter—we've never really been together—but in these past few weeks I've gotten to the point where it seems I've always had you behind me. Please—please—accept my deepest gratitude, and realize if nothing ever comes of our letter exchange you have done more to make one lonely guy feel like he's done something worthwhile.

I especially want to thank you because you never once berated me for requesting a transfer up here, while everyone else tore me down for doing so.

To sum it all up—I can't think of a better phrase than perhaps the two oldest words in the world—Thank you! I mean that, Pete, from the bottom of my heart. I didn't finish the bottom of the page as I felt after about 5 minutes of daydreaming that these next few lines would break the train of thought.

I'm glad you took the pocketbook to the wedding, and I'm thrilled everyone liked it. The one thing I don't like about these weddings is all the single males that always attend these weddings. Someday, I'm apt to receive a letter from you telling me about your wedding, and I don't think I'd feel any too happy. After this one in California—please don't go to anymore, or if you do than wear a veil, and a big sign saying "move on Buddy—" But for God's sake remember to take that sign off when I get home!!

I'm not going to say anything about the truce, because I won't believe it until I see it. However, I'll sneak in a quick word, and say it looks and sounds wonderful.

And also do you—

Goodnight, honey—sleep well and think of me as I think of you.

Yours always,

Ronnie

&OCR

At this time I had been relieved of all active duty as I was expected to recover from my injuries in the battery area. The big brass in the battalion and battery let me spend my days on my own, and as my wounds were so minor, it didn't take long for me to get back to being part of the outfit.

I lived in a hoochie that had room for about five or six of us. There was actually a small stream that ran through the floor and out under the front wall. The building (if I can call it that) was made of sandbags, and I cannot remember if there were any windows in it at all. It was cool in the hot humid air that pervaded Korea that summer, but the high moisture content from the stream kept us all damp and uncomfortable. I remember later, when I packed up to go home, I reached into my duffel bag and thought I was pulling out my Ike Jacket. All I got was the collar. The rest had rotted away.

I had plenty of time to write to Pete, and it sounds like I was falling for her without my realizing what was happening. The thought of such a pretty and exciting girl writing to me was almost more than I could believe. Letters from home are such an important part of your existence when you are in a situation like we were. And you can't realize what it means to either answer your name in mail call or slink away if there was no mail for you. I did not have a local newspaper sent to me, but many guys did, and that sufficed for their mail call in some situations.

My commanding officer, 1st Lt. Bill Crouch slept in the hooch along with Lt. Tom Curran, also wounded and resting like I was. Our Exec, Lt. Doug Gleason lived with us, but he was pretty much of a loner so that I never really got to know him.

My favorite bunkmate was Bernard C. Rulong, an old time grizzled World War II veteran. He was a Chief Warrant Officer and his rank was so high in his field that he never should have been assigned to us as he was qualified for a much higher position. Bernie was a fun person, and always had something interesting to say. One night he wrote a letter home to his wife, and when I mentioned that he almost got hit with shrapnel that day, and asked if he were going to tell his wife about the incident. He wrote something down, and then brought the page over to me so that I could see what he had written. It said, "Dear Schatzie (German for sweetie), read the headlines and you will see what I am doing. Love, Bernie".

During the day I spent time in our battery FDC as that would be my position if I were to become battery Executive Officer. Usually a Field Artillery battery travels on its own, and does not use a battalion FDC in most combat situations. Not only did this prepare me for the future, but because I am quite curious I was able to plot other flaps which we could hear occurring at that time. My job was to oversee the operation (the men were all better prepared for their jobs than I was), and to give the firing commands over the phones. Although I did not have much contact with most of the enlisted people in the battery, I did get to know some of the sergeants and corporals fairly well. Most seemed like an intelligent and decent lot, and as we did not have great turnover in our outfit most of them were combat-wise, and knew their jobs backward and forward. We never discussed why we were there, but spent an awful lot of time talking about going home and what we would do when we got there.

Today, people refer to the Korean War (notice I did not say conflict) as the "Forgotten War". That phrase was quite common in our discussions, and was amplified when we read that such and such an action took place. Usually that information was quite late, and buried in the back pages. If we knew people that were hurt in one of those engagements, and even if we didn't know them, we felt that they were being overlooked, and were of no importance. We were so far away from home, and in such an unknown place that it was almost like being on the moon.

Pete made me feel like the moon was part of my world.

Letter #18

Tues., 14 July

Dearest Pete,

Just a dreary rainy day which was very much brightened by a letter from you. You're really quite wonderful to write to me so often. The G.I.s have a new phrase which is used more than any other in their language. The phrase is "cooling it". It means to relax or shy away from heavy work. That is just what I've been doing these past few days—"cooling it". I've done very little, and hope to continue in this state for quite a long time to come.

I was getting over my fright when another wounded F.O. returned to the battery. He is very badly shaken up, and may be sent to a no-combat area. His story is so horrible I will tell you only that he was trapped in a 75 yard tunnel with 190 G.I.s for 14 hours. They were on Pork Chop itself, but luckily most of them were saved. We've been discussing it all over, and now I'm as jumpy as all hell. I'm sure I'll laugh at my nervousness someday, but right now it's a very big part of me. I hope you don't let anyone know I'm telling you these details as most people wouldn't understand my reasons. When I write you about it all, it's like putting my arms around someone and crying it all out. I guess I'm an over-emotional type of person, and I'm sure my actions wouldn't sit well with someone that has a stronger constitution.

I'm enclosing an article about a priest I've come to know up here. He's really quite a guy, and this article tells his story a lot better than I could tell it. Saw him after he hurt his arm. It was at the battalion aid station where we stopped for an hour before going up the hill. We talked for a while and he wouldn't tell me how he hurt his arm. What a guy!! He didn't ever say anything about being on the Chop.

Tom Curran (that other F.O. I mentioned earlier) is sitting opposite me while I'm writing this. He just told me that while he was at the battalion aid station a General came in and told everybody they had intercepted some Chinese radio messages. One said there were only 3 squads (about 30 men) left out of a whole Chinese Regiment that hit Pork Chop. The Chinks were supposed to be screaming to be taken off. The General could have been showing the troops to build up their morale, but it is known we did clobber the Chinks. Tom says out of all the horror he saw, one thing made him happy. He says the Chinks screamed as loud as our boys when they were hit. I've never hated anyone in my whole life—I may have thought I have—but now I know what real hate is like. You can't imagine my feelings toward the Chinese—I know also now why they say that hate and love are akin. There is no bottom to either. I'm sure at some time you've experienced a love, maybe for a doll, a boy, or even a dog, that you thought would never end. Well, that's what a true hate is like—I can't stop sinking into a greater hate for those people—I can't put my feet out and stop. Like I say—there is no bottom— what a feeling!

Before I started writing you so frequently, time went fairly fast, but now every day just drags by. When you mentioned about this girl's fiancé being in Tripoli for 19 months—I shudder. I've been here only $7\frac{1}{2}$, and have almost 8 more to do at the most. Maybe 19 months in Tripoli wasn't so bad a deal. I sure know it would be 100% better than 1 month over here. I really get to feeling blue when I think of summer back home. That quiet, serene feeling one has when a very hot day cools down around twilight and the sky in the distance is lighted by lightning. You may think I'm soft as a grape, but one thing I would rather do than almost anything is ride in a car through a driving thunderstorm—especially late on a summer's night. The sound of rain on a roof softens me like a puppy's whine or the sound of a far-off train whistle. I like lonesome things—and to me those three are the lonesomest sounds in the world.

It's now time for supper, but I'll wait until I hear the 6 P.M. news, then I'll eat, and then I'll come back and keep writing to you—if you don't mind. I'm in a letter-writing mood right now, and I got all my duty letters out of the way earlier in the afternoon— See you after chow—Love always—Ron

Well, now that I've eaten, and heard the news may I say the chow was real good, and the news the opposite.

I don't understand Joe—I'm sure he wants peace yet he hits with 60,000 men. It might be that the setbacks the Reds have suffered in Europe have forced them to gain victories if possible in this area. It's not established but the Chinks might hit our whole line quite hard. I'm being forced to agree with the Korean Admiral (I don't know his name) who said tonight Joe is only playing with us, and is in reality very insincere about a truce.

By the way, I'm going to see the Colonel tomorrow to recommend a medal for that Lt. who got hit quite badly with me up on the hill. He really deserves it as he did something he was told he didn't have to do. He stood by the aperture watching the rounds we were firing while Joe was throwing everything at us. I told him to wait until the barrage was over and so did the battalion commander, but he said it would only be wasting time as our fire was covering the G.I.s trying to get off of the "Chop". It sure was quite a feat in my mind, and quite a few of the higher-ups feel the same way.

Oh, how I pray that this thing will end before it starts all over again.

In regards to your question about getting a few days off I have but one answer—I sure would give anything for it, but that man behind the desk with the stars on his shoulder just says, "no can do." I'm sure you know what I mean. What a wonderful thing it would be to meet you in Hawaii or California! That would really be a dream come true. But—what's the sense of tormenting myself?

The rain is just pelting down now, and everything is a sea of mud. Maybe it will hold Joe back enough for the ROKs to get their balance back.

I've just had another interruption. This one lasted quite a while. We had a meeting of all officers and the top enlisted men.

We talked about the war situation, and discussed plans that have already been setup for a quick move. Apparently someone up high feels Joe is going to really drive in at us. I certainly hope not because when the battery moves back, I'm supposed to move forward, up to my infantry company.

It was mentioned by my battery commander at this meeting that the Chinese Radio in Peiping said today the war would end tomorrow. This is the damnedest thing—Nobody knows or understands just what's going on. I had some ideals when I got here, and now all I want is to get out—go home—I just can't see it. We've done what we started out to do—We've stopped Communist aggression over here, and now we're just sitting around getting stomped on.

Pete—when this is all over, I will come home and tell you some of the feelings and thoughts I haven't told you. I'll tell you some of the things that have happened that I've never mentioned. Those are the things I can't say, not because of security reasons, but because of personal thoughts and reasons. I've told you most of all that has happened, but not everything— Some things just have to wait. I'm sure you understand.

Well, I hope your wedding (the one you're going to) is a real ball, and that you have a wonderful time. I suppose the warm California climate will really add to the occasion, and make the ceremony a very beautiful rite.

I realize you will be busy probably every day and night while you're out there, but a few lines as often as possible would be greatly appreciated.

Take care, my Miss Smith, and remember I think of you all the time, and miss being with you very, very much.

Goodnight, honey—and sleep tight—Let's see, it's now 10 minutes past 10 on the morning of Tuesday, July 14—I'll bet the birds are twittering, the sun is shining, and Miss Nancy Smith of Longmeadow, Massachusetts—schoolteacher—hasn't even opened her eyelids. Hey—write and tell me if I'm right—I'll bet $10 I am—So long honey—

Write me—All my love is yours, Ronnie

ఞఇఙ

I can almost smell powder from exploding shells, and the odors given off by the bakers down near the mess tent. I think I can even conjure up the smell of the C-Rations, especially the franks and beans that were my favorite. The worst smell I remember was the plastic type of odor of the water in a Lister Bag. I really don't know how I existed with only sodas or Yoo Hoo to drink. Strange the things that cross your mind.

I was still resting after my episode on Hill 347. My commander and the colonel asked nothing of me so I spent a lot of time watching the gun crews doing their thing. In addition, I spent a lot of time in the battery FDC trying to polish my skills in that area.

Tom Curran was also recuperating, and we spent a lot of time together counting ammo in the ammo dump or sitting on our cots shooting the breeze. We became good friends, but unfortunately, we neglected to get a hometown address for later use. I know that he was from the Philadelphia area, and a few years ago, I found his name in the Social Security Death Lists. I am not positive it was he, but that person was a Philadelphian.

The rainy season was in full swing, creating many problems for the boys on the hill as well as for the registration of our guns. The hoochies and bunkers on the hill were mostly made of sandbags filled with local dirt. That dirt was heavy with clay and the sandbags had a tendency to flatten under their weight when wet. This caused a lot of construction to fail, and I remember getting a phone call to leave my OP until it could be rebuilt when the rains stopped. I didn't want to stand outside in the rain for 24 hours a day so I just stayed put in my bunker. Part of the rear wall collapsed, but we were still able to make do with the problem. Of course, all this happened prior to the Pork Chop flap.

I remember going to my window on a Monday morning after a weekend of hard rains when we could not even see the enemy hills in front. The sunrise was beautiful, and as I scanned out front, I noticed that the Chinks had built a small building out of white sandbags right out in front of their positions. I called the FDC and told Major Hawthorne. He said that because of the weather that we had to register our guns and that we could use that bunker as a target. He made me hang up and call in a fire mission.

For some reason I wrote down all the corrections which was something I did not normally do, but it was daylight, and I didn't need to worry about blackout conditions. I recall that after I told him where I thought they should fire the first round was "lost". Not unusual, and so I requested "red smoke , repeat range" which told them to fire a red smoke round and use the same setting that I originally gave him. I was told "Splash" which meant the FDC was telling me the round would land very shortly. I observed the red smoke about 1000 yard off to the right and maybe 300 yards above the target level. My correction was "left 1000, drop 300", and soon we were getting close to the target.

My phone rang and it was Major Hawthorne telling me to "Cease Fire". Normally, I would be the one to give that command as I was the only one who could see what was going on, but when a major says curtly "Cease Fire, Lt." I did what I was told. Soon he called back and had me recap my corrections. As I said I had written them down, and I think he was as astounded as I was that I could rattle them right off. After an hour or so, he called and said he was sending his jeep for me, and that I should report to him.

We drove back to the FDC, and I reported in. "Come with me, Lt. I want you to see what you did." He took me to a shell hole a number of yards away and said "You did that, and you are now known as Short Round Charlie"

He reconstructed for the chain of events that had just occurred. Our division was used to train Korean soldiers in artillery methods, and the novices were mixed in with our gun crews. Each 105mm artillery shell has between four and seven bags or charges of powder to be used when firing a shell. The number of charges is predicated on the distance to be calculated. On the weekend before this incident my battery had been firing at close range, and we were only using charge 4s. At the end of a fire mission, the crew is supposed to see that each round has seven charges, but in this case, the young Korean did not know this system. He put the round on the ready rack with only a charge four in it, and it happened to be the round that they used to fire my "lost" round with. Everything worked fine except the round only went a short distance and landed in the Staff Officers latrine, blowing it to pieces. Fortunately, no one was in there, and it became a joke. I don't remember whether we ever finished using that bunker for a registration, but it was not there the next day.

Pete was always in the back of my mind. I thought about her day and night, but only had those two occasions to remember. The first time we met was a blind date where I took her to a friend's nightclub. It was called Storyville, and was a Dixieland Jazz Mecca in Boston. George Wein owned it, and as I had known him from home, he met us at the door and seated us down front right next to the bandstand. It was not her idea of a fun place as she was suffering from a wisdom tooth removal that night.

I kept bringing up the memory of her wearing a Mouton coat while trying to enjoy the evening, but because of her lack of interest in me and anything I might have been involved in, I decided to classify her in my "gone but not forgotten" list of girls I had known. Her pretty face kept me interested for a while after that, but I had other things to do and see at that time.

I was a major in Public Relations through the medium of Television and Film at Boston University and was in my senior year. The department was brand new, and lacked many of the necessities that would have made TV production our basic course. We did a lot of filming and still photography work at that time. The cameras we used were the old Speed Graphics with flash attachments. It was great quality equipment, but big and hard to handle.

The Korean War broke on the 25th of June in my junior year, and in looking back I find it hard to believe we were still in school when that happened. It was only five years since WWII had ended, and here we were back at it again. Being young, I did not have the experience older people had regarding life, and sort of thought it would be a lark to be drafted, but we were all issued deferments to finish our schooling. Besides, the U.S. Army will clobber those North Koreans in just a few weeks, and it will all be over soon. Boy! Was I ever wrong!

Figure 53 - L-R John Christopher, Ron (with mustache), and ROK soldiers typical of those assigned to the O.P.

Letter #19

Wed. 15, July

Hi—

    Surprised I'm writing so often? I'm not—I enjoy it—If I'm snowing you under with mail, don't say anything about it because I won't stop. I know something good when I see it, and I'm pretty tenacious. At least I think so—

    Maybe you can notice by the first paragraph I'm in a pretty good mood. Even though the news isn't promising, I have a crazy hunch that truce will be with us very, very, soon. Maybe by the time this gets to you. Another reason for my good mood is the fact the sun came out this afternoon, and brought me four letters from my buddies. They hadn't written for so long, and I was afraid I might be losing contact with them.

They've all finished school now, and those that aren't in the service are on their way. It will be funny to get home, and find them not around. I'll miss them quite a bit, but it will allow me more time to spend with certain other people. I can get along with just a line from the boys as long as I know they're all right, but there are certain people I'm going to have to see in person. My relatives are the majority of this group—a couple of married friends and their children, and maybe a certain other person. I don't want to seem to be a pest of sorts, but, honey, when I get home I'm going to do some heavy pestering to a young lady named Smith. If she, at this time, has no desire to be pestered, then I advise her to start running now because the minute that ship docks, and the gang plank touches the pier I'm going to start chasing her. I think I told her in my last letter to buy a new pair of track shoes. If she's going to do it, she'd better start now, because the time for me to head home is not too—too distant.

By the way—teacher—I wrote a letter once to this particular Miss Smith, and we made a deal in which she was supposed to send me a picture. Just before she left for California she wrote a letter in which she said she would send one after she arrived out on the coast. She also wrote a very puzzling sentence. After she said that she didn't have any pictures at the present time, but she would send one after she reached California—she wrote, and I quote—"However, that shouldn't hold you back"—unquote. Maybe I'm slow and a little stupid, but I don't understand. I think I do, but I don't want to get into hot water because of a misunderstood statement. Do you think you might be able to persuade this young school marm to straighten out this poor, bewildered, tired old, soldier? I sure would be thankful.

Now that I've played around for two and a half pages it's about time I sort of quieted down—don't you think—I may have sounded sort of silly in these few preceding paragraphs, but actually all I said was true!!

It's a very funny thing to me, Pete—I sort of feel like I'm imposing with all my mail. I always did overdo things too much and was sorry in the end. It's like a lady who was told she had some very beautiful articles in her house; she promptly filled the house up with everything she could find, and pretty soon nobody would come to her house as it was full of junk. She overdid it!!

I can be like that—I know, and in this particular case I don't want to be—I very much don't want to be—so the minute I get on your nerves—I want you to tell me, and I promise to straighten up.

It's fairly hard for a guy in my position to get a situation like ours is, straightened out in his mind. I have always felt you were writing because you really felt an interest, and yet I've always harbored the suspicion you were just trying to be nice to a guy who is far away from home. Don't ever—ever think I don't appreciate it—no matter how you feel—because I'll just have to take you across my knee, and slap the daylights out of you when I get home.

I'm a pretty funny guy to understand. I'm sure of that—I'm moody—emotional—and probably the biggest day dreamer you've ever met or will ever meet. I irritate many people I'm sure, but have never met anyone I didn't like. I find something in everybody that impresses me, and never allow anything bad to overshadow my good impressions. One of my closet friends is always chewing me out because I'm that way. He calls me soft, and too easy. He may be right—People do need to get tough at times, but I just could never be that way. Once again my idle dreaming is a fault. It seems to me the world could be a lot happier if bad faults were overlooked sometimes.

A little insight to my feelings might straighten you out on a few of your questions you've probably formed in your mind.

Pete, I don't know anything about you other than the fact you appear to be interested in what is actually happening over here. You don't realize how happy that makes me feel, I'm sure, but I'm selfish and think maybe you're interested in my welfare just a little bit more than you are in the others that are over here. To think someone cares is a wonderful—wonderful feeling. It makes a dark—dreary day seem like the sun is trying to break through. I've sat through a few long and scary hours, especially at night, over here, and kept my mind and heart occupied with just thoughts of you. My only worry at those times was that you might not appreciate some of the endearing words or overfriendly terms I might use. I'd really feel terrible if I found out I was offending you—yet I would rather have you tell me you'd rather I didn't write as I did than not say anything at all.

Do you understand me a little better now than you did before? I certainly hope so. I'm in a writing mood, and nothing is going to stop me now—

I'll tell you more about myself, but I expect you to do the same—It will be another one of our deals.

Here's something I've never told anyone—I've hardly ever even dared mention it to myself—But I'm afraid I might not be thought to be all there, if I told anyone. Why I should tell you—a person I really only know on paper—is a very strange thing—I guess you just do something to me—I'm not complaining, either.

Would you think me weird if I told you certain things send actual shivers up and down my spine? Small things such as, I got to a movie, and at the end when the hero finally finds the heroine, and is amazed to see her alive—I get a shiver. In actual life when I see, for example, a seeing-eye dog—I get a shiver. I don't know why—that's the reason I don't ever like to think about it! Do you have an explanation?

If I've caused my parents grief, and if I've made enemies of my relatives because they found out I requested a transfer up here—I don't care—(that's not fair, is it?). I've proved one thing to myself—something I've always feared. That is—that I couldn't stand real fear—I found it is completely different from what I expected.

When I've been in a sweat—I've actually had my knees shaking so hard everything around me vibrated—or so it seemed. Then I found everyone else was shaking as hard as I was. My throat has constricted, and it hurt to swallow. Sweat poured out of me—panic ran through me right out of my fingertips. I couldn't even turn a flashlight on at one time. I was more afraid of being more afraid than anyone else. Then I found out everyone else felt the same way. All these moments of fear always lasted only until something actually happened. As soon as it did—then everything straightened itself out—I was too busy to be frightened.

After it was all over—I laughed at myself for my foolish

actions—and so did everyone else. I felt good—I was almost exhilarated. I stuck it out—It wasn't so bad—that's the way I felt after I got hurt—why—there's almost nothing to it. Then—after a while I got to thinking again—I said to myself, this sort of thing has happened before—why should it bother you so much each time? I've never found an answer. My only explanation is, I'm no different than anyone else. We all shake and quiver equally as much, and when it's all over we all feel as equally happy nothing happened to us.

Fear is a funny damned thing. When Lt. Barry fell across me—I had to get out from under him. I got myself out, and went for help. No, Pete—I didn't go honorably—It wasn't really to get help. I was so damned frightened after seeing that, I just had to get out of that place. I couldn't walk on my leg, but I didn't know that at the time. I just had to get out of there! Fear did it to me. I never even thought for a minute it was more dangerous to go outside. I just had to go—thank God for my mental state that I went back there—It proved to me I wasn't a coward.

That is one thing everyone must prove to themselves at one time or another. I know now how deep the workings of the mind are, deeper than any mortal will ever reach. It's strengthened my faith in something more powerful than man. I was an atheist before that day, but now I'm sure something more powerful or convincing than man made me do what I did. Are you as ashamed of me as I am of myself? Do you think I did wrong? I don't because something other than my own reasoning made me go. Everyone says I did the right thing by going for aid, but nobody but you, and I and God knows why I really went.

One thing, however, honey—that I'm pretty happy about is the fact I returned to the place, and most of all that I offered to stay after everyone left—I volunteered to stay only because I was ashamed I had left this place earlier. A Major ordered me to leave the hill. He said there was nothing further anyone could do. It made me feel like a human once again.

The human mind is a very involved mechanism. One fellow in our battery—an enlisted man—was with that F.O. I mentioned in another letter. He was trapped in that trench for 14 hours. They really had it rough. Believe me. This enlisted man—His name is Darnell. He told me what he did—only because he wanted to get it off his chest. He wanted someone to understand what was bothering him. He said he picked up wounded men—dismembered limbs, and worked through the 14 hours solid only because he was too afraid to do anything else. He too feels he was a coward because when the help finally arrived, he was one of the first to leave. He's to be decorated with the Silver Star for his bravery, however—<u>He deserves it</u>—as he says—"When it came time to leave—I just gave up—I couldn't stand it any longer—I had to get out of there."

You see—he felt like I did. He was so frightened he kept working all night to forget his fear. Even today you can actually see fear in his eyes. Yet, I would want that boy with me wherever I went. We're all proud of him, and can understand his feelings, but he's like me—He's not proud of himself.

Honey—do you see why I'm learning to hate like I told you I was. See what it does to people?

Well—enough—Let's put it this way and leave well enough alone. To understand me you must read between the lines. You'll find some very strange things written there. One sentence should be very outstanding, although it is completely invisible. That is, that I need your comfort—your faith, and especially your assurance. You mean ever so very much to me that I'll be in your debt always.

Pete, why do I write these things to you? Things I'm afraid to say to myself. I hardly know you. What irks me most is, after the letter is all written, and the envelope is sealed I still can rip it all up. I've calmed down by then—but still I mail it—what right do I have to torment you with my troubles?

Once again I beg you to forgive my extreme impositions and over familiarity, I don't know what's wrong with me.

Take care, kitten—and think of me—If I know that you are than these days go faster, and the nights don't seem so bad—Dusk and the time until I fall asleep are my worst hours—Sure wish I was one of these don't-give-a-damn kind of people. I'd be one hell of a lot better off. So would you …

G' night now—sleep well, and have a good tomorrow—maybe it will end then.

Can't think of how to end this except by saying, you're wonderful to take all this from me—I'll never-never forget you.

Promise you I won't—my deepest love to you,

And always I'll be yours, Ronnie

૭ᎧᏟᏸ

I never realized that I wrote such long letters until I started to reread the ones I wrote to Pete. I remember letting my thinking just flow to the paper as it came to me. It just seemed that I had known her all my life and that I could confide in her, as I had never done with anyone before. I guess I was falling for her, although I remember telling myself that that should not happen, as we truly did not know each other.

I told myself that I would wait until I got home before I made any decisions of that nature. She was, however, on my mind constantly as she is even until this day. As I write this I have now known her for fifty-eight years, and I still feel as I did then. But, enough of that stuff right now, as my thoughts should be on what I was doing all those years ago.

I had been sent to a Battery Executive Officers Course where I lived with around fifteen Marine lieutenants who were also taking the course. I forget where it took place, but it was some distance away. One night "Bed-check Charlie" flew his biplane down to our area. He flew so low that I could have hit him with a canoe paddle if I'd had one.

That got my tent mates all hopped up, and some of them started throwing bayonets around. Some Marines are either crazy or bored silly. Although we were not privy to the thinking of the high brass we all felt that the war would end soon, and we were counting the minutes. The rains were slowing down, and normal military life continued as before.

I was still limping on my bad knee, and so I took advantage of the situation by getting off my feet as much as possible. I was still given the job of counting ammo in the ammo dump, and running the battery FDC whenever we were involved in a flap. I often thought of Major Fritts, and was glad that he never knew what hit him. When I was hit and knocked out, I never knew what hit me, but if I had died like the major did, it would have been over just like that.

Ray Barry, on the other hand, was hit and knocked out, but when he came to, he knew he was in serious trouble, and that he couldn't help himself. Then he had the medics to bandage him up, which must have given him some solace, but the time it took to get us down the mountain side was, I am sure, intolerably long for him.

Years later, after we talked and wrote each other, he told me that he hadn't thought he would make it until somebody told him that he had great doctors working on him, and that all he had to do was believe in them and himself and that he would come through the ordeal.

He said he did not remember seeing anyone, but felt sure that it was a chaplain who spoke to him. He was sent home and ended up in San Antonio at Brooks Army Hospital where he spent a year recuperating. He told me that they fitted him for some kind of prosthetic for his palate, and over the phone, he removed it and said a few words to me. In all truth, I did not understand a word he said, but before his wound, I had a terrible time understanding his Oklahoma accent.

He wrote me and thanked me for saving his life. Although, I never thought of my actions in that sense it gave me great pleasure to read those words. If my children go through all the paperwork I have kept, they will find that letter, and I am sure they will be as pleased to read it as I did. I'm skipping ahead, but Ray and I formed a close bond on that day, and we remained friends for a long time.

I lost track of him for a while until I found him and his wife back near Denver. He moved back to the San Antonio area from Colorado, so that he could play a lot of golf. I called many times, but never got an answer. I looked up the West Point site on the computer, and found that he had passed away about a week before I found out he'd again been living outside of Denver.

He was about 80-years-old at that time, and had retired from the Army as a full Colonel. Two other friends of mine also retired as full Colonels. One was Lamar Daugherty and he and I were 2nd Lieutenants together back in Cape Cod. The other was John Brosnan.

Lamar's full name is Lucius Lamar Daugherty III, but we all called him either Lamar or Doc. Over his term of service, he has met a few people I know, and I discovered that they all called him Lu. If I saw him today I would probably call him "hey you". Lamar was in at the end of the World War II, and came home to graduate from Princeton. He went back in the Army, and that is where I met him. He wanted to make a career out of the military, and he did quite well for himself. He now lives in Douglasville, Texas, and adopted a Korean boy whom he brought to the USA.

John Brosnan's parents immigrated from Killarney, Ireland to the New York City area where John was born. His father died when John was four years old, and so his mother took him back to Killarney where he grew up. Realizing that he did not have a great future in Ireland, he opted to join the U.S. Army in Belgium, I think. John was smart enough to make it through OCS, and I also met him at Cape Cod. When Korea was over, he became a helicopter pilot. He also learned to fly fixed wing aircraft, and once came to my hometown in an Army plane and flew Bud Gaynor and me up to Lowell, Mass to see another Army friend, Bob Huntley. John also fought in Vietnam, and retired as a full Colonel.

Figure 54 - John Brosnan & Bud Gaynor

He went back to Killarney where he now lives. Pete, (now called Nancy) and I visited him over there, and had a marvelous weekend at his cottage down at the tip end of County Kerry. John has done very well for himself in Real Estate and other projects, which leads me to call him the King of Kerry.

I made many friends while I was over there, and have maintained contact with them ever since. Bud Gaynor and I met the second day at Camp Kilmer Reception Center and spent the next year side by side through all our training. After commissioning, we both went to Cape Cod, and saw each other practically every day. Bud became our anti-aircraft support as his unit was assigned to our battalion as backup. He was on the hill just behind mine, and often came up to my OP to bring me boots or underwear or whatever else I needed.

We have stayed in contact often, and in 2006, Bud and I went back to Korea on a "revisit program" supported by the Korean Government. Because it was the anniversary week of the start of the war we visited venues primarily in the Seoul area. We did get up to the truce site in Panmunjom, which we both found quite interesting. We wanted to go up near the MLR, but our Korean hosts did not give us an opportunity.

One afternoon, while at a Korean Army demo, I felt the heat and we both agreed to go back and sit in the air conditioned bus. As we were walking along, a thin, short U.S. Army Captain wearing the new photographic print fatigues (now called BDU's, or battle dress uniforms) stopped me.

"You're Jewish, aren't you?"

He must have seen my name tag, but jokingly, I answered, "No, my dad says we are Southern Greeks."

He laughed, and said, "I can tell that you are Jewish by your *Yiddishe punim* (Jewish face).

"I always thought I looked Mediterranean, but more Italian than anything else.

He introduced himself as Rabbi Horowitz, and told us that he was the only Rabbi in Korea, and because it was Friday he would like me to attend his Friday night services in downtown Seoul (at the Wonsan Encampment area devoted to the U.S. Army).

Again, in a joking manner I told him that I was with my Irish friend, and that he was an anti-Semite.

But the Rabbi said, "We'll have a good meal and drinks afterwards."

This impressed Bud enough to say, "I'll go".

I thought about the offer, and dropped my joking manner when I told the Rabbi that I couldn't participate as I had never had a Bar Mitzvah. (I came from a non-religious background), but he told me that if I attended that night he would Bar Mitzvah me.

And so, we went. There were more Korean Jews there than westerners, and Bud and I had a good time, even without all the gifts a Bar Mitzvah boy should get.

I have included the photo of me that one of the Korean Jewish men took with the smallest Polaroid I have ever seen.

Figure 55 - My Bar Mitzvah

Letter #20

Fri., 17 July

How do you do?

If you don't think I'm not amazed at myself for writing without answers so frequently—then you're in for a surprise. I don't know what's got into my pen, but it must be a new type of want-to-write-ink. The damned pen just goes by itself. I've always liked to write, but I've never written as much as I have in the past six or seven months. No complaints, however, as long as I get some in return.

Right at the present moment I'm Duty Officer in the Battery Fire Direction Center, or FDC as it is known. This is the place where all the commands are issued to actually fire the guns. The book says that normally the Forward Observer will send their fire missions directly to the Battery FDC, but in a static situation such as this, the Battalion FDC does all the computations, and sends the data down to us. We repeat it to the gun, and fire them. Every so often they let us plot our own mission to keep us from getting rusty. It's very interesting, but not half the fun as being an F.O.

Man, I eat that stuff up—provided Joe isn't shooting back at you. Sometimes, I used to pick out an old abandoned Chink bunker, and call up the Battalion FDC and tell them I've just found out Joe has reactivated that old bunker, and I want to fire at it. That way, I could practice, and also spend an enjoyable afternoon.

Being a good F.O. takes a lot of time, patience and practice. It comes naturally to some people, and to some it's harder than all hell. You have to have good depth perception, a quick mind, be a good judge of distances, and above all you have to have a cool nature. That's very important, as the idea of the whole thing is to get fast and accurate fire out there in a minimum amount of time. A man that gets excited usually gets all fouled up, and his fire mission is usually too late or very inaccurate. It's not too easy to keep your wits about you when you see those slant-eyed idiots out in the open. You forget everything except that you want to clobber them as fast as possible.

Sometimes the F.O.s get so excited when they see Joe out in plain view (a rarity—believe me) that they scream anything that comes to mind over the radio or phones. The language one hears is really funny at times. The other day on Chop—MacGrath was shooting at some Chinks in a trench. He didn't push the panic button, and was using excellent radio procedure throughout. He even went so far as to use the complete call sign "Blind Date Easy 5" before he said his number. We all remarked that something must have come over Mac as he had never been so military-like before. He ruined his reputation, however, when he was asked for surveillance of target "after he gave cease-fire". His answer was quick, concise, and really to the point. He didn't use a call sign or even his number. He just blurted out in a happy-sounding voice—"Christ, you clobbered the hell out of those ____'s." We all got a good laugh out of that.

It's funny now how things are really going to be with me the rest of my life. I mean little things like that call sign we used. I'll never say the words "blind date" any more without thinking of that day. Same with the word "Pork Chop" or even "Bone." "Bone" is the call name of our battalion. Each outfit over here has a call name like you have telephone exchanges back in the states. Every unit in the 7th Division has a call sign beginning with the letter "B". The division has been called the "Bayonet" Division for quite a few years now, and ever since it's been in Korea its call name has been "Bayonet". The 48th is "Bone", and the Engineers of the 7th Div. have the name of "Bulldozer" for example.

Making a phone call over here can sometimes be exasperating as well as humorous. If I wanted to call my old outfit this is what I would have to go through if I went the long way around. The short way would be two switchboards less. I'd go from Bone Charlie (the battery) to Bone (battalion) to Boss (Division Artillery) to Bayonet (division) to Jackson (corps switchboard) to Victor (Seoul) to Crocus (air airbase near my old outfit) to Cocktail tall (my old air base) to Cocktail (the intra-base switch board) and finally to Noose Baker (my old battery). That's quite a hookup, isn't it? Don't know if it particularly interests you, but I haven't got much of interest to say tonight as it was a very quiet day, and I feel like writing a little bit.

The news today has been so-so. I guess we're pushing the Reds back over to our East, but being the damned selfish G.I.'s that we are, we're more interested in what Joe might try to pull over in our area tonight. I guess the brass thinks he might try something to take some of the strain off the ROK push over to our right. Sure hope Joe decides to sit it out tonight as it's been a hot, hot day, and I'm quite tired.

The hot rumor is that tomorrow is the day they'll sign the peace treaty, but I'm not putting too much faith in it as I've been disappointed too many times before.

I've been drinking lukewarm beer all night trying to cool off. (We can't get extra ice to freeze the stuff). It reminded me of the promise of lobster and beer you made me, and I've suddenly developed a tremendous craving for lobster and beer. I'll bet I could get 2 dozen lobsters right now, and drink a case of beer with each one—Don't believe it?? I'm telling you I honestly think I could—I'd give it one hell of a try—anyway.

I'm enclosing a couple of clippings that are slightly out dated, and which you might have already seen. They describe, however, my feelings almost to a "T". I guess I'm just like any other G.I. in my feelings—

I've tried to keep away from my usual morbid type of letter tonight, as I'm sure they don't improve your morale. I'm sure you welcome the change—

The mail has suddenly stopped. All I've had the last two days are some old letters sent to my old outfit, and a delayed package. Sure hope you haven't been too busy to write me. I keep hoping each day will bring some sort of mail from you. Especially those pictures!!

I told you I was tenacious—and I can get worse—

Hey Pete—I'm gonna flake out for tonight, but even though I'm closing this letter—I don't think I'll be forgetting you tonight for quite a while.

Take care, honey, and make sure you're only a bridesmaid at this wedding. Please give the lucky two my long distance and belated congratulations. Goodnight, honey—miss you

Love always, your Ron

ৰ০তক

Letter #20 was written on the 17th of July 1953. I'm quite sure that the info I sent to Pete regarding the telephone connections were beyond her interest, but I just rambled on as I wrote, and hoped she would accept all of it as if I were really talking to her. Although our field telephones were of World War II vintage, heavy and cumbersome to carry, they managed to work well, especially in the rear areas where the lines were protected from being cut or run over by vehicles.

On the hill, it was a different story. Shellfire was quite often the problem. Shrapnel cut the wires easily as most of them just lay on the ground. Also, wet weather caused us many crossed lines, and quite often you got more than one conversation at a time. I recall a rainy night when I received a phone call to pick up Line 2 at 1600 for an explanation where that evening's patrol needed preplanned concentrations.

When I did pick up the phone, I heard someone say "they're at the bottom of the hill, Captain".

I said, "Who's at the bottom of the hill? Chinks?" Just as I said that two other FOs picked up their phones and heard only the remark that there were Chinks at the bottom of the hill. They both immediately got on their other lines and called the FDC to prepare to fire defensive fires circling our hills. We called those missions "Flash Fires", and they were designed to encompass an area with air bursts to drive the enemy back.

Fortunately, we got the problem straightened out when I learned that the mess Sergeant was telling his Captain that the Chow trucks had just arrived at the bottom of the hill. The wet weather had caused our lines to cross, and I almost started a major flap over nothing.

When I think about flash fires, I think about the command when one of our positions was over run. The FO supposedly sent this final message as he called fire in on himself: "When you no longer hear my voice, your range is correct." Even today, when I read those words, although the story is probably just a story, it sends shivers down my spine.

Firing at targets was almost like being in a shooting gallery at an amusement park. I don't recall ever thinking about the death or destruction I was creating, I was only concerned with my ability to get on target as fast as possible.

One morning, I awoke to see what looked like a rectangular opening in the front wall of the Lower Horseshoe, which was to my immediate front. Although it was larger than it looked at that distance, I thought the Chinese had opened a horizontal door in the hillside. I could see movement inside as they were wearing white uniforms. We use to joke that the enemy across from us were what we called "Mongolian Marines". We rarely saw them, but when we did, they all seemed to be very big men, not your typical Chinese "shorty".

I called in a fire mission on the target, but could only drop in a few rounds near the opening without any effect. My sergeant heard all the noise and came running down to the OP to find out what I was doing. When I let him see the target through my BC Scope he asked if he could call in a mission. I agreed, and the first round he fired went right into the opening.

He looked at me and said, "That's how to do it, Lieutenant," and walked away.

The Chinks closed up the opening right after that, but I'm sure we did some damage. Those people were known to dig out hills and use them as shelters. They had the manpower. They had a very poor transportation system and hand carried everything all over at night on their backs.

We, of course, had every type of vehicle to carry our goods for us and our rear area was always buzzing with noise and traffic. We used various colored panels to mark out our areas so that our fliers knew who and where we were. Even so, we sometimes got strafed and bombed by our own planes. I remember when a group of Marines were playing volleyball and a number of them were machine gunned down by one of our fliers. We never found out any more about that situation. Fortunately, this was a rarity.

The weather was very much like home during the summer. The 38th parallel also runs through lower Pennsylvania and Maryland and we were only a few miles north of that line. High heat and high humidity, and of course we had no method of cooling down other than a shower. We had what was known as a "shower point" a few miles down the road from the battery area, and when you went in you removed your brass, belt and boots, and kept them separate from your underwear and fatigues. After the shower you were issued brand new underwear and a brand new uniform. We were told that our used clothing was given to the South Korean Army for their use.

If there had been a particularly strong rainstorm, the water taken from a local river or stream was quite muddy or sandy and I often felt dirtier after the shower. The relief from the heat was worth all the trouble and effort, however.

Unlike the army in the WWII, we had air mattresses to sleep on and a folding cot to keep us off the ground. During the winter we all had down sleeping bags made in a "mummy" style, but in the summer they were too hot to sleep on, not in, and so we used to sleep on our air mattresses. They were made of plastic and the humidity made them stick to your body. Some people just slept on the canvas cot, but I used to turn my poncho over to the fabric side and slept on that.

I almost always slept fully clothed and with my boots on at night when I was up on the hill. During the heavy rains, I even wore the raincoat I bought in Japan on R&R. And I didn't remove my flak jacket, either, as I became quite used to wearing it. I thought I would never get used to wearing my helmet, although its weight was not that great. However, it was enough to give me neck aches at the end of the day. After a while even that became comfortable. I remember the strange feeling after the first few days of the truce when we didn't have to wear them any longer. I was almost light headed.

The summer of 1953 was miserable from a weather standpoint, but the thought of a nearing truce kept us hopeful and happy as could be expected under those circumstances.

Figure 56 - Shell landing on Hasakkol Ridge behind Pork Chop.

Letter #21

Sunday, 19 July

Dearest Pete,

Today started out to be one of the nicest I've had over here. It was a nice, warm, clear summer morning, and we were expecting to get the afternoon off. A letter from you was handed to me, and that made everything just right. I even thought they might sign the cease-fire this afternoon. As it stands right now, we all missed the newscast, and are still in the dark.

After dinner, I went back to our hoochie, took off my shirt, and tried to cool down. No sooner had I got comfortable than I was told to see that the motor pool and mess hall were squared away as the new commanding general of the Division Artillery was on his way over to inspect us. After I sweated up a storm, got things pretty well cleaned up—the general arrived. He looked at one gun pit, remarked on the heat of the sun, and then took off. Needless to say, I was quite thoroughly disgusted. At 5 of 6 we had an officer's call, and I was informed I had better check all my F.O. equipment as I was still Reserve F.O. for Blue Battalion. It seems we're expecting the Chinks to hit the Arsenal outpost tonight, and I've got to be ready. I don't know, this is about the third time the brass has pushed the panic button this week, and I'm getting sick and tired of it all. If I was shaky a week ago Friday night, then I'm twice as shaky now. In all truthfulness, I don't really think they'll call me out, but one never knows. Nevertheless, if I do go—I'm sure I'll be back in a few days quite safe and well.

Well—here it is now 9:30 P.M., and I was writing this at 7 P.M., originally. I'm no longer in C Battery area. I am now in the BOQ (bachelor officers quarter) of King Company. After I finished the last paragraph, I was told to pack up and move out. I went down to Battalion HQ, picked up a new map, radio, and field glasses, and reported directly here. These people know absolutely nothing of any Chink attack. See, I told you somebody pushed the panic button. Well, if nothing happens before 12, I'll be much happier, 'cause I don't think Joe will come after that.

Sweetheart, you'll never know what all this panicking, button pushing, scaring, and general all around messing up does to a person's nerves (pardon the paper, I had to borrow it, and the guy had nothing else). Some night when we're out riding, and the moon is full, the breeze is warm, and I'm in a talkative mood, I'll try to tell you exactly what went through my mind when things occurred. It would be impossible to write it all down.

I was just told Joe agreed to sign the truce, and that the negotiators are working on it right now. Darling, if that's true, all this worry and sweat will then be worth it!!

To get back to the same side of life—I just reread your letter, and I have one thing to say right away—No honey, "getting married isn't too awful bad after all."

You mentioned your full moon on your walk by the beach. Then you said you wondered if it was as calm and clear where I was. Well, as the letter was written on the 11th, and you said you took your walk a few days earlier I assumed I must have still have been on the hill. Sure, the moon was out, the air was warm, and there was probably a layer of fog 10 feet thick over the valley floor. But as to the gun smoke—I don't know—it probably mingled with the fog. It's funny, I never noticed the smoke, and the noise. I can never remember it other than there was a lot of it. It's a constant thing, and usually you're concentrating your mind on something else. The one thing I will always remember is the color of the explosions. They turned the fog a beautiful golden crimson.

There's a fight going on in the next tent right now. It sounds like the ROK is drunk. He's yelling in Korean, and interjecting American swear words. The guy he's yelling at hasn't answered as yet, and it is quite humorous. It's really funny. All he can say in English is S.O.B., goddamn. We have a certain percentage of Koreans attached to each American unit. They usually cause some kind of trouble. The company commander just went into the tent, and told the Korean (they call him Colonel) to go to bed. Very nicely he answered "yes Sir," and now he's quiet.

Pete, I'll never be the same. I swear I won't—Things are just completely all screwed up over here—everything.

I don't really know whether I'm coming or going. It's just

that everyone is keyed-up and tense—nobody wants anything to happen to anyone, themselves especially, and they get into more trouble trying to stay out of trouble.

I had a lot I wanted to say to you tonight, honey, but since this alert came up my mind has been confused. I get panicky myself, and sort of lose all power to get back on a quiet and normal plane. It's a funny thing to say I know, but it's oh so true—I know you'll find it hard to believe, but I'll tell you because I think you might know and understand what I'm trying to say—I miss you terribly—How can I miss something I never had? I don't know—I'll be honest with you—But I feel that I miss you, and I miss you very, very much—Do you understand?

I've got to close this now honey, but I'll be thinking and dreaming of you the whole night through. Make sure those pictures come right along.

It's now morning in California, and it's Sunday—The wedding day—Have a wonderful time, Pete—Give my love to the bride & groom. Remember what I said about that sign I told you to wear!!

> Goodnight—Treasure—See you real soon—
> Love to you as always,
>
> Your Ronnie

&OCB

It is pretty difficult to explain how we all felt at this time in our Army life. Here we were 8000 miles or more from home in a pretty much un-civilized world living closely with people we had just met a few weeks ago, and unsure of our future. I was a typical young man and quite sure that it would be somebody else who would be the next to die, as it just could not be me. I had too much to look forward to when I got home.

We knew the truce was just around the corner, and nobody wanted to be the last to die, especially in a war that was hardly even recognized back home. It was called a "Police Action" when it started, but that was quickly forgotten when we had our bottoms kicked back in 1950.

MacArthur had been fired by President Truman, and Matt Ridgeway took over. He turned our Army's poor attitude around, and made us into real soldiers. In all truth, I was very fortunate that I did not get to Korea until January of 1953. 1950 through 1951 was a terrible time to be over there, and 1952 was only somewhat better.

By the time I arrived, the soldiers lived pretty well, and we really had little to complain about. Just because the milk we drank (I did not) was powdered in form, and we had to float ice chunks in it to cool it down was no reason to complain. I do not think the GIs in the WWII even had dry milk to drink. However, complain we did or we would not even be thought of as soldiers if we did not have something to scowl over.

Mail delivery was quite good, but if we did not get anything, we did not complain about the writers back home, we complained about the delivery situation. It was the Army's fault. My mom sent me some brownies. She wrapped each piece in wax paper and aluminum foil, but by the time the package got to me, we could have used the squares to shell the enemy, as they were brick hard. I think that package took over a month to reach me, and must have sat at the bottom of a ship's hold that whole time. I think we dunked them in warm beer one afternoon to make them soft enough to chew. The chocolate taste was marvelous as I recall.

Pete at this time went to California to be in a wedding of one of her friends who had married an airman, and that was where they lived. Her letters were my whole life at that time, and the 3000 miles closer to where I was made me feel more as if she mentally was nearer to me. I was so happy that someone back home, besides my family, had any interest in what I was doing or where I was.

My dad's older brother, my Uncle Simon, traveled to Asia back in the mid-1920s when he was a buyer for a sausage manufacturer in the Boston area. There were many family photos of him often dressed in native costume. I remember one of him dressed as a Mandarin holding an opium pipe, and one on the back of a donkey wearing a pith helmet. It seemed to me that he was visiting lands that were far more developed and civilized than the Korea we were living in.

He was there twenty-five years before we got to Asia, and he went to Tibet and Outer Mongolia, which at that time was like space travel is today. The Korea we occupied in 1953 had no paved roads outside of Seoul or Pusan, no electricity, no running water, no streetlights. It did not even have the basics of life, as we knew it. It was real country living. The large cities did have some of the comforts, but they were mostly in ruins when we were there. They had nothing other than their mud and wattle houses, and maybe a Yak in the yard. Most of the trees were gone, as they had been cut down to make charcoal for their cook fires.

Little children were carried around in a cloth tied around an older sister while Mama-san took care of the house and maybe helped the Papa-san in the rice fields. They ate rice as their main staple, and fertilized their fields with their excrement. The smell below the military zone was unbelievable to our gentle noses. It was almost worth going into combat to get away from the odor.

Figure 57 - Seoul as seen from Nam San Mountain. Spring 1953

I was sent up to Seoul a few times to pick up supplies, which always meant a trip to the Post Exchange in that city. It was about the only place to see or do anything, as the rest of Seoul was a pile of rubble. I recall the only restaurant that we could find open was Chinese. Here we were fighting the Chinese, and all I could find was Chinese food. We even bitched about that. The trip to Seoul was only 42 miles, but the roads were so bad that it often took three hours to get there. We drove up in jeeps or three-quarter ton Commo trucks. The jeeps had their tops down while the Commo trucks had an enclosed cab. I always opted for one of those especially in cold weather.

One time I was sent down to the city to order nametags for our battery. I don't know how my CO, Lt. Crouch, or Colonel Kimmitt, our Battalion Commander, found out where to buy these, but I got an address and brought down a list of names. The tags were made of raised letters on an aluminum bar with a red painted background. I suppose they got the aluminum from downed American planes, but we never questioned that. I still have mine in a mounted frame along with some other devices.

The weather was hot and the war just rambled along with fewer firefights as time went on.

Figure 58 - Inchon man wants the shell (bottom left). It's made of solid brass. The Koreans would salvage anything and make the metals into all kinds of goods to sell.

Letter #22

Tues., 21 July

Dearest Pete,

The sun didn't shine today, and there was no mail. I wonder if it might not come in late. Sure hope so—I could use some.

I'm back in the battery again. I only stayed that one night with King Company. They sent me back the next day in time for dinner. Nothing happened in our area at all. Let's hope it stays that way until they sign that damned piece of paper.

There was an expected sweat all last night, so I went to bed quite early so I could get some sleep in case they called me out again. It's just as well I didn't write you last night, as I probably would have written a pretty dejected-sounding letter. So far today there has been no news of an expected "sweat", and I haven't started to panic. That's why I'm writing this now. I've caused you enough grief and worry to last a lifetime! It's pretty hard to take such things as that when we're so close to the end. I just can't see it—no kidding!!

When first I wrote you I remember telling you I was firm in my belief we should stay in Korea. I really felt that way, but now that I've seen what it is really like I've changed my mind. I was a fool I guess, in many ways for requesting a transfer. I've gained a lot, however, out of the deal. I had to satisfy my own ego by proving I could take what other people were taking. I guess you never know how big a shadow you cast until you stand up.

When I read of a war in the future I'll know myself what it can really be like. It seems to me to be sort of like visiting foreign places. You never know what they're really like until you've been there yourself.

Well, it's now about 3:30 A.M. on Tuesday morning back where you are. I'll bet you're still tired from the wedding. Sure hope everyone had a good time. Maybe you're just getting over a hangover!! That's one thing I could see right about now—A good drink—Here you are probably dreaming of a nice, clean, sunny day, and I can only think of an ice cold beer. Not very nice am I??

I still haven't forgotten our deal with the lobster and beer.
I saw a picture of a lobster and a can of beer in a magazine
today, and it nearly drove me crazy. Underneath the picture was
a recipe telling the reader how to have his own New England style
lobster anywhere in the states. Oh—brother I could almost see
that animal swimming before my eyes, and if I had about 5
minutes more to think about it I would have had the thing boiled
live and dripping with melted butter, sitting on a white tablecloth
in a big serving dish with a frosted can of beer and a plateful of
steaming fresh sweet corn right nearby—

Boy—how I can daydream?

I'll bet we're having stew or something delightful like that
for chow tonight. It seems all we've had this past week has been
stew, hamburger, sweet potatoes, and rice. Rice, I like, in fact
I'm crazy about it—but the other three—Never happen, G.I.
That stuff like stew, hamburger and sweet potatoes don't show
me much. We eat in about 15 more minutes, and if I'm still not
done with this, I'll tell you what we have—Aren't you thrilled??

A very close buddy of mine who was in my OCS class, and
who I came overseas with, finally got his transfer out of the
398th. He has one of the softest deals possible now. He's Air
Advisor for the 5th Air Force, and is stationed down at 5th Air
Force Headquarters in Seoul. He works an 8 hour day, and has
every night and weekend off. He called me up today, and we
chirped for a few minutes. He wants me to come down for a few
days, and won't believe me when I tell him I can't ever leave the
battery area as I'm on 15 minute alert notice. I'd run down there
in a second if they'd only give me a chance. He told me even
though they have movies every night down there he hasn't been
to one of them. He says the club is right near the movie hall, and
somehow he never quite makes it to the theatre. Besides, he says
the club has a floorshow every night!! How tough can life be??

His name is Jim Gillen, and you'd get a big kick out of him if
you ever met him. He's one of these big, tall, handsome, black
haired, brainless Irishman, who gets a big kick out of life. When
we were stationed together in the same battalion at Camp
Edwards on Cape Cod, last summer—we had one of the best
summers I've ever spent. We found the nicest cocktail lounge in
all the world, and practically lived there.

The piano player was Eddie "Gin" Miller, maybe you've heard of him. He made the record of "Music, Music, Music" and stuff like that. He got to be quite popular at one time. Jim and I got to be real buddies with him, and every night after all the people left, and the waitress started to sweep the place out, Jim and I would sit up on the piano, and have Eddie play all our favorites. We'd all sing, and we really loved it—Eddie was disappointed because the management would only let him play some songs from the various New York shows. He hated that stuff, and liked what Jim and I liked—the old favorites, Irish songs, dirty songs, rag music, etc. I liked in particular the way he played "If I Loved You". It was the only show song he played I liked. Jim and I would never get back to camp until 3 or 4 in the morning, and were always tired and hung over the next day. Thank God the summer season ended around Labor Day, and the place closed down.

Have you ever been to Cape Cod? If you haven't, that's one place I'm going to take you next summer—Lord—what a beautiful, quiet place—You'll go crazy about it, I know. Well, it's just about time for chow—Koreans call chow "chop-chop". Someday I'll give you a lesson in the Korean-English slang. So long, hon—see you after chow!!

Well, what a surprise! Southern Fried Chicken, corn, potatoes, gravy, etc. We even had iced tea—what's this army coming to—

Heard the six o'clock news while at chow, and though they still haven't signed anything it sounded encouraging. I tell you, honey, it is really a crime the way those people are taking their own sweet time about reaching any decision. I realize, of course, that our negotiators are as desirous of signing the truce as soon as they can, but I can't understand the Chinese. I guess lives mean nothing to them.

The battery commander just mentioned another field artillery battalion in our division caught some unarmed Chinks trying to break into their supply room. What kind of people are we fighting against? They sneaked through our lines without weapons, and only to try and get supplies. We know they are the wiliest, most treacherous people in the world, but yet they seem so foolish at times. One day when I was on the OP, I saw five of them walk down a valley to a little stream and go wading. There they were only 1800 yards away from us. They didn't seem to even think any G.I. was going to shoot at them. I watched them wade for a while, and then after they walked back up the valley, and sat down to have a smoke, I let them have it. I got two I know of, and might have wounded the other three. What silly people they seemed to be. Did I ever tell you about the time they yelled at us one night? I was with *George Company*, and the *Chinks* were yelling "*George Company—32nd Regiment—Eedewah. Eedewah* means "come here" in Japanese or Korean—everyone uses the word—I was scared silly it sounded so eerie.

Well, sweetheart—the people just came in, and the place is getting real rowdy—I just can't concentrate at all—as much as I want to. I'm way up on you in letters anyway, but I don't mind as long as I'm not boring you or overcrowding you—

Take care, Pete honey—and think of me often—It would sure help a lot if I knew where you were—

> Goodnight—treasure—
> > I'll try to write again tomorrow—
> > > All my love to you hon—always,
> > > > Yours, Ron

⁎⌘⁐

The letter I sent Pete was dated 22 July 1953. We had to wait another six days before the truce was signed, and I remember how long each day seemed. The heat, the dust, the feelings of frustration, the lack of cold, clean tasting water, (and I missed having a refrigerator to open and rummage through), were all weighing heavily on my mind at this time. Almost the lack of everything we knew and appreciated finally made us understand what we were missing in our lives.

In this letter and the one previous I mentioned that I was sent over to King Company, but I didn't explain why or what happened. We heard the guns of a neighboring unit firing so we went over to our FDC to plot where they were firing. It appeared that the outpost on Westview, which was a little south and west of Pork Chop was being hit late in the afternoon and early evening. I soon heard my name being called, and I was informed that I was being sent over as the FO for a planned counter attack on Westview.

When I arrived at the appointed place, the officer in charge, a big black

First Lieutenant, greeted me and introduced himself. He was to lead the attack, and I was to be his artillery observer. I told him that my crew and I were ready, and would await further information from him. That was when he told me that he didn't need a crew, and that I didn't really have to carry a radio or anything else as he figured that he would use me as moral support only. He felt that his mortars were sufficient to do the job, and anything heavier wouldn't be needed.

Good grief! I was superfluous, and could be killed for no reason at all. I was sure I was going to die, and my story would be written up or told by a guy like Paul Harvey. I went back to where my crew had settled down on the ground near the assault company, and informed them of what Lt. Armour had said. It was at this point that a runner came over to me and told me that if I needed a call sign for the evening that I should use 'Cancer 3 zero' for my name.

That did it!! Now I knew I was going to die. What kind of a word was that to use? The Communications Officer should have picked something else, but then he wasn't going to be in the attack, so what did he care. You can see the foul mood I was working up to. I could even see the headlines in the Boston Traveler. "Lt. Freedman, of Newton, Mass. dies needlessly just before the war ends."

Sitting there, stewing, the order to load up on the trucks came. We were to be driven to the jump off point, but before I could get up I heard my name being called. It was a runner from King Company reminding me that I was to use "Cancer 3 zero" as a call sign. It didn't matter as I was not bringing a radio or phones with me. I jumped up on a truck and was handed a bandolier of ammo for my carbine, and two grenades. I was putting the bandolier over my shoulder when I heard whistles blowing and someone yelling, Dismount! The Chinks have pulled off of the hill," and I was free to return to my battery. The weight was off of my shoulders, and I was going to live another day. Although I had the fright of my life at least I had a few hours away from being bored silly.

Back at Battery, life continued as usual. Living in that hoochie with a stream running through it made everything smell moldy. As hot as it was outside it was better than being in that humid sandbag bunker. I began wishing I was back in combat where at least I had something to occupy my mind. Writing to Pete was my only diversification, and I used that time to write about anything and everything that came to mind. I could not wait to go home and see her.

****

Letter #23

Thurs., 23 July

Dear Pete—

Heard from you today after a lapse of a day or two, and I was quite happy. I've been haunting the mail clerk lately, and have been threatening to shoot him unless there is mail for me. The other day he asked me if "Pete Smith" was that picture guy from Hollywood. I said no, it wasn't. Then he said, "Smith must be a pretty close buddy of yours—you write him so often." His mouth dropped when I said this particular Pete Smith was a female. I guess he's still wondering 'cause he's always looking at me as if to say—"You're not kidding—are you?"

Today was cloudy and damp again. I was wakened at 6 A.M. by a 21 gun salute. I was sure Joe was coming until I found out today was Haile Selassie's birthday, and at 6 A.M. here it was noon or something in Ethiopia. The Ethiopian Battalion is attached to our regiment, so our battalion fired the salute— actually, the front has been fairly quiet of late—though I understand the ROKs are still being clobbered over to the east. That deal on Arsenal is still expected, but as yet hasn't happened. Sure hope it never does. I'll even knock wood on that!

I've picked up some funny superstitions these past few months, and don't think I'll give up on them for quite some time to come. I won't even tell you what they are as I'm superstitious about telling my superstitions—No, honey—I'm not soft in the head—I've just got to think of something besides getting home—

The last letter I wrote you was cut short at the end by the entry into the hoochie of our battery commander and a few other people. They wanted to have a small party of sorts, and I was ordered to cease all letter-writing. The Battery Commander or B.C. is a West Pointer-class of '51, and is about a year older than I am. His name is William E. Crouch Jr., and although he's only a 1st Lt. I've never called him anything but Sir or Lt. Crouch. He's sharp as a tack, but quite a good boy. I enjoy working for him. The two other 1st Lts. in the battery are Doug Gleason and Al Adickes. They're both good Joes also. Doug hopes to go home next month, and Al expects to leave in September.

I'm the other Exec, although I'm only a 2nd Lt. If I stay in C Battery, I'll probably end up as the Exec. We also have a Chief Warrant Officer in the battery. His name is Mr. Rulong, and he's a real old soldier. I get a big kick out of him as he has no use for what he calls "citizen soldiers". All day long we ride each other— He claims the Anti-aircraft is useless, and I claim the army should get rid of Warrant Officers—especially the aged and decrepit such as himself—

The situation over here has me all confused. I've just about run out of patience with regards to the truce. It's pretty damned exasperating to sit here—not knowing what they're talking about—and just wait for either the signing or the Chinks to come strolling over the hills. I've not given up on our purpose over here, but all my driving force seems to have run out.

Naturally, it being summer back home—vacation time and everyone having a good time—also makes this place pretty unbearable. It's like dusk or twilight to me—that's the part of the day that affects me the most —it's "going home time"— That's the best part of the day, especially during the spring and summer.

You always talk about dreaming, etc. Well, if you haven't noticed as yet, I'm sure you can see I'm probably the world's greatest day-dreamer. I've come to realize my imagination is also apt to get the best of me at times. I do a lot of day-dreaming, Pete—probably quite a bit more than the average person, and although day-dreaming and imagination go hand in hand—I really go way out of my way in some of my ideas. Some things I think of are really wild—I don't mean weird or abnormal, but rather impossible. At night while trying to fall asleep I usually can pick out one day, and completely plan how I'm going to spend it. Then other times I pick out a day when things went wrong, and I go over the day, and re-do it sort of.

It's taken me over an hour to write the last paragraph because of a debate that has been taking place. We've been discussing the war, but mostly the why and wherefore of our being here. One thing we've all agreed on is that none of us can actually put down our feelings in words. Mr. Rulong feels (as an old soldier) we don't have any real army men in the younger ranks. He is really afraid our country and our younger generation are on the road to ruin. He says he's afraid to die because he doesn't know what will happen to those he leaves behind. He's not being a braggart about it, but he sure makes some pretty positive statements.

Honey, I'd sure like to be with you right now so I could really tell you what I feel. I think people are so damned ignorant as to what is actually on our minds. I feel it is the fault of our newspapers, and maybe it can be traced back to our primary educational system.

Well, by now your wedding has been over for quite a while, and you should know what you're going to do in the next few weeks.

Honey—the guns just started up, and a hurried call to the fire direction center tells us the Chinks are attacking on our left. As yet I've had no word on my expected actions, but I'd better close off in case something comes up.

Please keep writing, hon, and I'll try to keep you informed.

Good night—Pete—
All my love to you—
Yours—Ron

ଚଟ୍ଟ

I just realized that in the last letter I mentioned Jim Gillen, but did not follow up with anything about him. Unfortunately, Jim passed away a number of years ago; we have many fond memories of him, and some of his antics. Pete only met him after his marriage when he was still in the Army, and even then didn't get to spend a long time talking to him.

Jim came from North Andover, Mass, and was the son of a late Army Colonel. I met him in OCS, and when we realized we came from the same area we became fast friends. We were both assigned to the same battalion on Cape Cod, and it seemed like we spent every night at a bar somewhere near the post. Jim was a tall, good looking guy, and was constantly looking out for good looking women. It turned out that the only one that caught his eye happened to be a high school friend of mine who had a summer home on the Cape. She was engaged at the time, and that created a problem for Jim.

After I transferred up to the front, Jim got a job as the flak analysis advisor to the Fifth Air Force in Seoul. I was sent down there for some reason and had lunch with him and spent that night as well. While we were eating, two

Canadian officers came to our table and after the introductions were made they invited Jim and me to spend the evening with them. We picked up a jeep and were driving to the place we were to meet when a Canadian jeep pulled up on my side and the driver reached out and punched me on my right arm. He yelled "You're it!" and sped away. Jim goosed our jeep, but we could never catch them.

We ended up at the British Commonwealth Club which was a private building with a walled in swimming pool attached. We went in and walked out to the top of the wall. I was suddenly handed three uniforms and the three guys jumped in to the pool. They created a ruckus, and a British officer was sent out to quell the disturbance. The three guys were, by this time, standing next to me when the Brit demanded their names. Apparently the British Brigadier General was sitting by the picture window overlooking the pool, and when he saw what occurred he sent his aide out to get the names of the culprits who caused all the nurses in the pool to squeal and jabber like a tree full of monkeys.

The boys were drying themselves down with their T shirts when the officer arrived and demanded their names. The senior of the two Canadians mocked the British officer's accent and when asked for his name and number he answered, "I shan't tell you." That ended that and we ran to our jeeps, planning to meet at Jim's room in the Seoul City University where he was billeted.

The drinking went on up in Jim's second floor room, and the conversation led to post war plans. Jim said that he was staying in the service and planned to go to Parachute School. The Canadians volunteered that he should switch over to the British Army if he wanted real parachute training. They reasoned that whatever the American Army did the British Army did better. As an example they said that the British jumped off twenty-foot towers to toughen themselves up. Jim said that the Americans did better, and he could prove it. He walked over to the window, and I watched him jump out and land on the sidewalk below. He did a roll and walked back upstairs.

I couldn't believe he hadn't hurt himself, but he was fine the next day. He took me to his office and after I gave him the location of my OP he pulled out some photos of the area. They were exactly what I could have used to plot and pinpoint targets of opportunity, but Jim could not part with the pictures. Why the Army and the Air Force could not get together on something like this has always bothered me.

Jim did go to the Airborne School, and eventually served in Vietnam. He came home and was discharged after twenty years of service. He was on the road selling eye glass frames when we last saw him. It was just before Memorial Day, and he told us that his home town was planning a parade and that they wanted him to parachute in and start the festivities. He said that he would do it if they paid him $1,000. They, of course, refused, and Jim said that he never even wanted to go up in an airplane again let alone jumping out of one. Jim's wife, Marylyn, didn't like us as she felt that he spent too much time in our company, and we were not a good example for him. He died of cancer soon after that.

I also mentioned Bernie Rulong in my latest letter to Pete. He was a grizzled old soldier, and really felt that our current Army was too young, and that we could never be the soldiers that his age group was in the Second War. Bernie was a Chief Warrant Officer Grade IV, and really should have been assigned to a much higher unit than ours, but he was there and we all truly loved having him and his comments around. We figured him out one night when we were getting shelled in our battery area. He said we didn't have to worry about anything as what we heard was "outgoing". We young soldiers argued that it was "incoming" and that he should take cover. He sure was surprised when one round landed nearby and nearly knocked him down. Score one for the young guys.

****

Letter #24

Monday, 27 July

Dear Pete—

Well, in just one hour and sixteen minutes it should be all over. I've waited quite a few days for this occasion, and now that it's here I don't seem to feel any elation at all. We were all expecting it to be signed in the very near, but were still amazed when the radio actually said they were signing it at 10 A.M. the next morning.

I guess it's all true, however, but for some reason I don't trust Joe—I find myself actually wondering if he'll cease firing at 10 P.M. tonight. So far today he's been clobbering our front lines with artillery and mortars. We expected to be attacked last night, but I guess our prayers were answered as he left our area alone. The poor guys on our right and left caught it, but I'll be honest with you—I'm sure glad it wasn't us.

Today I took some men, and went up to our forward gun positions. We pulled the bunkers down, and tomorrow we'll go back to police the area up—We're trying to do everything as soon as possible as we don't know whether or not we'll have to move from our present position. We're behind the demarcation limit line, but it still may be too near for some of the higher brass.

There was very little emotion displayed when the news came out they had signed the truce. First and foremost on everyone's mind of course, is "how soon do we get home?" I don't think it will be for quite a while, but I'm willing to stay as long as Joe will keep his part of the bargain. Sorry for my "citizen soldier" attitude, but I gotta get back—I've got a few things I want to do, and some certain people I want to see—

The mail situation over here has been quite bad. I've had one letter in 5 days, and that was from home. Nothing from you in that time. Sure hope it's the fault of the postal system! I guess I've told you enough times about the importance of mail so I won't go into it again.

Should be happy tonight, but one of our F.O.s, Lt. Dixon, hasn't been heard from all day. He's on a little hill that hooks onto Pork Chop, and it's been getting hit every day since we lost the Chop. We can't ever get him on the radio. When he went up there he was told he shouldn't expect to get off alive if ever the Chinks hit the hill. He's a little "spooky" at times, but when the sweat is on he's an 'A' number one F.O. I guess he'll be alright—though—He can take care of himself.

Well, only 45 more minutes to go! Way off to our left down near Big and Little Nori; Joe is shooting up a storm. That's just like him. I'll bet when the clock strikes 10 P.M., all the noise will cease.

I wrote my folks tonight, and told them I was confident of a complete Armistead. I'll bet they're two happy people right now. I'll bet there are a lot of happy parents all over the country— Can't say as I blame them—

The weather here has been miserable. It rains for 2 or 3 days, and then the sun comes out, and we wilt in the hot, humid air. All the leather goods are getting covered with mold, and we're throwing things away by the dozen—Can't quite feature the country. Remind me never to come back here after I get home.

Well, hon—I've just been invited to join the Battery Commander in a beer, and I guess it wouldn't be wise to go against his desires—Besides—I'm thirsty!!

Please see what you can do with my mail situation—I'd

appreciate it.

Take care, Pete, and let me know where you're heading after you leave California.

Goodnight Pete. I still miss you.

My love to you, always!

Ronnie

ꙮ

I would think that a letter about the proposed truce should have sounded more exciting than it did. It was what we all had been waiting for, and here it is more than 50 years later, and I feel more elated about the truce now than I seemed to have felt back then. I guess I am more mature now, and understand better the misfortunes that could have come to me at that time if the fighting hadn't ceased.

The news about the truce happened in a funny way. I didn't hear it on the radio, and neither did someone run around yelling "Truce". I had been informed that I was to relieve Willie Dixon on Hill 200 that afternoon, and that a jeep would be by to pick me up around 1600. Hill 200 sits right next to Pork Chop to the east. Although it is right there, the Chinese ignored it completely during the six-day battle that had just taken place.

It seemed a strange thing for them to treat it as they did. If they had taken that hill they would have completely flanked our right side, and left us with no easy way to get to Pork Chop. They left it alone, however, and after the fight Dixon was sent up there to be the FO. I spoke to him a couple of times, and he told me that he spent much of his day trying to figure out a way to rid himself of the smell of all the dead and dying soldiers that lay on the right side of Pork Chop. He tried covering the bodies up by firing artillery nearby which would hopefully throw a blanket of dirt on all the bodies. He said that they would not give him the shells he needed to do the job, and besides that system did not work very well. He was excited to hear that I would relieve him as it was getting to him mentally.

I was in our hooch packing my clothes into my "war bag"—a pack that slung under our field pack—when Doug Gleason, our exec, came in with the news that his orders to go home had just come in. We all congratulated him, and went back to whatever we were doing when he added, "Oh, by the way, the truce was signed and goes into effect at 2200 tonight." With that I dumped everything out of the bag, and went to the phone to call Willie to tell him that I would not be out to relieve him. I checked with my CO and he had told me that if the truce was signed that Dixon would be called back into battery, and I wouldn't have to go.

That night we drove up to my old OP as it was easy to get to, and had a commanding view of the area. We sat on the top rear edge of the trench line and watched all the 'fireworks' from both sides. At exactly 2200 (10 p.m.), the firing suddenly stopped, and the nearby searchlights that lit up some of the enemy positions blinked off. I took off my flak jacket, and sat there in only a T shirt while I lighted a cigarette. Nobody shot at us, so we guessed that the truce was for real.

The next morning we were told that we had three days in which to dismantle all our positions within two miles of the truce line. We were all sent out with parties to do whatever we could to police the area. There is a photo in my collection, given to me by an unknown sergeant, showing the dismantling of OP 13 looking down at Pork Chop. For the next few days we were all involved in this dismantling work. To me, the greatest relief came when we were told that we no longer needed to wear helmets and flak jackets. I felt like I'd been reborn.

All in all, it was quite an event, and I am happy to say that I was there to see it all. My part in the Korean War was minor and limited, but I'd "wanted to see the elephant", and by golly, I did.

Figure 59 - On Hill 347 the day after the truce.
Pork Chop in the background

Letter #25

Wed., 29 July

My Dearest Pete—

I really can't decide just how to start this letter as my mind is slightly confused. I'll probably amaze you when I tell you I'm quite ashamed of myself. I am—honestly. Why? Because of my stupid imagination. I didn't hear from you for five days, and during that time I only wrote you once. Maybe you noticed my last letter was a bit reserved. I didn't quite know what to think. I couldn't figure out why your letters should suddenly stop.

First, I thought you were probably too busy, and then I figured I had bad luck with the mail service, but then I got the brilliant idea I had over stepped my bounds, and you just decided not to write anymore. I was pretty red-faced this morning when I got 3 letters from you—I certainly hope you'll forgive me for not writing, and for assuming such a damned stupid attitude. I'll try not to let it ever happen again. You have been so wonderful in writing me as often as you do that I should never complain about anything you do.

As I reread these letters you wrote, I find myself very glad I have told you the things I have. It really makes things go right when you have someone to tell your troubles to. To me, the knowledge a certain somebody that isn't a blood relation and who hasn't any obligation to you —is interested in your doings and thoughts is one of the most comforting feelings a person can have.

It makes me feel so damned glad I'm alive and it warms me down deep when you write, you just know I'll be back safe—I know that, too, but when you say it, it makes me feel all better. When I say it to myself I always wonder if I'm saying it to bolster my own confidence. But when you say it—in exactly the same way I told myself—then I know you must really feel it. Do I confuse you, honey? You told me you know I'd be back safely, but you didn't know why or how you knew it. Well, that's what I used to tell myself at night as I tried to fall asleep. I didn't know why I felt that way—but I just knew I'd make it all right.

It's all over now—no more nights of waiting to see if you'd be able to see the sun the next morning. The danger is gone now, but I'll never rid myself of the fears I once held. No matter how bad I thought things were, I always remembered somebody was having it worse. It didn't make me feel any easier, but it sort of quieted me down an awful lot. To me, the whole thing was like a game of chance. No one ever thought that their turn to die would ever come up, and when it happened they were the most surprised people in the world. Of course, they never realized it. The day our O.P. got hit I was very sure they'd never come near hitting us. Joe had missed me so many times before; I didn't think he'd ever get close to getting me—

I had many, many hours to think about it all while I was sitting there at night by the window. The way it seemed to me was, if you were in the wrong place at the wrong time then it was unfortunate. I also learned to believe in the power of prayer. That was something I never thought I would live to believe. I never was brought up in a religious atmosphere, and naturally never believed in prayer. I sort of thought there was a God, but He appeared to be more of a name than anything else. I knew there was one, but as I say—it never interested me.

Then one night when things were getting a little active, and the rounds were coming close I found myself begging God to make them stop it all. They did soon afterwards, and I felt quite ashamed of myself for begging. I began to think about God more often, and now although I'm still not a believer in any certain type or form of religion, I'm getting so that I realize more and more how much I depend on Him. I don't think it's very fair for us to ask Him all the time for different things. We should give things to Him, but being a novice at this sort of thing maybe I'd better stop my mouthing off. When I learn more about it then I'll tell you what I believe—

Since I wrote that last sentence I have been forced to eat tuna fish sandwiches, drink 8 cans of beer, and have been thrown in the little creek that runs through the area. It was all pretty funny, and we all had a good laugh. It's now 5 of 12, but I'm not going to put this pen down, until I've told you all I want to tell you.

The people here think I'm crazy trying to finish this letter tonight—But they just don't know who I'm writing to. If they had someone like you I'm sure they'd be up writing a letter also.

Hon, I'm still trying to answer all the questions you've put in my mind in that first letter of the three, I got today. You said you didn't want to get burned again now that you've been burned once. I think I know how you feel, and believe me, Pete, the last thing I would ever want to do in this world is to hurt you in any way—You've been too good to me!! I'm glad you were frank with me for I want you to be no other way.

I feel differently towards you than I've ever felt towards anyone. It's a hard thing to do by mail, but I want to know you—know what you think, and how you act—I want to know all about you so when we are together when I get home—we'll feel like we've been together for a long time. I never realized someone had hurt you before, and now that I do, I'm both sorry and glad at the same time. No—darling—I'm not being cruel when I say that—I'm sorry, probably a lot more than you can realize at this time, that somebody wronged you, and yet in a sense I'm glad because now you know just how bad things can seem.

It's not good to see the rosy side of life all the time. And now the next time your heart is turned you will know what it's all about—I've been burned myself, but it wasn't anything too serious. I guess I thought I was in love, but I couldn't have been because I've forgotten her. However, I think it's a mistake for anyone to deny their feelings in any way because they only leave scars. You are much too young, too sweet, and too beautiful to force yourself to shun anything that might turn your way. I would be very happy if some day you wrote and said you had found him, because you'd be happy, and that's the way I want you to be—I'd also be disappointed, but that's another thing. I suppose you'd better go on being my Pete Smith, and let ever thing come as may—however—I'll brain you if you don't want me to come home!!

Honey—if you had "your little jet plane," and did hop right on over to see me, I'll guarantee you I'd have no more depressed moods. I don't get them too often, however, and they usually disappear quickly. They always come with spells of loneliness and thoughts of people I hold dear—Maybe that's why my letters to you are sometimes depressing—You just keep writing me, and you will be doing all that's possible for anyone at home to do, and in my case it will be a little bit more.

I just went out to check the guard, and what a beautiful night it is. What a shame to be wasting it on checking a guard. I'd much rather be walking down the road with you. I know you'd love it outside. It's warm but not hot, and a big full moon is lighting everything up with a silvery gleam. It's too peaceful to believe 50 yards away there are guns. The silence seems so odd. May it always be that way—

I told you once before you could do so much by teaching those little ones the proper way. I'll tell you again. It's so important to our future, and even more important to theirs. I'll just leave it at that, Pete or else I'll go off into another of my long lectures. I'm sure you realize what I mean, and I know you'll do a wonderful job with those kids.

It seems like I got you a bit angry by saying I hoped you didn't tell anyone I've been writing you frightening things. I guess you got me wrong—or else I didn't word my statements properly—what I meant was I hoped nobody thought you were being scared or depressed by what I was telling you. I've tried only to tell you my inner thoughts because I feel so much closer to you when I share those thoughts with you—

Do you remember I once told you I had some superstitions, and someday I would tell them to you?

At that time I didn't want to tell you because I was superstitious about telling my superstitions. That's changed now that it's all over, and I can tell you of some of the silly things I did. I was like those baseball players who won't change their uniforms while their team was winning. After the season is all over things were different. Well, now the season is over, and I can tell you. I know you'll laugh at them, and I guess you should 'cause some of them are rather stupid.

One thing I would never do is throw my helmet on a bed. Right now it's lying on the floor under my bed where I've put it ever night. Another one is, I wouldn't use one of the common G.I. sayings. When somebody got killed up here nobody said he "died" or "got killed" instead they said he "was wasted". I just would never say that word. My Grandmother gave me 18 cents for good luck before I came overseas, and I won't go anywhere without that same 18 cents. Another thing I did was promise my mother I would write to her every night. That was way back in May when I first got up here. She only asked I write a couple of times a week, and I, in a fit of madness, told her I would write to her every night until the war was over. I never missed a day, either—although I have to admit some of the letters were pretty poor.

That's just some of the weird things I've done, and now I hope by telling you, I won't change my luck. I don't think it will because you've been lucky for me—

I understand what you meant now about the pictures not holding me back so I'm reciprocating. Mainly because I promised something better than those mustache pictures. However, I want more of you. I got one today—but I WANT MORE!!! Okay??

Well, my honey—time to go to bed and dream of you. I guess I've written enough to make up for the last few days—

Take care of yourself, sweetheart, and know I'm thinking of you constantly. You're on my mind always, Pete and I wouldn't want it any other way—wait for me, for my love

Is yours for always—

CB80

This letter to Pete was long and probably reflected on the workings of my mind at that time. The immense relief of the end of the shooting war is apparent in my words. In some respects I think that the letdown from the excitement created by being in a combative situation was almost more than I could bear. What would I do with myself if I couldn't play "Shooting Gallery" anymore? I had thought that perhaps after the war I would stay in the service and probably attempt to go to helicopter school. But if it was going to be a boring existence until that happened, perhaps I should just go home, get my discharge and see what my future with Pete might be.

I was at sixes-and-sevens thinking about that subject when we were ordered to move back into new positions. I can't tell you where we went, but I do remember it being very, very hot and humid, and we were living in a squad tent. Those tents were made of a very heavy canvas fabric that had been treated with a flame proofing material. I also imagine that they incorporated a water proofing substance as well. The fabric and the coatings caused the tent to be windproof, and we didn't get any movement of air inside. Sleeping was difficult, and the lack of exercise led to short tempers and anxious thoughts about the e future.

At this time, my thoughts turned more to the why and what Pete Smith really meant to me. Apparently, I was falling in love with someone I hardly knew, and that fact sort of frightened me. Was I that shallow a person that I couldn't even reason with my thoughts? How could a supposedly sane man fall in love with a thought or even a memory? Maybe I wasn't mature enough to figure things out. There were, however, compelling ideas in my head. She seemed to be interested in me, and she did open up a bit by telling me that she had been "burned", and that she was being careful about her future. Well, whatever would be, would be. I decided I'd wait until I got home and saw her before making any rash decisions.

Still, life in Charlie Battery went on as usual. Joe Chink left us alone, and we left him to his own devices. We could not go up on the hill to see what he was doing, and I think he would be as bored as we were if he had an opportunity to watch us in our daily routine. The men in the battery held "Cannoneers' Hop" daily where they practice their aiming and loading skills.

I never had any training in this area, so I often went over to watch them drill. We were still training South Koreans, and some of the antics by both groups of men were fun to watch. I think the Koreans knew more than they let on, but the longer each session lasted the longer they could stay in our unit, and be well treated.

I don't know what transpired in their outfits, but on the day after the truce when we were policing areas I watched as South Korean officer talked to a group of his soldiers. They were all in a single line and he walked down and spoke to the men individually. He came face to face with one of his men and they had something of an argument. The men were standing there helmetless in a line when the officer took off his helmet and bashed the soldier on the head. I was more surprised than the Korean soldier whose knees buckled a bit, but he came back to attention as the officer moved down the line.

I had not seen anything like that since we were aboard the General Hersey and had picked up the battalion of Columbians in Cartagena. On that occasion I saw an officer take off his gloves and slap a Columbian soldier across the face. We had not been allowed off of the ship, but all the GIs lined the starboard side of the Hersey, and witnessed the slapping. The sound of surprise echoed off of the nearby buildings as the GIs were astonished to see how other armies behaved. In fact, while on board ship, the men had to stand "fire guard" at various places on the ship. Our GIs and the Puerto Ricans we had picked up often stood guard reading 'funny books' while the Columbian boys stood at attention. The difference in some attitudes is amazing.

Figure 60 - Cannoneers' Hop:
Each man on the team practiced at each position on the gun.

Letter #26

Sun., 2 Aug

Hi Honey—

It's only 5:30 P.M., and I hate to start this letter so early in the evening, but things are piling up a bit and I do want to get something off to you today—I'm being forced to start this against my will. I normally like to write later in the evening when I relax, but tonight there may be a party as the Major will be over (all officers will be there), and I also have to compile a check list for inspections. I'm in charge of a team that has to go around and inspect the battalion for certain items of combat material.

According to the terms of the truce neither side is allowed to bring in any more weapons or arms, and as we've lost quite a few items due to enemy action we are allowed to requisition replacements from our reserve stockpiles. We're to go around and find out what we need. It's a lousy detail, but at least I'll be busy for 5 or 6 days.

Our battalion commander, Lt. Colonel Kimmitt, is a number one boy. This outfit is supposed to be one of the outstanding field artillery units in all the Army, and it's largely due to his efforts. Since July 6th, however, he's changed. Nobody can figure it out or give any explanation. That was the first day of Pork Chop, and the battalion headquarters was shelled quite heavily. Some boys were killed, and that bothered him considerably. We all think it's because of that, plus the fact he's been in command for over 13 months. Over here, normally, commanders are changed every 6 months because that type of a job is a strain during combat operations. He's on call 24 hrs a day, and never can go anywhere that won't allow him to control his unit properly. Our colonel normally stayed up 18 hours a day, and often even longer. It's time for him to go home. He's becoming strange. His whole attitude has changed. He used to call all the junior officers either by their first name or by the word "lad", but now when he calls you it's just "Lieutenant", and it's said in the most derisive manner possible. He's no longer friendly or good-humored, and everyone is afraid of him. Sure hope they get him home soon.

I got 4 letters and a paper today. Mail comes during coffee call every morning about nine, and I brought mine back to the hoochie to read there. First, I looked at the home town paper, then I read the letter from the folks, then the one form my kid brother Steve, then I read my 'buddy Jim Gillens' letter (he's down at Seoul).

I saved yours till last, and was mildly surprised to find it so short. However, I know just how you feel when you want to write, but are too tired to do it. So I'll forgive you—the peace news is wonderful, of course, but it's not real enough to suit me. I won't believe anything until I get on that boat for home. It may not be for a while, but I'll stay as long as Joe doesn't start anything. I'm like everyone else now—I've had enough.

I'm no longer the hero I was when I was back with the 398th. I'll be truthful with you Pete—maybe it would be better I didn't mention this, but you have a right to know—Before we started writing in earnest I didn't much care what happened. I really didn't have anything to make me want to come home other than my family. Oh, I wanted to get back—sure, but not like the guys who had wives or girls waiting for them. It just didn't make that much difference to me—But now, whether you want it to be this way or not—you've changed everything.

I've only been gone about 8 months but it's surprising how much I've forgotten in that short time. Things I always took for granted now seem so far away because I never attached any real importance to them. I miss little things like going to a movie—Sunday nights—the beach—warm summer nights—I'm not being a copy of those movie heroes who always say things like that. I really do miss those things now that I don't have them. But one thing I miss more than anything is the sweet simplicity of an American girl—I don't mean that physically—It's just like I said—when you don't have things you normally take for granted, you realize how much they mean to you. I would like to be able to just hear your voice on a telephone now—I'd like to be calling for you right now—I'd just like to see you in a summer dress, or maybe in a suit getting ready for some big function—

I'm tired of these people I've seen over here—They're not

clean, and they're all out to take you for what you have—The
difference between you and an oriental girl is enormous—Again I
don't mean physically. Of course, I realize there are differences
due to geographic location and environment, but underneath,
everyone should have the same basic qualities. Maybe I'm
particular, but I don't think any foreign girl could stand up to an
American girl—Because of the memories I have of you, and
mainly because of your letters you typify that American girl to
me, and I know now I want to come home as soon as possible to
see you—You've made me change whether or not you know it.

But, no matter how important it is to me now—it's really
worse on these guys who are married or engaged because they
have someone who is waiting for them to come home. I don't know
who it's tougher on—the guy that's here or the people waiting at
home for him. I know how my mother must feel—worrying 24
hours a day—she can only live from letter to letter, and my
mother is a very strong woman when it comes to things of this
sort.

The guy over here doesn't worry so much. He knows he's
safe and alive, and he can feel reasonably sure everything is well
at home. I'll bet you've felt that way—When you're driving a car
you are in control, and you know you can pass other cars or do an
intricate maneuver, but the guy sitting next to you always puts
his foot on the imaginary brake on his side when he gets
frightened. I'm over here, and I know I can take care of myself,
but my folks are both jumping on that brake pedal when they
read the news. I don't see how they can take it, but I guess I will
when I have some kids.

Well, honey—I've got to go and write up inventory lists, and
then get ready for the "party." These parties consist of 8 or 10
officers sitting around a case or two or three of lukewarm beer
in a hoochie filled with the biggest bugs in the world. Everyone
gets sick about 10 P.M. from the DDT that gets in the beer from
the spray bombs, but nobody dares to leave because the Major is
having a good drunk on the bottle of Scotch he brought for
himself, and him alone—So we all stay, slap bugs, and drink beer
that's been liberally mixed with DDT. Tomorrow I have to be up
at 6:15, but the Major won't get up till 9 or 10—we both have the
same headache, but mine wears gold bars, and his wears gold

leaves—so much for the old Army maxim "rank has its privileges."
    Take care, sweetheart, and dream of me tonight, because
I'll be dreaming of you—

My love is yours, always—

Your Ronnie

�☙

The time that I wrote this letter was in early August of 1953. The weather was still as hot as can be, and of course, air conditioning was not available to us as it was in its early stages of use back in the states. Our uniforms were made of fairly dense cotton so as to be tear-proof and wear-proof. Each piece also had to be dipped in a miticide which helped close the pores of the fabric and added to its weight. Our shirts had to be tucked in and our boots bloused.

We didn't have to carry weapons or wear flak jackets and helmets. Thank God for little favors, but the sun continued to burn down all day, and being under a tent was impossible. There wasn't much to tell Pete about, but I just couldn't write to her and tell her that we had nothing to do except train, train, and train some more. My letters reflect that tenor in my thoughts, and I started to think more deeply about her. Prior to this time I had been involved in a war, and I could put off any serious thinking until sometime later. Well, it appears that "serious thinking" time had arrived, and it is seen in my writing.

I really had a hard time visualizing her face, except that I remembered she was about the prettiest girl I had ever dated. Her mental capabilities also appeared to be of high quality as her letters were well thought out and well written. I knew nothing about her family, and was only concerned regarding our religious differences, and what her family might say and do if and when she ever told them about me. The religious aspect didn't bother me as I had no religion whatsoever. We were a Jewish family, but never followed the precepts of the religion.

I remember once we had a Passover dinner, and because my best friend Bill was Irish, my mother had invited him over for the meal. Guess what? Grandma Cele had made a baked ham that night, and not one person said anything derogatory about it. The ham was delicious. Sort of interesting as my mother's mother, my Grandma Newman, lived with us, and she kept Kosher, using own dishes and utensils. (Her father was a Chief Rabbi back in Vilna, but she allowed us to live our lives the way we wanted to live them.)

If things ever got truly serious with Pete, I was prepared to tell her that any kids we had could be brought up in any manner she so desired. I didn't realize that my thinking had come to such an advanced state, but there it was

… I was thinking that maybe I would marry her. I tried to put that kind of thinking out of my mind, but I recall wrestling with that situation for a long time. In any event, she was my girl, and that's the way I thought of her. Did I ever think of her? All day and all night, that's all. At the time, I had nothing else to do that was as important.

****

Letter #27

Tues., 4 Aug.

Dearest Pete—

Tonight I'm in a very, very, happy mood. I don't know why, but I just am. As a matter of fact I should be a little disgusted because I was told my promotion papers have been fouled up, and will be delayed. One of the other officers in my battery got his promotion today, and I'm in grade longer than he is. It doesn't matter too much, however, as my pay will be retroactive as soon as I do get that silver bar.

It's early evening right now, and it's wondrously cool both outside and inside my hoochie. I'm sitting on my cot in just my pants and boots, and I've got my pipe going like a steam engine. The damned mosquito netting is tickling my back, but I'm too lazy to get up and fix it. I did some laundry today, and am glad I've gotten it out of the way.

I've been singing at the top of my lungs since 5 P.M., and plan to continue until I can't sing anymore tonight. Everything is going just the way it should with Lt. Freedman tonight, and he's mighty happy—Haven't been that way in a long time, darling, and I'm really enjoying myself. I've got a case of beer by my side, and you on my mind. The only thing I lack is about 11,000 miles of space.

If I had that then you and I would be out tonight, and I'd see to it that we'd both be in a happy frame of mind. I wonder where I'd take you—there's a million things we could do—what do you say to supper at Locke-Ober's—upstairs, of course, as they don't allow women downstairs in the Men's Bar except on New

Year's Eve, and the eve of the Harvard-Yale game—For supper we'd have either rare prime ribs of beef or just a broiled live lobster—You can have white wine with your meal, but I'm just going to have me a cold, cold glass of beer.

After supper—about 8:30—we'll go any place you name, but about midnight we're going to go for a walk along the Charles down near the Hatch Shell—Don't plan on getting home early, 'cause you'll have to walk—I'm staying late tonight!! Then when we're too tired to walk any more we'll drive out towards Weston or Norumbega; we'll turn on the radio, and we'll just sit and listen to that nice quiet music. You'll just have to put your head on my shoulder or else you can't come with me!! Then whenever you say—we'll go home—

What's that song, "But I can dream, can't I?"?

Oh well—that's only 8 months away from now—Maybe I can think of some better way to spend an evening in all the time I've got left to think about it.

Things over here are the same from day to day—Every night we sit around writing, and shooting the bull. Tonight I think Bud Gaynor is coming over. Maybe we'll have a party—Sure could see it. His fiancé is the one who wrote me that wonderful letter the other day. They're to be married in April, and she wrote me a personal invitation. They're wonderful people! I definitely expect to be home by then, and will be there with rings on my fingers, and bells on my toes. Maybe I'll even press my dress uniform for the occasion, and maybe I'll even take some girl—One never knows!!

I've been with Bud since the 3rd day I've been in the Army. We were in the same squad together all through basic training, leadership school, and OCS. We were both assigned to the same post after we were commissioned, and it was only a month and a half before I was transferred to his unit. We came overseas together and applied for transfer up here together. Mine came through about 2 $\frac{1}{2}$ weeks before his did, and we were sure the two of us would be separated. One night, however, I got a phone call and it was Bud—We jabbered like a couple of school girls, and the next day he came up to the O.P. to see me. He's really a great guy though at times he's inclined to be quite set in his ways. We throw many sarcastic remarks at each other, but I really think the world of him. I've met some wonderful guys since I've been in, and have made some lifelong friends. I believe that alone makes up for the three years out of my life that have been taken from me—

Bud's girl's name is Eileen, and she's a beautiful little blonde, and I'm really crazy about her—Maybe sometime you can get to meet her.

No mail for me for three days or so, but I imagine that tomorrow there'll be something. I sure hope so—no mail sort of spoils the day, and especially when I don't find one there from somebody named Pete Smith. If you ever run across her—tell her to write often and long—would you? I'd sure appreciate it.

Well, honey—another day, and another dollar—I only hope you're in as good spirits right now as you read this as I am in writing it to you—

I won't tell you how much I think of you, Pete, or how much I miss you as you'd never believe me anyway. It's more than you imagine.

Take care of yourself, sweetheart

And write for I'll be thinking of you—
        Good night and God bless you, hon,

                    Yours always, Ron

                    ⊂⊗⊃

This letter to Pete was sort of short, but as we didn't have very much to occupy our time, at this period of our military life, there wasn't much to write about. I mentioned Bud Gaynor and his girlfriend at that time, her name was Eileen Hawkrigg, but he never did marry her. I don't know exactly what happened, but just after Pete (Nancy) and I were married Bud showed up at our door in Connecticut with his new wife Sue. She is still as nice today as she was back in 1954.

When Bud got out of the army we stayed in contact, and as he was only about a two hour ride away, we got to see each other quite often. He worked for Mobil Gas, at that time, and travelled around inspecting sites for their "Mobil Travel Guide". He then went into the insurance business, and ended up as a vice-president of Northbrook Insurance which is a division of Allstate. We have maintained contact with Bud and Sue over the years, and Bud and I went on a Korea Revisit program back in 2006.

When Nancy and I eloped in 1954 we went to New York City for a weekend together before we both had to be back at work. I spent quite a bit of time trying to get hold of Bud, but it was not until the second day we were there that I found him. We drove out to Brooklyn and spent an afternoon looking at slides of Korea. Guess who wasn't too happy about that scene? But, in all truth, I knew more about Bud than I did Nancy, and had spent almost three years at his side. Besides, I was so proud of my new wife that I wanted everyone I knew to meet her, and Bud was at the top of that list. The Korean slides were an unwelcome subject in our married life for many years, and I am still reminded of them upon occasion. If I become somewhat technically proficient I will try to add them to this writing effort for you all to view. I almost wrote "for you all to enjoy", but I think I would be put down for that remark.

Other friends I met in OCS and afterwards are still friends, and we communicate through email. Bob Huntley and his wife Gini live in Ipswich, Mass, but travelled extensively in their motor home every winter. Bob took over his dad's hardware business in Lowell, Mass, and eventually turned it over to his boys. They had 6 kids, and our kids enjoyed being with them as much as we loved being with Gini and Bob. Once he flew down with his whole family piled into a Piper Cub type of plane and landed in an unpublicized field near our house. When they left, I remember, Nancy, her mother, our two children, and I were sure that they would never get the plane up over the trees at the end of the field, but they are all alive and well today.

Another friend is Ray Kalil and his wife Rosemary. They live in Nashville, and own the Weight Watchers franchise for Middle and Eastern Tennessee. Ray owns his own plane, and sits in his office doing what, I don't know, while Rosemary and their two children run their business. We get to see them upon occasion, and love visiting their gorgeous mansion in Brentwood, Tennessee. (They won't like the word "mansion", but that is what it is.)

Ray is very active in The Korean War Vets programs in his state, and was a Colonel in the Tennessee Governor's private Air Force. Unfortunately he has a bad heart, and has trouble flying his plane as often as he would like.

I have other friends with whom I have maintained some sort of communication over the years. Lamar Daugherty was last living in Douglasville, Texas and was a retired Colonel. Ray Barry, my partner in the Pork Chop flap lived through his severe wounds, and retired as a Colonel in the Army. Unfortunately, he passed away just before I tried to contact him in September of 2010. John Brosnan, also a retired Colonel, lives in Killarney, Ireland, and is as elusive as can be. Bud and I suspect that he is, or was, involved with the CIA, but we have no proof.

Bud and Sue have been over a few times to visit both John and Bud's family sites. Nancy and I went over for our 40th Anniversary, and spent a lovely weekend with John in his home and down at the southern end of County Kerry where John had a cottage near the ocean. I am in constant email contact with a man named Bill McWilliams from Las Vegas. Bill was a West Point grad and a veteran pilot who flew in Vietnam. I met both Bill and his wife Ronnie during a trip to Vegas where he was a speaker at our 7th Division reunion.

I received a phone call from him one day. He asked if I would tell him of my involvement in the last battle for Pork Chop Hill. He said he was writing a book about that fight, and he found out through the internet that I had been there. I told him my story, and about Ray Barry and Billy Fritts. The book was published, and there were my words in a whole chapter dedicated to my efforts. I bought enough copies to send each family member, and also a copy to close friends. My story was also published in our local paper, and in a book that the newspaperman, Don Moore, wrote. He has also put that story on the internet, and can be viewed by going on to War Tales by Don Moore[3]. I also organized a reunion of my OCS class in 1999 which we held in El Paso. Got to see a lot of old friends, but those reunion days might be over as there are fewer and fewer of us left now.

****

Letter #28

Fri., 7 Aug.

Dear Pete—

It's only about 12:45 in the afternoon, but I won't be able to get a jeep for an hour or so to continue my inspection, so I just thought I'd start a letter to you.

I haven't had any mail from you for a number of days, but finally I got one today. The last few have been short ones, but I guess you're pretty busy. By the time you get this you'll have been home a few days, and maybe you'll find time to write some longer letters. There's probably not many exciting events going on around home, and you'll be at a loss for things to say, but anything will do me fine.

I, myself, have very little to write about, but I like to write—so I usually fill up the pages with uninteresting things.

I haven't done or seen anything of interest since the war

---

[3] Go to http://donmooreswartales.com and "search" for "Ron Freedman" to read the account of the July battle of Pork Chop Hill.

ended, but I have no complaints. I'm quite disappointed the stateside papers and magazines devoted such little time and space to the ending of the war. My folks were quite happy, of course, but they only wrote one page, and your letter was quite short. Even the people over here seemed to be unenthused. Maybe I'm more emotional than the rest of them, but so far the truce is the biggest thing that ever happened to me. Nobody can ever realize how horrible a thing death or mutilation can be. A person that dies of old age doesn't convey anything to people that look into his casket. It's just too bad—but he was old, and was expected to die. There's no horror or anything. The person is dead—and looks peaceful—

It's quite different over here to see a young kid of about 18 or 19 lying on a stretcher in a stiffened pose—there's no peaceful look on his face—It's usually one of surprise or one of agony—He's not dressed in a blue serge suit, and his hands aren't folded on his chest like you usually imagine people to look like when they die—He always seems to be caked in dirt, and in a filthy uniform. That bothers me the most—Then you see a kid leaning up against the wall of an aid station. He's been wounded—probably not seriously, but he's so damned amazed he actually got hurt he's dumbfounded. I know how he feels—It just doesn't seem possible.

But all that's stopped now—You don't see things like that anymore—You used to see them every day—but nobody gives a damn outwardly—That's the horror of this whole thing. This week's edition of Time had an article under the <u>WAR</u> <u>IN</u> <u>ASIA</u> section in which the writer expressed some terrific sentiments. He said the boys after the last war had suffered but won—the boys over here have just suffered, and he's right. It's very discouraging to think nobody realizes this was a war. Real bullets, etc. It seems no one back home will admit it to themselves—don't say I'm wrong, Pete, because I felt that way when I was back home—I felt the guys in Korea were just the unfortunates of the situation.

I didn't know just how unfortunate they were until I became one of them. I don't for a minute think the world should stop because Ron Freedman is in Korea, but I do believe that everyone, no matter if they know anyone over here or not, should be made to understand the situation, appreciate what some of these kids have done for them, and should make some display of their interest and appreciation. I think it insulting for newspapers and magazines to give first priority to Joe McCarthy's political funding. The realism of what was going on over here never was brought to the fore, and the public was never made to care.

You can't imagine how miserable life can be when you're unwillingly brought 10 or 11 thousand miles from home—sure—somebody's got to go—but damn, how about a little encouragement or outward show of appreciation by those who stayed behind?

Hey—hon—don't get the idea I want you to sit down and write me a thank you note for being here—It's just I've got quite a bit of time left to do, and I'm feeling pretty low about it all—I'm just letting off a little steam, and will be all over this mood in a few hours. It's a combination of things and events that get me like this. This inspection deal is a pain-in-the-neck, mail is slow—The sun is hot—The chow is the same, rice & sweet potatoes—I've seen one movie since sometime in early June—no good books to read—R & R a long way off ...

It's things like that—they all add up, and I get irritated and disgusted for a while. It will all blow over when I get a few minutes to sit down, relax, drink a can of beer, and reread your letter.

(My jeep just arrived to take me on the inspection, so I'll finish this tonight—so long, hon—I'll be thinking of you all afternoon.)

And I did!! I also saw another movie—"The President's Lady"—and I thought it was quite good—I'm also over my irritation for now—I made my inspection, came back and ate, then hustled up to headquarters for a shower, and the show—It turned out to be a good day after all.

The inspection I've been making of the battalion's equipment was completed today, but tomorrow I start on another one. I've got to check the clothing and equipment of every man in the battery to see they still have everything they were issued. It will be a long and tedious job, but I think it can be done in a day.

I've also been told I've been promoted to 1ˢᵗ Lt, but it's all unofficial. My orders got fouled up, and went to the wrong outfit so nobody will commit themselves and tell me—It doesn't make too much difference as I'll get the back pay that's due me, anyway—I believe my promotion is retroactive to 23 May—that's the day I had one year's service as a 2nd Lt. Normally the amount of time required in grade for promotion to 1st is 18 months, but I'm getting it in only 12 as mine is classified a "battlefield promotion." If you serve in a combat area you can get this. They stopped it, however, if you weren't put in for it before 28 July—I made it by about a month.

I'm glad you saw Gen. Clark, but I'm even happier that your meeting didn't end up in a romantic manner—He didn't mention me, did he? I work for him you know, and I thought maybe he said something about me—It must have slipped his mind or something—

I got a letter from Bud Gaynor's father tonight, and am real pleased. It was a nice one in which he thanked me for the note I sent him. Bud was over last night, and gave me his camera. Mine is broken, and I want to get a lot of pictures of this place, and all the people. I have a roll of black and white I took up on the hill, but I haven't sent them to be developed yet. Just plain lazy I guess.

Well, in just a few days from now you'll be cooling it back home in Longmeadow—sure wish I could be back that way myself—These rice paddies are a hell of a long way from any long meadow I know of—

That's about it, Pete—Time to flake out—It's been a long day, and my bed looks quite inviting. So if you'll pardon me, I'm going to trundle off to beddy-bye. Take care now, hon, and write to me often. I'll be thinking 'bout you, and dreaming of you in the meanwhile—Goodnight, Pete—

My thoughts are with you always

Ron

ଓଚ୍ଚ

Now that I am retired, and have some medical problems, I find that I spend a lot of my time doing absolutely nothing. It's almost like being back in Korea fifty-eight years ago. Here I am with nothing to do except write about how I had nothing to do back then. Truth be told, the Army kept us occupied by coming up with ideas like counting all the equipment in the battery. If something was lost during the war, say an airplane or a rifle, we filled out a form, or had the supply sergeant do it, stating that the object was considered a KCL or Korean Combat Loss. That way an accounting of our TO&E, or Table of Organization and Equipment, could be kept up to date. There was always, however, a slip up somewhere and so I guess there was a good reason to have an accounting.

Back in 1952 when I was in my first duty assignment with the 44th AAA Gun Battalion on Cape Cod we had to count every single item in the battalion. We were an all-black battalion, except for the forty-eight white officers, and President Truman ordered all segregated units to be disbanded, and all the men incorporated into the rest of the Army. In our battalion we had four radar vans. These were almost as big as today's trailers that you see on the highway. They had big rotating radar receivers mounted on the roof, and stood out like sore thumbs. Someone, however, painted over the serial number of a particular van, and we could not prove it was ours. Also, my battery was supposed to have over 100 pairs of field pants, but I could not find one pair.

The day of the inspection I could not find one blanket in the whole battery. It was an amazing situation, but our commander, Captain Owen Doherty, told us later on that the Army accepted our count on everything including the missing radar van and that the 44th AAA Gun Battalion was no more. That unit had fought at Gettysburg in the Civil War, and had a fishhook to denote that fact on its battalion crest which we all wore. The fishhook was the symbol that characterized the Union lines in that battle. The unit was field artillery at that juncture, and later was transferred to the Anti-Aircraft.

In the letter that I wrote to Pete, I mentioned what it was like to see dead people. When our ship anchored out in Flying Fish Channel off of Inchon we had to be brought ashore by small landing craft because of the 30-foot tides in that part of the world. We disembarked from these little boats, and trudged (I use that word because we had to hand carry all our own clothing and equipment up a small inclined ramp). I had to stop to catch my breath, and I noticed just off to my right there was a small cabin cruiser painted white with green lettering on it that said USS Repose. That was a hospital ship, and on the front deck there was a body covered in a poncho with only its feet sticking out. It was the first thing I saw in that country and it shocked the hell out of me. I'd like to think it was a mannequin placed there just to get our attention, but I don't think I believe it was.

Dead bodies were not commonly seen unless one went down to Graves

Registration to buy or borrow ice for our drinks. When we had a big flap or even a little one, you would see the dead, usually on stretchers, or just covered up. The closest I came to feeling sick to my stomach was when Major Fritts was decapitated. That was like being hit in the solar plexus by Joe Louis. It still bothers me today, but I am trying to get over the thought.

We had a total of 58,000-plus killed or dead from other causes in our three-year war. The same amount as in Vietnam in their ten year war. However, that war was fought in the age of television, and people could see what was happening almost as it occurred while they sat in their living rooms. That opportunity was not around during the Korean War, and we only saw correspondents rarely. Also, we had just been through a horrendous war with 400,000 dead. People were tired of war and war stories. We would see the papers that parents sent over usually weeks after there was an action. The stories always seemed to be short in length, and never found on a front page. If you had been in a particular flap it was the biggest thing in your life, and yet nobody seemed to care, except your family and friends. It was disheartening to say the least.

Today, things are a lot different. The people stand behind our troops, and best of all, they tell those troops how they feel. I mentioned Joe McCarthy in this letter, and cannot recall having any feelings regarding this man until after I got home. I was recuperating from an illness in the hospital, in the early spring of 1954, and listened faithfully every day to the Army/McCarthy hearings. He sure didn't seem to help this country heal from all its wounds.

I was promoted to 1st Lieutenant around this time, and sensed that my Forward Observer days were at end in the event of a resumption of the war. Going back to fight the Chinese was on our minds most of the time, but I think we were more concerned with what the remnants of the North Korean army might do. We did not trust them at all, and I guess we still feel that way today. They have committed two shooting events in the Truce Area, and have dug a number of tunnels under the truce line. I wonder what else they are doing behind our backs beyond their building an atomic bomb, and selling advance weaponry to our foes. That truce is still in effect, and should not be construed as an armistice by a gullible American public. We are not done with them yet.

****

Letter #29

Tues., 11 Aug

Dear Pete,
     Haven't very much to write about, and without your letters to answer, I'm sort of at a loss for words.

A couple of things have happened, however, in the past couple of days that might interest you. First, my promotion finally did come through, and so now I'm a 1st Lt. Second, and perhaps the biggest news of the war other than the Truce, is the Army's plan to release all Officers who have served for more than 24 months. I fall into that category and have already sent my application for release to Washington. I asked to be separated by the 30th of Sept., and so I might be home by then. I'm not counting on it, however, as I'll be quite disappointed if it falls through.

I'm already planning on that new blue convertible. I'd like to get either a Chevrolet or Pontiac. Both are pretty nice—I think— If I get home early enough I think I'll take me a trip out to Albuquerque. I've a friend out there who wants me to come and live out near him, but I'll go see what it's like first.

We're moving down towards Seoul about the 20th of the month, and then our problems will begin. Our V.D. rate is now negative, but I'm willing to bet it will be anywhere from 4 to 8% within 3 weeks after we arrive. We'll have AWOLs, drunks, and our court-martial rate will go up. We haven't had one since I've been in the battery and that's about 3 months.

This VD is what bothers me the most. I can't understand why grown men or even 19 year old boys can't see the after effects. Some claim they can't help themselves, but I don't believe them. Personally, I can't look one of these women straight in the face without getting a little sick to my stomach—They are the ugliest girls I've ever seen. A letter from 8th Army came down today, and it said 80 to 90% have some form of V.D. I wouldn't doubt it.

It's quite a sad thing. As you drive through the village you see only old men, old women, and little kids. All the men and boys have gone to war, and all the girls have gone to Seoul or Pusan to survive. They can't find enough work legally as Korea has little or no industry now, and they're just another mouth to feed if they stay at home—Besides, they can make good money in the city. If I were a girl I'd rather slave to death than do what they're doing. The Korean people call them "U.N. poo-yin," or U.N. Ladies—this same sort of thing must happen in every country that's been racked by war.

I got thrown in the creek again tonight and for no reason at all. I didn't get a chance to take my clothes off, and I got completely soaked—What-the-hell, it's a lot of laughs.

The weather has been real nice—a few thundershowers now and then, but otherwise, I can't complain. My mail has been slow of late—Nothing from you for the longest time. I wrote last time to Longmeadow. You should have that by now, and maybe you have the last one I sent to Calif. That one had the pictures in it, so when it arrives you'll know that there are no more going to Calif.

I sure hope your stay there was pleasant, and you had a good trip home, I worried about you travelling around like that. I just don't trust airplanes for some damned reason.

I should be moving off to bed by now, but Bud Gaynor is coming over to get his camera, and I have to stay awake till he gets here—Some buddy of his wants to take it to Japan with him tomorrow on R&R. I'm quite tired myself, and am tempted to leave the camera next to my bed, but I know Bud—He'd never let me sleep. He'd probably dump me out of bed—so I figure it's best to wait up for him.

Boy—I'm quite excited about this early release—Sure hope it comes through. If I do get out I won't have to come back in unless they call the Reserves, and if they do that then we'll be in a big war. By staying in the Reserves I can keep my commission. I wouldn't want to come back in as an enlisted man. They have it too rough—

If you're still willing, honey—we've a few dates to fulfill when I get back—I'm still thirsting for that cold beer and lobster, I hope you haven't forgotten—When I get an offer like that—I'm not going to let anyone forget they made it.

I wish I had started this letter earlier—I want to write, but I can hardly keep my eyes open—It isn't fair to write when I'm like this because it doesn't make for an interesting letter—But you know ... I'm trying—

How about letting me know when you start school, and where you're going to live? You should have found a place by now, but if you haven't, how about sending your "little jet plane" over to pick me up, and I'll go looking for you? I'm sure the Army would understand—

Well, Pete—forgive me if the letter seems to be dry—Conditions just ain't right for writing tonight—Bud hasn't shown up yet, but I'm going to sleep anyway—

Goodnight, honey—sleep well—

Maybe I'll see you real soon—

But till then—remember, I miss you, and am thinking of you all day and night—

My love to you, always – Ron

CR&O

The truce is in effect, the war is over. Now what do we do?

Everyone was bored, but there was no place to go to let off some steam. When the day ended beer call started. Each enlisted man could get two cans of 3.2 beer, which had to be opened and drunk on the premises. In this case "the premise" was the little stream that ran through our sleeping hoochies and down through the battery area.

Early in the afternoon someone put the beer in empty sandbags and dunked them into the stream to cool until beer call. The stream, however, was about 85 degrees Fahrenheit, and the beer only got down to the lukewarm stage. The men drank it, however, and seemed to enjoy the time.

Some of them adopted puppies, and played with them. It seems that all the dogs are named "Sukoshi" which is Japanese for "Little or Little One". Dogs are a delicacy to the Korean people, and the GIs want to save all of them that they can find. I don't think I ever saw a cat during the whole time I was over there. I bet they were even more of a delicacy. As a matter of fact, I don't remember seeing any small ground animals, not even a rat or a mouse.

The big topic at that time was Early Release for Officers. We junior officers were a surplus to the Army, and instead of serving our 16 months as originally proscribed there was talk of sending us home early. You can well understand what that meant to us. I did have Helicopter School in the back of my mind as I knew that my weak college background in Television production would probably cause me great concern when I was out looking for a job. I enjoyed Army life to a certain extent, but I had to straighten out my Pete Smith situation before I could make a decision. I knew that I would have sometime before and after my discharge to re-enlist for Helicopters, and I knew that that was one area the Army was looking to enlarge. My buddy, John Brosnan opted for it, and retired at age 47 after thirty years of service as a full Colonel. I envy him living in Killarney, Ireland.

My oldest friend back home, Bill Hacker, was planning on visiting another old friend, Teesie Rosenthal who lived in Albuquerque, New Mexico. We had made plans to go out there after the war, and see what it was that Teesie raved about. Bill did go out there, and met his future wife, Sheila, an Army brat, while he was in New Mexico. (More about what I did in a later letter.)

When I was back at the air base earlier, our battalion had a very high VD rate, and there was talk among the officers that that situation could raise its ugly head if the men had nothing to do. At that time civilian traffic was very limited in our area, but we could envision a loosening of the rules, and we had to prepare for it beforehand.

This letter ended with my remarking that I was waiting for Bud Gaynor to pick up his camera. Mine had broken and I'd been using his to take photos. Our deal was that he could keep all the originals while I got copies. (Over the years my copies have taken on a greenish hue, but I will print them in black and white so that they can be seen properly.)

I keep mentioning Bud, and I think I should say why. I entered the Army on Friday, May 23, 1951 at 10 a.m. in the morning. After our being sworn in we entrained for Camp Kilmer, New Jersey arriving there about 7 p.m. Unknown to us, the noncommissioned officers had drawn up an alphabetical list of our names to be used as a duty roster. On Sunday the 25th, my name was drawn to be an area guard during Visitors Day. My last name beginning with 'Fr' was just in front of the next man in line whose last name began with 'Ga'. He, too, was assigned as an area guard. In fact we two had to police a line in a large field keeping the visitors out of a group of unused barracks. It poured all afternoon, and the visitors sat out in the rain on that muddy field while this 'Ga' guy and I patrolled the sideline. We each took one half of the field and proceeded to walk towards each other wearing our civilian clothes under a helmet liner and poncho supplied by a sergeant.

The first time we met up we acknowledged each other with a brief "Hi".

The second time I said, "I'm Ron." He said, "I'm Bud."

The next time it was, "I'm from Boston", and "I'm from Brooklyn", and so on.

That night we realized that we slept near each other, and I guess we were happy that we each had made a friend. Bud and I had both contracted to attend Officers Candidate School and eventually spent every day together, side by side alphabetically and by height, for the eight weeks of Basic Training, the following eight weeks of Advanced Basic, the next ten weeks in Leadership School followed by four weeks of cadre.

We were sent to Fort Bliss Anti-Aircraft OCS where we roomed, studied, and marched together for the next twenty-two weeks. Upon graduation we were assigned to Camp Edwards on Cape Cod, Massachusetts. He went to the 398th AAA Aw Battalion, and I went to the 44th AAA Gun Battalion. The desegregation order from President Truman closed down our battalion, and I was transferred to the 398th. Bud was in Charlie Battery, and I was in Baker. Again, we spent practically every evening together, and even went overseas in the same stateroom.

In May I transferred up to the 7th Infantry Division, and two weeks later Bud transferred up to that division as well. Each Artillery Battalion has an anti-aircraft platoon assigned as its support. Bud was sent to Dog battery of the 15th AAA AW Battalion which supported my unit, the 48th Field Artillery battalion. His platoon headquarters was on the hill directly behind my Observation Post, and we maintained contact daily. I even called on his unit to act as artillery upon occasion. We came home together on the same ship, and flew to NYC together. We revisited Korea in 2006, and our families have maintained a close relationship over all these years. The Army did something right when it put us together.

****

Letter #30

Sat., 15 August

My Dearest One,

Seven o'clock on a beautiful summer night is no time for a guy to be writing letters. He should be combing his hair or straightening his tie for the millionth and last time before he goes to pick up that beautiful girl of his. No, honey, it's a shame he has to dream of all this instead of actually being able to live it. That's the way it's been with me for the longest time now. Mentally, I see myself fixing that striped tie, telling the folks I'll see them in the morning, rolling the car out of the garage, and then picking up that beautiful girl. Someday real soon I'm going to do all that, and it won't be a dream.

I'm sitting outside in sort of a speaker's stand that we use sometimes, my feet up on a bench, my pipe in my mouth, the sun going down behind me, a cool breeze, and a little running brook just below me. To make it complete, honey, I need only you—then I wouldn't have to write this letter—I would say it all to you. I got two letters from you today, and they just—I can't put it into words—but let me tell you this—If you keep writing like that

you're gonna have me falling in love with you real-real soon—
Those two letters did more for me than any other letter I've
ever received. You couldn't have made them any better no matter
how hard you tried.

I've been moody all week—a combination of the heat, the
work, the chow, and the lack of mail. I know my attitude showed
through my last letter or two, and Pete—I'm truly ashamed of
myself. I know myself to be moody, but sometimes when I get
that way I don't want to get out of that mood. I do my best
thinking and daydreaming then, but I cause trouble for myself
and others.

I've learned to care an awful lot for you in these past
months, and it's my nature to be afraid that whatever part of
your heart that I might call my own will be someone else's if I
don't hear from you all the time. It's purely a selfish act on my
part, and I realize it, but I don't want anything to hurt what we
have built between us. When I don't hear from you for a few
days I actually get sick at heart. And yet, I have no right to
expect you to write all the time. I feel so damned low and foolish
when I read your letters that tell me not worry because if I had
any brains I'd realize you wouldn't stop writing without an
explanation. As mixed up as this page may seem I know you
understand what I'm trying to tell you.

Have faith in me Pete, and try to forgive me for all my
mistakes. I make many of them, but none are with any intention
to do the slightest harm. When I write and the letter seems to
be all wrong—you just sit right down and write me two words—
smarten up. I promise it won't be long before I do.

I wrote you a 10-page letter this afternoon, but I won't mail
it as it was one of the poorest examples of the English language
I've ever seen. Last night our battalion entertained the Horace
Heidt USO troupe, and we all got quite drunk. I got to bed about
3 A.M., and at 5 I had to take a convoy on a 6 hour trip. You can
well imagine how I felt when we returned at 11. I came into the
hoochie to find your letters, and as soon as I finished reading
yours I started to answer you. I was tired, hot, and still a bit
drunk from last night, but I just had to write you. In it I tried to
tell you some of the things I've already said in this letter, but
they just wouldn't come out right on the paper. Actually, I could

write you a 50 page letter every day. All I'd have to do is write down my thoughts because all I do is dream of you all day long.

When you wrote you closed your eyes, and could see me on that steamer you probably made me the happiest guy in the world. I "see" you everywhere I go. I even get the crazy idea I might bump into you in Seoul or maybe it will be in San Francisco when my boat does dock. Wherever it is I do find you Pete, I don't care, but I pray it's soon. I've got to get home now, and most important—I've got to get home to you. That's all I'm living for now, sweetheart—getting home to you.

Pete, where would I be today if I didn't happen to see two girls in Camel Hair Coats in front of the Riverside Apartments one afternoon last November? I had been over to school to find you, but I was told you had left with your roommate. So I left too, but as I drove down the Riverway, and saw you there I really felt funny. I was sure you wouldn't remember me, and I was afraid that I might embarrass you, but like a good trooper you came through and remembered my name.

Sweet—I just got a call, and I have to go to Seoul immediately. I don't want to go—I'd rather stay here and be with you tonight, but it's an emergency, and I couldn't get out of it. I'll continue this tomorrow night when I get back. Goodnight, darling—I'm going to miss you real bad until I get back to this letter, then I'll probably miss you more—

Love you always—

Ron

প৪০

It is hard to recall right now exactly how I felt in getting two letters from Pete, but if I think about it, and all the things I probably had rumbling through my mind at that time, I can most likely go back to that time in my mind. I was counting something, somewhere, I am sure, as that is all we seemed to do when we weren't training or having "Cannoneers' Hop". That, by the way, is where the gun crew moves from one position on the gun to confirm that everyone knows what to do in case of an emergency. As mentioned before, every soldier learns the first thing in the service that it is a "rifle" not a gun, and that a cartridge belt is just that and not a "bullet belt" as one of our Italian immigrant draftees in basic used to call them. Also a weapon can be called a "piece", and our howitzers were often called just that. The men also practiced "laying the battery" which encompasses the installation of the piece and it leveling, etc.

We were finally notified that we were going to have some entertainment, which was sorely needed by all. Horace Heidt and his Musical Knights were coming to our area, and the whole division was invited to attend. Heidt was the leader of his band which was known as one of the "big bands" in the musical world. They were not in the same league as say, Harry James or the Dorsey brothers as far as big name recognition was concerned, but they could be heard on the radio all the time. We were told that he was bringing eighteen young lady banjo players, and Colonel Kimmitt mentioned that the junior officers should be on their best behavior because we should be escorting the girls as they were in our age bracket.

Our battalion was selected to meet and greet the group at a steak dinner party which was held in some sort of a nearby building. I didn't think there was a place like that anywhere in the area, but I do remember the Colonel calling me over and pinning on my silver bars while we stood next to a bar. Either that actually happened or I've made up a good story. In any event, the junior officers never even got near the young ladies as the senior officers (what we call Field Grade officers, majors and up) took over our jobs. Somewhere they got their hands on eighteen ambulances, and each girl was driven to where they held the show. Most, if not all, the young guys were disappointed, but like the song said; "Que será, será".

Figure 61 - Training on a 105 Howitzer.

The whole division, I think about 16,000, sat in a hillside bowl to watch and listen to live music. The show started when an announcer came to the front of the stage and informed us that our Commanding General Arthur Trudeau would make a special presentation to Mr. Heidt. The audience was as quiet as could be, and he said, "Let's hear it for General Trudeau."

Before the applause started we all heard a solitary voice from way back at the top of the hill holler down a very derogatory two word commentary. It must have been heard on the stage as a soundman who was recording the show at the side of the stage, whirled about in his chair and dropped his earphones. Trudeau, however, either did not hear anything or else he chose to ignore it, and so he made his presentation of a chrome plated bayonet mounted on the base of a 105mm shell to Mr. Heidt. If you will remember from earlier in the commentary, each division in Korea had a name attached to it and all the units had names that started with the same letter to use as their designations. The 7th Infantry Division was called "Bayonet" and my unit, the 48th Field, was called "Bone". Other units were "Blaster", Boxer", etc.

I remember that Heidt's vocalist was a young man named Hal Derwin. He had a pleasant voice, but I never heard of him again. He sang "I'm Walking Behind You, On Your Wedding Day" which was a hit for Eddie Fisher as I recall.

The evening ended, and we went back to our units to wait for the next day. That was the only USO show I ever saw, and only the second time I witnessed any entertainment. Back in Leadership School, or La DI Da School as some called it, we had a 48-hour field exercise, which knocked us all out. After chow, when the day was done, we had to watch as they backed up a flatbed trailer, on which a solitary girl did a tap dance for us. It was the last day of that school, and I think that was the toughest ten weeks I ever spent.

One night our platoon had KP duty, and the meanest captain that ever lived refused to release us at the end of the day. He said we were the poorest example of "future leaders" he'd ever seen, and ordered the walls to be washed down with the fire hoses. Well, the paint peeled off the walls and clogged all the drains in the mess hall. We had water over our ankles before he attempted to call a civilian plumber. A hard man to find on a Sunday night. We stayed there until the next morning, and were advised a few weeks later that an Inspector General had reviewed the situation and that the captain had been court-martialed.

I was the pot boy for that duty, and I'll bet those pots were never cleaned so well. The next weekend I visited my friend Margie Lantos and her husband Ray in Philadelphia, and while waiting for Ray to get home from Medical School, I showed her how to clean pots and pans the Army Way. Ray Lantos, by the way, was wounded severely in Italy during the WWII, and left for dead. Fortunately, he was found and his life saved. He went on to be a well-loved heart doctor in the Johnstown, Pennsylvania area, and I am still in contact with

Margie. Our families grew up together, and she has always been a dear and close friend.

If the Horace Heidt visit was the biggest thing to happen around that time you can well imagine how bored we were.

****

Letter #31

Sun., 16 Aug—

Hi, Honey—

I'm back, and I'm quite tired and dirty. It was a very tiring ride, and the road was just clogged with convoys. The dust was like a fog the whole 60 miles. I saw my boy Jim, and we had a few pleasant hours together. I got to Seoul about 10 P.M., and found Jim at the 5th Air Force Officers Club. We stayed till 11 or so, and then went swimming over at the Canadian Officers Club with some Canadian Officers we met. Today we took the 1st Sgt. to the hospital, and while we were there the doctors were trying to pump the stomach of a colored boy who had eaten rat poison, and swallowed a bottle of methylate. He died just before we left the ward. He was waiting to be court-martialed for desertion, and I guess he was trying to beat the rap.

We came back about a half hour ago, and the dust was just as bad coming back. I got the 1st Sgt. mad at me because I wouldn't stop to take a shower—I had to hurry back to write to you. I ran up to the mess hall, grabbed a handful of cold turkey, and washed it down with a beer, and now I'm in the BOQ and I'm not going to do another thing until I've finished this—no matter what comes up—

While in Seoul, I had some pictures developed, and I'm going to send you 2 or 3 every letter. I think there's a total of 17. They didn't come out very well, but they'll give you an idea of what this country, and our own area looks like. I also got me one more silver bar—They're scarcer than hen's teeth, but Jim dug one up some place. Now I have one for my hat and one for my collar.

I spent an hour trying to find you a pair of earrings, but there isn't a thing to be had over here. The main PX usually carries a line of jewelry made in Thailand. It's real pretty stuff— You know—dragons and dancers, etc.—Maybe next time I go down they'll have something.

I found a letter on my bed from my mother when I walked in, and I got soundly chewed out for not writing—That was about 2 weeks ago—Man, wait till she gets this past week's mail—She's in for a surprise. I think I only wrote once—

Coming back today I got to thinking, and I'll bet you're pretty disgusted with me because I complain about the lack of mail, and then I don't write myself—as the saying goes around here, "I'm nothing but terrible." In the future I will, however, be different—I hope to write you more letters than you know what to do with. You make me feel good when you say you've been saving all my mail. Someday, we'll reread them together—so hang on to them—

I got something to tell you, but I have to tell you in a roundabout way or else I'll spoil it all—Last night as we left the club I stopped on the front stairs to look up and see if it was going to rain—Just as I looked up I saw a shooting star fall behind this big mountain. So I made a wish. Now, this is the ticklish part because it won't come true if I tell you what I wished. I'll tell you, however, in a way so I won't have to come right out and say it, but you'll have to close your eyes, and put yourself in somebody else's shoes—Sorry, size 9D combat boots.

All right—now picture this—You're standing on the stone steps of a patio, and there are about 100 people sitting outside at tables having their last drink. You're quite tired, and the only thing you can think of is the fact you're quite mad because you had to leave a letter you wanted very much to finish. It was to a certain somebody you would have liked to have had right next to you, and you were quite blue because you knew it couldn't be true. You're thinking how wonderful it would be if you could go home right away to her. Mind you now—you're only, only idly dreaming when all of a sudden you see a shooting star—You're still thinking of how you want to go home to her as soon as possible when you see this star—Quickly you make a wish. Now, if you were standing in this person's size 9D combat boots—what would you wish?

Remember now—you're thinking about going home real soon to her …

Well, if you came up with the answer I think you will—then you'll know what I wished, and I've often been told if you wish on a shooting star it <u>always</u> comes true.

I sound like a girl in junior high school, don't I?—but I really did that—and I wanted you to know—

Sweetheart—you just put me up in heaven with those two letters, and I know the feeling will never go away—I don't want it to go away—You've really made me feel so wonderful—I feel like a heel because of the way I've acted, and I apologize. You and your letters have been the most wonderful thing that's ever happened to me—If I could only in some way show my gratitude I'd be very much happier, but no matter how hard I try I can't make my pen say all my heart feels. If you'll wait for me then I'll be able to tell you, and then I know the words will come as they should. It seems now I've known you all my life, and when I come home it won't seem at all possible to believe I've hardly ever seen you-

Well, honey I hate to close this, but I have to write home—I'll be dreaming of you tonight—let's see in about 45 minutes or so. Wonder what you're doing right now? Well, no use in tormenting myself—goodnight, princess—take care of yourself, and write me—

I miss you very much, Pete—More and more each day in fact-

You're always with me, darling.

All my love to you—Ronnie

Cﾃﾞꕥﾞﾞﾞ

That weekend with Jim Gillen probably tired me out more than it shows in the letter I wrote to Pete. Jim was always an on-the-go kind of a guy, and he never seemed to slow down even when it came to a bottle of booze. He drank a lot, and I foolishly tried to keep up with him. When we served together at our first duty station on Cape Cod, he and I had adjoining rooms in the BOQ (Bachelor Officers Quarters), and ate at the same mess table every day. At night we always ended up at the Coonamesset Inn, Falmouth, and then usually on to the afterhours joint called the Alibi Lodge, which was somewhere in the nearby woods.

One night Jim was late for chow, and said he would meet me at the Alibi around midnight. He arrived as a passenger in John Chruney's Nash automobile. We stayed at the Alibi until early morning, but when I awoke the next day there was no Jim Gillen at breakfast. When he finally arrived for duty he said that he and Chruney had a disagreement about a left or right turn on the way home. Apparently it was a wrong turn and they ended up in the soft mud of an outgoing tide on some beach. Jim said the car couldn't maintain traction, and there was nothing else to do until they could get a tow out of the mud in the morning.

The Nash people had invented reclining seats in that year's model, and so they both put their seats down and took a nap. Jim said that the rising tide woke him when he felt cold water around his ankles. They jumped out, and found a garage that was able to pull them free, and get the car started in time to meet the troops for that day's activities.

The only time I found Jim to quiet down was when he found out about Paint-by-Numbers which was a craft toy that one could use to make a painting look personally made. We both went out and bought the Nude subject, and for days after noon chow we went back to the BOQ, and spent a half hour or so pretending to be artists. My finished product looked so false that I threw it away, but Jim had his tacked up on his wall for all the world to see. After I came home I introduced Pete to Jim, and she always liked him as company from then on.

In this last letter to Pete, I remarked that she told me about keeping my letters, and I said that maybe we would talk about them at some future date. Well, here we are almost sixty years later, and we finally got around to talking about them. That old Lord & Taylor shoebox sat untouched on our closet shelf for all those years, and never once did we open it to look inside. Now, as I write these commentaries I re-read each letter that I wrote, and it brings back some wonderful thoughts and memories. I sure wish I were 24 again instead of 82, but then, don't we all?

That scene of the GI who drank the Merthiolate, I think was written about in an earlier letter to Pete. I don't think it happened during that weekend with Jim, as I wrote in this last letter to Pete. Maybe I had more to drink than I remember! But in any case, I am quite sure it happened earlier. Drinking with Jim was always a problem for me.

****

Letter #32

Monday, 17 Aug—

Dearest Pete—

Nothing much has happened since last night, but I'm sure I can find something to write about. I'm in a writing mood, and can't think of a better way to spend an evening than with you. That's the way I get to feeling when I write to you. So sit back while I do some rambling on—

Today was the hottest and sultriest yet, but as I had to move into the FDC this morning I stayed fairly cool all day. Now that Lt. Gleason has gone home we have to have a duty officer who will live in there every night. We're moving to our new position on Thursday, and it seems foolish I had to move everything for just a few nights. The battery commander, however, wanted it that way, and as Alfred Lord Tennyson once wrote, "Theirs not to be a reason why—theirs but to do or die". So I moved—It's not bad in here—cool, and I have a little room to myself. I've got a nice table to write on and an electric fan blowing down my back—

I got one letter today, and it was from a little kid about 7-yrs-old I know from camp. He's really the cutest little devil, and I got quite a kick out of it. I never told you about camp, did I? My folks have been very friendly with this couple for almost 25 years now, and the man has been running this boys summer camp up in Maine for about 29 or 30 years. I started there when I was 4 yrs old, and went every summer for 18 years. The name of this place is Brunonia, which is brown in Latin (the owner of the place was once a famous football player from Brown University) and it's about 35 miles west of Portland, Maine. It's really a beautiful spot, and someday I'll take you up there.

Every year the same kids went back every summer, and I'm still friendly with about 10 or 15 guys I met when I was only 4 or 5 years old. Zeke Levin is one of them. Right now my kid brother is spending his first year as a full-fledged counselor up there, and he's given my address to everyone. I think this is about his 12th or 13th year up there—By the way—his name is

Steve, and he's 18 years old. You couldn't meet a nicer kid in the whole world—He's really terrific. You'll like him I know—Gonna be a lady-killer, too—Give him about 2 or 3 more years. He starts at Mass. State this fall—My folks must have been reading funny books when they picked out our names. Mine is Ronald Kenneth, and his is Steven Leslie. Originally his name was Stephen, but he writes it as Steve or Steven. After 24 years now, I've gotten used to Ronald, but every so often I get fits of laughter when I write it down or someone calls me—None of my kids are going to be tagged like that—They'll have plain and simple names—Vladimir, Casper or something like that.

There's a fellow sitting outside playing a guitar, and some other guys are singing along with him. My radio is broken, and I'm hurting for good music. I can't sing worth a damn, but I'm continually singing. I get a song on my mind and I don't stop for months. I like good music—none of this bop, etc., for me—just slow pretty tunes. I don't know if you ever heard "China Nights" or "Gomenasai" They're both very popular over here, and we all sing them. The last one means "excuse me" in Japanese, but it is used to mean "I'm sorry" in the song. I think it's real pretty— Another thing I'm crazy about is Gilbert and Sullivan—I could listen to them forever. I liked Dixieland, but only in doses—too much of that stuff can drive you bananas.

Remember the night we went to "Storyville"? We parked on Marlboro Street, and had to walk for miles in that freezing cold—We sat way down front in the left hand corner—Our one date—honey—Seems so long, long ago—I think I called you a million times after that, but you were always busy—I was crazy to have given up—look what I've missed, but as you wrote—"it all works out for the best—". You probably would have tired of me, and then I wouldn't be writing to you now—I'm very glad that it's worked out the way it has.

You remember Zeke Levin, don't you? After he went to Marine OCS he wrote me and asked me to take out Frannie Levine for him—So I obliged one night, and she happened to mention your name—I asked her who was still at Wheelock that I might know—When she said Pete Smith I was amazed—I thought you had graduated the year before. That's when I came down to see you last November—It's funny how things work out,

Pete—isn't it? You don't know how glad I am that I sent you that Christmas Card—Another thing was that pocketbook—I walked into the Hotel Kyoto, and saw it in a shop window. I just walked up to the lady, and had her wrap it—for some reason it had to go to you—It's one of those strange things—It was like it had a card on it saying "this belongs to Pete Smith." I'll be honest with you, darling, I went into the hotel looking for the bar, not for presents, but I saw it, and just had to send it to you—That's the way my mind works—Sometimes it's good, and sometimes it's bad.

Well, honey—I've been rambling on for an hour and a half now, and it's about time to close—I hope you don't mind the way I switched from subject to subject, but it seems we're just sitting here batting the breeze around—I don't think I could write in any other way—

Before you fall asleep tonight would you tell yourself that Ronnie is thinking of you at that very moment—I will be too, honey—asleep or awake—I miss you more and more all the time, darling, and even though each day does bring me nearer home—that day won't come soon enough—Goodnight, Pete—

My love will be yours, always—Ron

ᬠᬠ

The remains of the summer were dragging along, but I was told to move into the Battery FDC as it was a battalion rule that an officer had to be on duty there at all times. I was allowed to leave for chow, and to perform other duties in the battery area, but I had to be available in the event of an emergency. Actually, living in a sandbag hoochie that did not have a stream running through it was a lot more comfortable than one would think. Although it was damp, the humidity was lower than in the BOQ, and the air seemed quite cool in comparison. It was also a lot quieter as the FDC personnel did not have to be there all day every day. We weren't shooting at anything, and thank goodness, the Chinks weren't shooting at anything either.

I had known Zeke Levin for almost 20 years. He and I attended a boy's camp together, and eventually his family moved to Newton, Mass., my hometown, and we spent a lot of time together. Zeke died quite unexpectedly at an early age, and it happened at the same time that my cousin also passed away, and when my dad was in his last stages. I went to Zeke's funeral, but just could not go inside the building. It was just too much to bear at that time. I hope his mother, sister, and wife can find a way to excuse me. I did call on his wife Patty, a few weeks later, but she refused to see me. Pete and I were with them on their first date back in Hartford where Nancy and I lived.

My purchasing a handbag for Pete is mentioned in this letter, and that little item probably brought me more happiness than anything else ever did. Nancy still has the little silver handbag, and I still think it was a good deal.

In 1978, Nancy and I spent a night in Kyoto, but I never thought to look for the hotel where I had bought the little handbag. Nancy probably still has information on where we spent each day, at that time, and can tell me what hotel we stayed in, but I don't think it was the same one. We shopped on Kwaramaguchi Street in Kyoto, and I recall not wanting to walk too far down that street as that was where John Christopher and I met our Japanese girls at the Cabaret Den-en back in 1953. I'm sure it was no longer there, but I didn't want to have to explain anything at that time.

I flew back to Korea that day, and back to the humdrum life of the Anti-Aircraft. However, that R&R was a fateful one for me as it soon set me up to be a pen pal, and to an event that has lasted almost sixty years.

****

Letter #33

Wed., 19 August

Hi Honey—

At 8 A.M. this morning, I heard someone lift up my mosquito netting and say—"I think you're waiting for this—aren't you, sir?" I didn't even open my eyes—but said that if it was from 130 Westmoreland Ave—I was —It was from you, and so I was awakened in the best way possible—

It's only noon time now, but as I might be busy all day I'm writing this as soon as possible so I can be sure it gets off okay—We move tomorrow at 12:30 to our new position. I probably won't get a chance to write tomorrow, but I sure will try—

I'm glad you had a good trip home, but wish you could have stayed a little longer out west, as it also made me feel closer to you—It may be, however, that as soon as you start teaching the days will go by faster, and the time won't seem so long—I'm sort of dubious about this early release deal, and would rather nobody planned on my coming home any too soon—Maybe you won't hear it on the radios like you did about the prisoners of war, but when they tell me to pack up for home you shall receive either in letter or cable form the same message you wrote—"Lt. Freedman wants Miss Smith to know he's coming home." Or would you rather pick up a telephone someday, and hear somebody say, "Lt. Freedman wants Miss Smith to know he is home and he'll be right over to see you." Which do you prefer?

If I don't go home early—I'll probably go on R&R to Japan very soon, and then one day you'll get a call from an operator telling you to be near a telephone on such and such a time on such and such a day because there will be a trans-oceanic call for you from Japan—and when that call comes through you might hear me say "Lt. Freedman wants Miss smith to know he isn't home, he doesn't know just when he will be home, but he wants her to know he sure is wishing like all hell he was home."—I say that you might hear him say that because he'll probably be too excited to talk—You'll probably have to do all the talking as a matter of fact—Pete, honey—I miss you so very much!!!

I've been thinking of a name for your new car all morning, but I can't think of one—So here's what we're gonna do—if you're agreeable—all the guys in the FDC are gonna think of a name—the prize winner will get a case of lukewarm (is there any other kind?) beer. First, however, we have to know the type-year-kind, and color, so send the info along as soon as you can, and you should have a name pretty soon.

It's funny you should write about the time I saw you in front of Wheelock, when I just mentioned it in a letter—I'm quite sure you remembered me, but maybe I just think you did because I wanted you to—However, it better not happen again!! Charlie and Connie must both be thrilled he hasn't received his orders as yet, and I don't say that I can't agree with them—he sure is lucky, and I wish you'll tell him I hope he remains that way. This place is bad enough for a single man—My battery commander—Bill Crouch—class of '51 says he knows Charlie—Crouch is one hell of a good guy—career man, etc.

I originally planned on staying in, Pete, but I've sort of

changed my mind. First off—I've seen all I want of war—It was only a little bit, but it's left something on my mind I'll never forget—secondly—the army is reducing the number of officers now, and is giving us a chance to get out—third—maybe you don't realize it, but I've really missed you—how do you think I'd feel if I were married—In the army you never know when they might ship you someplace you can't take your family—and honey—when I marry I don't want to leave my girl for a minute—Even that would be too long.

The only catch to the whole thing is we'll probably be caught in another war soon, and as I'm in the reserves I'll have to go—If they do call me, however, I won't feel I'm leaving here willingly, and that will be half the battle. As for plans for the future—I don't know—I just want to get home to you, my family, and some of the things I've missed. I think I'd like to go out west, and see what I can see—I want to settle down, but I've always had an itch to travel—I'm going to have to think of some get-rich-quick scheme so I can have enough money to do all this, and I'm going to have to find me a girl who'd be willing to do all this with me—Best thing to do, I guess, is wait till I get home, and then decide—maybe you'll give me some help?

I sure hope you send those pictures along—I need something to help keep my morale up—I'll send some of myself to you as soon as I can get them taken—I'm afraid to send any home to the folks as I've lost quite a bit of weight over here—Naturally, I don't look any different when I shave in the morning, but I know Mother would notice the difference in one second—

That's about all for now, treasure. I'll close my letter but not my thoughts of you. I think of you constantly, and pray I'll be with you soon—

Theirs a song my mother always used to sing, and its title fits you perfectly—It's "My wonderful One"—maybe you know it. That's the way I feel about you, and I want you to know it—So long for today, sweetheart—Take care of yourself for me, and remember I miss you.

My love will be yours always—Ronnie

ଓଔଔଓ

The truce was in effect, but we stayed just where we were until word came down that we were moving to a rear area position. Apparently the Army wanted to make sure the Chinese were not going to make any sudden moves and attack us. As I had been in a stationary situation during my part of the war, I had never been involved in a shift in position where we had to make a move as our Army did earlier in the fighting. At times a unit had to move everything every night, and it was not an easy thing for them to do.

I remembered my old AAA outfit that was "semi-mobile". We had sixty-four weapons in the battalion that either had to be towed or trucked, and we only had less than half the vehicles needed to move us just across the street, if that were the case. At least, here in the Field Artillery, we had enough equipment to transport everything and everybody.

We moved out one morning, and only went a few miles south to our new position. The guns were placed properly, and all the other things that were necessary to set up our position were also done. We were not, however, under a real combat situation, so I noticed that things were done almost in slow motion. There was no need to hurry, and the troops knew it. We didn't have to build any sandbag hoochies, but we did live in a squad tent. As I have mentioned in an earlier note, living in an army tent that did not breathe under severe heat and humidity, was difficult for us to bear. The drinking water still tasted terrible, the beer was still warm, and that damned Yoo Hoo had that sickening sweet taste that made me drink the miserable water to wash down that awful aftertaste.

The two major powers were setting up a prisoner exchange over near Panmunjom, about sixty miles to our west. The few photos we saw of the returning POWs really riled me, as those people had suffered more than one can imagine. At this date in 2013 there are still 8000 missing from the Korean War, and I have a theory as to where many of them are. Koreans ate rice as their main staple, and rice paddies are to be found throughout the whole country. In some areas they are side by side for acre after acre, and as they have been worked for countless years, or even centuries they do not have true bottoms to them. I am sure that many of our missing are lying in those paddies and have sunk down in the mud to where they can't be found. In a later commentary I will explain where that theory originated.

The hard ground in many parts of Korea has probably been worked as a vegetable plot at some point in its life. One night, again back in the AAA area, we were all called out at about 3 A.M. as many of our gun positions were sinking in the mud as a sudden spring thaw took place. Some of our vehicles had winches on them, and that was the only way to get them out and on to hard ground. It took all night and the next day to reposition everything.

The "Early Release" program was on all our lips, but we knew nothing of how it was going to work or who would be eligible. Naturally, as citizen soldiers, most of us expected to be on the list, but guys like Gillen and Brosnan , who were what we called "RA's" or Regular Army, or career soldiers, were probably a little concerned, and hoped that their names were not on the Early Release roster. We just had to sit and wait to see what happened.

Pete wrote me about her new car. She was excited, and I couldn't blame her. It was a light blue Chevy convertible with a stick shift. Even today she won't have a car without a stick. I'm lazier. I like the automatic. Her dad, who knew everybody in town, had a connection and helped her find the car. Later, when he helped us buy a car it was a four door Plymouth that I am positive was pre-owned buy a little old lady. I was almost embarrassed to be seen in that car. Thank God, it caught fire and we had to get rid of it.

In the cooler fall weather Pete would drive around with the top down, but with the heater on full blast. Women are strange!

****

Letter #34

Thurs. 20, Aug.

Dearest Pete—

As far as I can find out the mail that was supposed to have been sent out this morning never left the mail clerks hoochie. We were supposed to get mail today, and at the same time the outgoing was supposed to be picked up. As yet we've neither received mail nor sent any out. However, we're supposed to get mail tonight. If we don't you'll find yesterday's and today's letters arriving at the same time—

We got up at 4 A.M., and the battery was loaded and ready to go by 7:30, but as is the usual case with all army doings we just sat around and waited. Finally during a terrific rainstorm— old Charley Battery 48th Field moved out smartly—We got about half way down here when the rain stopped, and the sun came out—the dust was terrific, and it caked over everything. When we arrived we were all quite at odds with the world, and after one look at the new position we were ready to give up—I won't go into details, but take my word for it—this place ain't fit for the birds—it's not good enough for them!!

The terrain down here is much, much different from what it was back there—The hills are real small, and there are very few streams. We're on the right flank of the Marines, and the left flank of the British—It seems funny to see these big, bronzed men stripped to the waist marching down the road in berets or tams. Instead of PXs they have what they call "roadhouses" along the roadside. They're made out of white stucco or something, and are trimmed with dark wood. They're real English looking, and have names like "Newcastle," or "Northland" Roadhouse.

My stomach is grumbling as I've had nothing to eat all day—both dinner and supper were C-rations, and I can't quite see them—Right now I can either starve until breakfast or eat a can of crackers, jam, instant coffee, dehydrated milk, sugar , and water purification tablets. That's one of the components of the C-ration.

Skoshie just came into the hoochie, and crawled under my bed to sleep —She's the cutest damned thing—always on the go—chewing shoes, brushes, and continually nipping at Butterball—I'd love to bring her back home with me—

I wish that mail truck would show up. Our mail goes from the APO (army post office) to battalion headquarters. The clerk up there sorts it all into the proper batteries, and then drives it over to us. Our clerk sorts it into the proper places, and then gets out in front of his hoochie and yells "MAIL CA—" He never finishes his yell as he's swamped by a galloping herd—Seems hard to believe there's somebody else that wants mail as badly as I do—

Writing to you tonight reminds me of when I used to write to you while on the hill. All the light I have is a flashlight just like it was then—Only before I used to sit in the tunnel or hang a blanket up so Joe wouldn't catch any reflections. Now that the pressure's off—I don't care how many Chinks know I'm writing. This letter's to my Pete, and Mao Tse Tung could be right behind me, and I wouldn't even care—let him go write his own letters—

I wish I were home with you now, and didn't have to write any more letters—I wish I could see you instead of just looking at your pictures—I wish—I wish—I wish. Doesn't help much, does it, darling?

Whatcha doing right now? Let's see—it's about 9 P.M. over

here, that would be … 8 AM on Thursday morning the 20th of August back in Longmeadow. You probably won't even get up for an hour or two—Pretty soon I'll be home, and I won't be getting up until maybe 3 or 4 in the afternoon. I'm going to make up for all this lost time.

I'm in a funny old mood tonight—I'm dead tired, and yet I'm not—I'd give anything to be near you right now. I'd probably put my head down on your shoulder, and sleep for a million years—that would be quite thoughtless of me, wouldn't it? But I've told you I'm selfish—Just to be near you is all I need—If you don't mind, tonight when I do go to sleep I think I will put my head down on your shoulder—I bet I could even smell the perfume in my dreams—if I knew what kind—

I guess you think I'm crazy with all my strange ideas—Maybe so—but that's the way I'm actually feeling and thinking right now—Somehow—my letters to you write themselves, I just hold the pen on the paper, and it goes by itself. Quite often I find I have to restrain it as it goes a little too far —someday, however I'll tell you in person all I didn't say on paper, but just for now, darling, I want you to know you are all that is on my mind both day and night. These things I tell you I feel all the time—not just when I write—missing you as much as I do is one of the best things that's ever happened to me.

Goodnight, sweetest one—

my love is with you always—

Your Ron

Figure 62 - Nancy "Pete" Smith

CROSO

I'm pretty sure that everybody was writing a letter to someone at the time that I wrote to Pete. There was nothing else to do, and certainly no place to go. Chief Rulong probably found a quart or two of something to drink, and Lieutenant Crouch was probably spit shining his entrenching tool. That is how boring it was.

By this time I had been writing to Pete for almost five months. I am sure that I was convinced that she was the girl for me, and it all came out in my letters to her. I never asked her if she understood my thinking, and I guess that I just assumed she did. In any event, I just continued along those lines.

I would have gone over to visit with Bud, but I did not know where his outfit had set up. In fact I didn't even know where we were, and had to leave everything up to our Battery Commander, 1st Lt. Bill Crouch, a West Pointer, as was Ray Barry. I think they were in the same class at the Point, and had a lot in common. Bill was a no-nonsense kind of guy. At first, I didn't think he had a sense of humor, and that all he did was scowl all day.

*Figure 63 - The part of the Wyoming Line we would fall back to
if we needed to do so.*

One afternoon I had to go make some sort of a request from him, and after I saluted, and said "Sir" he just looked me in the eye and said, "Dress yourself down, Lieutenant!" I think he thought I wouldn't understand that command, but I had heard it a number of times in OCS, and was prepared to show him that I knew what he was talking or scowling about. He wanted me to see to it that my shirt button line was directly above the fly line in my fatigues. To this day, I always check to see that there is only one straight line down my front. It's a lesson that has stayed with me all these years, and I have now Retired Colonel William Crouch of Panama City, Florida to thank for that. When I phoned him for Ray's address his wife yelled "Willie, it's for you!", but I wouldn't dare call him that even now.

Figure 64 - Road back to the Wyoming Line from the Jamestown Line.

When the United Nations manned a permanent type of possession or line across Korea they gave that line a name. Two of the names I remember are Jamestown and Wyoming. I know that the Wyoming line was behind the line we occupied when the truce came about. I think that our new positions were just behind the Wyoming line to the south. This line consisted of pre-built bunkers, trenches and barbed wire, along with other types of fortifications. If we had to pull back during the war this would have been our new Main Line of Resistance (MLR).

I am sure that Chinese line crossers had already inspected this line and knew exactly where we were. Our line crossers (we called them TLO's (Tactical Liaison Officers) knew what was going on behind the Chinese lines, but usually we lower ranks were never informed. The Chinks sent people over to our area, and they must have stayed for a while. One day back at the battery area, we were getting shelled, but fortunately it was not in an occupied area. They were shelling a wooded piece of ground, and it became noticeable to us that they were trying to knock down our communication lines. The shelling followed the lines, and in places even made right angle turns to knock down certain telephone poles. The Chinks were known for their accurate mortaring, and also their artillery. They didn't have big cannons like we did, but they made very good use of their 122 mm mortars. That was what got us up on Hill 347.

Sometimes, when they fired their mortars at night I would see sparks come out of the tube. That was the only way I could approximate where they were located. We had radar in our lines that supposedly could follow the trajectories of enemy weapons and deduce where they were located. That information was never handed down to us. In fact, that brings me to a complaint that I have harbored for many years. I was attached to George Company of the 32nd Infantry Regiment, and occupied a position in that company's area. There was little or no communication between the Infantry Commander and me except for the one night I was brought over to his Command Post (CP) to meet him. I never got his name, and he only spoke after I offered my services to any of his units that might need help. He grunted his thanks and that was the only time I ever saw or heard of him.

I did become familiar with a sergeant in George Company who hoochied near me—Louis Rothrock, of Louisville, Kentucky. He appeared to be a very Gung Ho (a Chinese term used in the WWII meaning "anxious to fight or work) leader. I was told that one night while patrolling in Chinese territory he actually yelled out "Here I am, Joe Chink. Come get me". His men thought him a screwball, and I agree. I never did get the opportunity to go out on a patrol with the Infantry, but I did offer. I think maybe I was lucky they didn't ask me.

****

Letter #35

Sat. 21, August

Tap kung-ni, Korea

Hi Sweetheart—

I put the name of our new location on this letter just so you'd know where we are. I'm sure you know now exactly where Charlie 48th is in position—Please don't tell any Communists!!

The letter you said you would write on the 11th didn't show today, but as our mail is fouled up I guess it will be here soon. I did get a couple from the folks, and they are slightly angry because I took them at their word when they said only one letter a week would be enough. I planned to write them a couple of times a week, but as there was very little news, and we were involved in getting ready for the move I never quite fulfilled my plans. My letters to them are real masterpieces—"Dear Folks, am fine—am hungry—send food—see you soon—Love, Ron."

You, I, can always find something to say to each other, but it's tough trying to keep the mail going home full of interest. They don't really care what the letter says as long as they know I wrote it. I didn't mean they're not interested in what we're doing, but you know how parents are—I could tell them we've been building sandbag skyscrapers until 12 midnight every night, and Mother would still answer "That's nice, dear. Don't forget your raincoat when it rains."

I'll bet your folks are like that too! My Mother is the sweetest, gentlest woman I've ever met or known. She's about 50, and only looks about 35. Her name is Celia, but naturally everyone call her Cele—except Dad who usually has a different name for her every ten minutes. His favorite is "Kathleen" or sometimes "Mary." I've had people I hardly even knew come up and tell me to give their regards to "that sweet Mother of yours." One of the biggest thrills I ever got, and I know Mother was pleased, too—happened one day when we stopped for a hamburger—A friend of mine saw us (he didn't know my Mother), and later asked me where I got the new girl.

It might seem to you mom is sort of a domineering type of person the way I write of her. I realize I sometimes say she wants this done or that done. Actually, she has never forced me to do anything in my life. I think I once told you she wanted me to write every day. When I wrote that to you I was sure it might give you the idea she demanded a letter a day from me—No, honey, all she said was, when she gets a letter every day or every other day she's much more at ease—I knew it would please her if she got one every day, and so I just wrote every day—It was a good luck charm with me. At the end of each letter I wrote this sentence, "I promise to write you tomorrow." As long as I wrote that every night, and did it the next day then I knew nothing would go wrong.

Dad is somewhat different—His name is Jack, and he's about 52 or 53. When he was young (before he married) he was a silent picture star. That was out in Melrose when Louis B. Mayer was just getting started. Dad worked for him, and almost went to Hollywood with Mayer. However, my grandmother wouldn't let him go as Wallace Reid (a famous star at that time) had just committed suicide, and she was afraid all actors ended up that way.

Dad's business kept him in New York for 3 or 4 days out of every week. When I was a kid at camp—my Mother did all the writing, and so when I came into the Army she just continued. Dad's only written about 5 letters to me since I came in, but I don't mind because I'm sure I know how he feels. You'll really like him. He's real friendly, and is one hell of a lot of fun.

I don't know why I went on about my family—I just started, and didn't stop. Hope you found it interesting!!

Tonight we all went down to the river for a swim, and was it ever good. The water was just cold enough to make you tingle. The truck stopped at the movie on the way back, but I wanted to get back to write you. I really look forward to these letters to you. It's almost like a phone conversation with you that lasts for a couple of hours every day. It's funny what a person can imagine. If you close your eyes, and think hard enough almost anything can seem to be real. When I actually do get home, and am within seeing distance of you I'll have to keep pinching myself to make sure I'm still not imaging things.

How nice it would be if I could be walking down some of these roads with you on a night like this. Its cotton dress and button-down-the-front-type-sweater-over-your-shoulders weather over here for you, and it would be an open-necked-long-sleeved-sport-shirt-rolled-up-about-one-turn-at the-wrist weather for me.

That kind of talk really makes me lonesome for you. I'd better get along to bed before I go AWOL, and start swimming home to you. I'll probably write you again tomorrow—so till then—take care, and remember I miss you, want you, need you, and that you're with me in thought all the time. You're too wonderful to be true, and if you wake me from this fantasy—then you've had it.

Goodnight again, you—Write me, darling—

All my love as always—

Ronnie

CR80

I must have received a letter from my folks reminding me to write more often, because in this latest letter, I wrote about them to Pete. I know that everyone says that their mothers were the greatest that ever lived. Mine actually was. I never heard a complaint either to me or my brother, and never an unkind word about anyone or anything. I think I only ever heard one four-letter word emanate from her mouth. That was when she giggled about that song that I think Phil Harris sang about "Get outta here with that boom, boom, boom," and she said she knew what that phrase was. I could not believe it was my mother saying something like that. She lived to be 95, and passed away one afternoon right after my visit. I only hope she knew how much she was loved by everyone, especially me.

My Dad was a little different, but still quite a lovable man. He came to this country at the age of six, and became very Americanized at an early age. He had to quit school in the 4th grade, and worked at an ice cream cone factory trimming rough edges from the cones. I believe he worked for the Chelsea Baking Company which was still in business the last I knew.

Dad's mother, my grandmother, did not speak English except for a few words, but boy could she cook and bake on her wood-fired kitchen stove. Whatever humor there is in my family, came down from her. She was apparently quite earthy, and whenever she told a story I had to leave the room although I could not understand one thing she said.

She wrote and acted out short plays and stories which she recorded on a wire recorder. My father took after her, and became quite proficient as an actor in a local dramatic society. One night, when he was doing King Lear (at 17) in Yiddish, a man by the name of Louis B. Mayer was in the audience. He was that same LB Mayer later of film fame. He hired my dad as his star, and they made four films in the Boston area together.

Mom said that she remembered seeing the films in our home, but my brother and I never could find them. In any event, Mayer invited Dad to go to Hollywood, but Grandma found out that Wallace B. Reid, a well-known actor, had died of dope poisoning, and she wouldn't let Dad go west. Mayer then invited her to come out with Dad, and be Mayer's cook, but she wouldn't leave the rest of the family.

When I was older and told friends about that period in my dad's life, I used to say that maybe he would have gone out there, and my mother would have been an actress like Myrna Loy. Years later, in OCS, I was talking one day with another candidate and he mentioned that his last name was Hornblow, and I said that that was an unusual name. He replied that his dad was English (which accounted for the name), and a movie producer in Hollywood. And then he offered that his mother was Myrna Loy. Gee, he could have been me! Or I could have been him.

Day dreaming about being home with Pete occupied a lot of my time, as this last letter shows, but we brought along our little puppy to the new site, and she occupied much of our spare time. Everyone tried to teach her a new trick, and in the end we got her so confused that I don't think she ever even learned to shake hands. Actually there were two puppies, Skoshie being the small one and Butterball, who was a little older. They were the only two dogs I ever saw in my year in Korea.

Also, at some point I wrote to Pete about my mom singing the song "My Wonderful One" to me when I was quite young. Many years later, in fact about 50 years later, I asked Mom if she remembered singing it to me. She looked at me, and said "No, I never sang that song to you!" I must have had two mothers because I have carried that thought in my head for almost 80 years now, or maybe I got senile at an early age.

****

Letter #36

Sunday, 23 Aug.

Dearest Pete,

Today is a hot, muggy, and showery Sunday, and the whole battalion has the day off. There's nothing to do, however, except sleep, and that's practically impossible because of the heat. It's been like this now for a couple of weeks, and it's quite oppressive. I can only liken it to spending a month in a Turkish bath.

We had a party for Colonel Kimmitt last night as he's leaving the battalion. It was quite a wing-ding. I ache all over because Lt. Crouch decided I should learn to be a paratrooper, and made me jump off of a roof. I guess I had a little too much to drink. Not as much, however as some other people. The Colonel was talking to Captain Green and Lt. Crouch when he turned to Green and said, "Charge." He was pointing at Crouch, and Capt. Green just looked at the Colonel. The Colonel said, "Dammit, Green that's an order—charge". Green did so—Crouch sidestepped, and Green went full tilt head down into a wooden wall.

It was so hot inside we all stayed out of the hoochie. It was quite a sight to see 40 officers sitting around tables eating charcoal broiled steaks with their bare hands (somebody had thrown away all the silverware, and broken all the dishes) during a downpour—However, the rain didn't dampen our spirits 'cause we stayed and sang till quite late. I remember marching a 2nd Lt. home. We got about a mile from headquarters when a truck pulled up and drove us home. It was a patrol wagon sent out by a disgustingly sober officer.

I sure hope you're not getting the idea I'm coming home a drunken bum. We don't have these parties very often. When we do, however, they're great—After all, we have no other way to have a good time.

I have been anxiously awaiting those pictures you were supposed to have been sending me, and was a bit disappointed not to find them in today's letter. You won't forget them, will you?

The people that work in here are having a good laugh over my antics last night. They claim they could hear me marching Lt. Evans over the hills, but I think they're only kidding—because we were a couple of miles away. They said when I came in I said I didn't want to hear any more noise all night. Nobody said a word, and I took off my clothes and lay down. All was quiet and still until I sang a Korean song at the top of my lungs. They also said I kept asking them if I had ever told them about "Purty Pete" the new schoolmarm from Longmeadows. I must have been in a real gay mood!!

Just took time out to light up a smoke, and to reread your letter. If you're not planning to become a hermit down in Hartford then maybe we can make some sort of arrangement to spend that one evening in Boston. You'd better not decide to hide away in Hartford because I won't let you!! There's a lot of places I want to go, and things I want to do when I get back, and unless you're with me to do them then they won't be what I want them to be—I promise none of it will interfere with school, and we'll do these things only when you can get the time. It's not fair of me to plan all these things because you'll have other plans I'm sure, but I'll just wait until you can come along—after all, I've been waiting long enough to come home to these things, and I'm sure I can find the patience to wait a little longer. Going out to these restaurants and other places just wouldn't seem right without you with me.

You make me quite envious of your little nephew the way you lavish attention on him, but seeing as he's only 1$\frac{1}{2}$ and a relative to boot. I guess I won't have to write him any poison pen letters.

I've got a lot of little cousins, but two in particular I want you to meet. They're brother and sister, and the world's cutest kids. Johnny is about 8 and Nan and about 3 or 4. They're going to have another brother or sister very soon, and I'll bet it will have strawberry blonde hair just like the other two—I have another little cousin in Norwich, Conn.—that's Janie, and she's a little doll. She's about two, and as I recall she has jet black hair and eyes. Her father has the same coloring, but her mother is a flaming redhead. She is the younger sister of John and Nancy's mother. The third and oldest sister of that family has two daughters—Barbara and Ruth, but they lived in Denver until recently, and I've only seen them once. They live in New Jersey someplace now—Man our family is just packed with little kids. On my Dad's side there are 11 and one on the way, and on my Mother's side there are 3 and one on the way—that's all I can think of offhand.

However, I have one "nephew" about a year old that's no relative of mine. That's little Jeff the son of Margie Mishel—now Margie Lantos. I grew up with her, and look upon her as almost a sister. She's married a doctor from Philly, and that's where they live—It's almost strange to say Jeff isn't a real nephew—I don't think I ever thought of Margie not being a real sister. I think you might know her—Do you remember Joyce Allen? She was a friend of Evelyn Kravits'. If you remember Evelyn then I'm sure you know Margie as she was a very close friend of hers. Why I brought Joyce's name into this I really don't know, but I thought she might help you remember Margie. Speaking of Joyce—She's a weird one—Always got a laugh out of her—I tried to take her out, and 3 nights before I left for the Army I introduced her to a friend of mine at a party. Five months later she married him. I was sort of shaken up by it all, but it was for the best. I'm sure, as I couldn't quite see eye to eye on many things with her. She was a character though.

Oh me—I've got all afternoon to write to you, honey, and I think I'll do just that. Writing you is one of the pleasantest parts of the day. In fact the only thing that beats it is getting mail from you. Pete—I know I've told you many times how much your letters mean to me, but I'm sure I could never tell you enough to

make you fully understand. Being over here is something like a
dream.

When I was stationed in Texas it seemed as far from home
as Korea does now except that I could call home just about
whenever I felt like it. If I wanted to I could make myself think
I was only a few miles from home now, because it doesn't really
matter how far away you are form home. It's just the fact you
are away—10 miles or 10,000 they're the same. Still in all,
however, when you were on the coast you seemed to be nearer to
me, but that was because I measured the distance mentally
every time I thought of you. I'd miss you as much as I do now if I
were only 1 mile away from where you are now. Your letters have
helped me to get over the long mental distances.

The thing I look forward to most of all is mail call because
there might be a letter from you. You make me feel wonderful
when you say you enjoy writing to me, but it must be an
imposition on you at times. Over here we have nothing to do but
write so it's never any trouble at all to write your folks or
friends—But when I sit down to write you it's almost like a
special privilege to me. It's a funny things, but every time I write
I look around for something to send you—So far I've found
nothing not even a good cartoon from the *Stars and Stripes*—
Someday soon I'll find something you'll appreciate like a flower or
some such item. One day I wrestled with the problem of how to
send you this beautiful red lily, but I couldn't figure out a way to
get it in the envelope. If I could find a way to get it past the
postal inspectors I'd send you a jeep so you wouldn't have to go
out and buy a car.

Time out to light my pipe ...

Heard from Steve last week and he paid you a fine
compliment. Said he'd seen you a number of times before he
shipped over here, and had a really good time with you. I was glad
to hear that because I know if you're with The Fenn, and he has a
good time then you must have enjoyed yourself also—It's hard
for anyone not have a good time with him—I'm going to get
together with him if I go on R&R again. I told him I'd take off my
bars, and make like a lowly enlisted man with him.

It's taken me 2 hours and 48 minutes to write this letter so
far—so I guess I'd better start bringing it to an end.

I hate to leave you so early in the day, but I imagine I'll be back again tomorrow. In the meanwhile I'll be thinking 'bout you, honey—as a matter of fact, when I seal this envelope I'm going to lie down, close my eyes, and do some real thinking.

I miss you more and more as the days go by, Pete, and feel I've come to know you almost as well as I normally would if our letters had been conversations, and my dreams realities. I don't know if I've proved it to you, but I've learned it myself by the fact everything I plan or think about includes you—I certainly hope I'm not being over-presumptuous when I write all these things, but I just can't help writing what I feel. There is a lot I've left unsaid, and they will remain that way until—Well—just until—I'm sure you read more into my letters than I actually write, but I want you to because they're meant that way—So long, sweetheart-

As always I send you all my love—

Ronnie

CB&O

I can just imagine what that Sunday afternoon was like, having nothing to do except write letters home. It was August in Korea, and we sweltered wearing long pants and long sleeved shirts. Army regulations forbad us to walk around in anything other than a military uniform. We were just north of the 38th parallel which is the same line that runs just below New England, and the weather approximates what we were used to back home. We didn't have the ocean to cool us down. There wasn't even a lake we could jump into. There was the Imjin River, but its current in our area was so fast that it was best not to use it as a swimming pool. One of our drivers drowned in the river when he brought his jeep down there to wash it off. He was on some sort of a sandbar when he lost his footing and fell in. He was not a swimmer, and could not save himself. What a terrible way to die, especially after coming through a war without a scratch.

I vaguely remember the party for Colonel Kimmitt but not much else about that evening. We were all upset that he was leaving, but hoped that his new assignment would be in line with his wishes. He eventually went on, in civilian life, to become the Secretary of the U.S. Senate and lived in Washington, D.C. When I received my Silver Star I called to inform him, and he was as excited as I was to receive it.

Parties like that one were fairly rare as getting steaks for everyone was a difficult problem. I'll bet a lot of bartering went on with other outfits such as the Marines, who were just down the road. Booze for beef was an axiom that each unit lived by during that time. There was plenty of beer available, and we officers were able to get our booze from the Air Force. It was only $2.00 a bottle for any brand or type of liquor, but during the hostilities I never saw it on the hill. However, back at Battery it was available. Fortunately for me, I didn't drink anything but beer at that time, and waited until I was much older before I developed a taste for the hard stuff.

There were no permanent structures in our area, and so all of our work and social affairs had to be conducted under the tents. Almost all of these canvas affairs were either squad tents, meaning that one could house up to fourteen men, or a small wall tent that was used for other purposes. The latrines generally were tent covered or small wooden affairs with screening along the upper walls. Back at the air base, I started off living with my platoon in the squad tent, but the noise and the crowding was too much, and so my supply sergeant was able to get me an Arctic tent. This was a pyramid-shaped unit that had a white cloth inner tent liner. There was room for me and a gasoline-fired heater only, but at least I was able to sleep without radios blaring in my ears. The gasoline heater sort of got me nervous because of its volatility, so I only used it to warm the tent up before retiring or in the morning to melt the ice from my pan of water so that I could brush my teeth and shave.

In later years, when I first saw the movie MASH, I thought I could actually smell the inside of a tent whenever one was in a scene, and I distinctly remember the opening scene of that movie which had a Red Cross jeep careening around a tent corner through a mud puddle. I was sure that this was going to be an authentic movie about Korea, as that scene was so realistic, but as the movie went along it turned out to be a comedy, and nothing more. It was a great show, however unrealistic as it was.

My letters to Pete were quite long and involved. I considered her to be "my girl" whether she realized that fact or not. She never did send me any photos, and all I had were memories to fill the empty picture frames in my mind. She often mentioned her nephew, Donald, in her letters, but I had a problem trying to conjure up his visage. Pete's sister Carolyn lived in East Longmeadow at the time while her folks owned a home in Longmeadow. Being from eastern Massachusetts, I had no idea where those places were, but Pete was in college in Boston, and I knew exactly what that place looked like and where it was.

Later on, our daughter attended the same school, and actually lived in the same dorm room that Pete had lived in, and slept in the same bed. When our daughter first went to the college I was allowed to carry things up to her room, which looked different from when Pete went there. At that time, no male was allowed out of the guest area, and any extra-curricular activities were not allowed. By the year our daughter Lynn entered the school, men were not allowed to stay in the dorms longer than four nights. Wow! Had things changed in the new world we lived in.

Figure 65 - It must have rained a little!

****

Letter #37

Mon., 24 Aug.

Hi Pete Honey—

Wonderful news!! I've fallen in love—Yup—she's a Korean, and whatta little doll. She has brownish blond hair—big brown eyes, and she weighs about 10 pounds. Her name is Skoshie, and she's my honey—

No kidding Pete, she's the cutest little puppy you'd ever see—chasing butterflies—chewing grass—climbing all over you— Even as I write this to you she's nipping at my shoelaces. Wish you could meet her.

Went to see "Where's Charlie" tonight, but the damned projector broke down, and we only saw one reel. I was talking to the Battalion Exec—Major Trubey, and he sort of informed me I was coming up on the Colonel's staff soon—as battalion supply officer—I hate jobs like that—all you do is sign your name 500 times a day. Sure hope the deal falls through. I don't want to leave Charlie Battery—

Came back to find a package from my Dad. He sent me some silver bars, and when I asked if that was all the mail I got, the switchboard operator said 'Sorry, sir, but "Purty Pete"—the schoolmarm—from Longmeadow—done forgot you today. I guess my exploits of the other night have made their rounds of the battery.

Last night I had a very funny dream. So help me, it happened, and I woke up laughing my fool head off. You remember writing me about the swimming pool your Dad gave your little nephew, Donald? Well, I dreamt you and I were watching him swim—when he looked up at me and said, "I don't mind you seeing my Aunt, but keep the hell out of my pool!" It just struck me funny, and I've been laughing over it all day—

Today was the hottest and muggiest one so far, and I really suffered—I don't like cold, but heat like this just about drives me insane. On top of all that heat we had some rain showers, and I'm covered with mud from the knees down. This place must be the "Inferno" of Dante's poem, but I rather doubt it as his Purgatory couldn't be half as bad as this country is. One might say I'm beginning to loathe the "Land of the Morning Calm", maybe you've noticed it in my writing.

The days are going by fast, however, and soon it will be September. Here it is the 24th of August, and I've been away now for 8 months and 15 days and approximately 7 hours. It certainly seems hard to believe it's been that long and yet when I remember writing that Xmas card to you—it almost seems like centuries ago.

Tomorrow General Trudeau will approve all the applications for early release, (he's required by the Army to approve them) and he'll send them on to Washington. There's a rumor he has requested the release dates to be adjusted to the dates the officer is supposed to leave Korea. I sure hope it isn't true, but somehow I can't help but feeling that is just what will happen. Good things like early releases just don't happen to people like me—That's why I get a feeling of amazement every time I see a letter from you in front of me. Good things like Pete Smith just don't happen to people like me. As a matter of fact—things like Pete Smith happen to very, very few people—

It's going to be real strange actually talking to you when I get home—Every time you say something I'll probably get out my pen and paper and write you the answer—To be honest with you— I probably won't say very much for the first few minutes—I'll just look—no stare would be a better word.

Well, sweetheart—I'm going to bring this to an early close as I'm sort of tired, and I've got some minor things to do before I flake out—Boots to polish—brass to shine—etc.

Do remember I'm with you in thought all the time, and I miss you more than anything else in the world—

Goodnight, darling—
All my love will be yours for
As long as you want it—and longer—
Ronnie

CS80

This letter to Pete was written the next day, and is fairly short in length when you consider the other letters I wrote to Pete. I don't know why I hadn't mentioned the little dog in earlier letters, but as she grew older she became more of a mascot than ever. She kept everyone amused, and was instrumental in keeping up our morale. She belonged to everyone, and was as spoiled as you would imagine.

Major Trubey was our Battalion Executive Officer, and although he was a quiet man he was well liked by everyone. When we were on the hill, I noticed that I fired a lot more missions than the other FO's. Maybe I had more targets of opportunity than they did, but it seemed that the hot loop was almost a private line between me and the FDC. It may be that I made more of my Gung Ho attitude than the rest of the guys did, and that is what brought me to their attention. At the party that night, Major Trubey told me that I would probably be brought up to battalion to be an Assistant Supply Officer. Any place up at battalion was considered to be a step up in one's career, but I knew that it would be even more boring than what I was currently doing. I would rather have stayed in Charlie battery, as we all got along quite well, and the more I thought about going home, and "my girl" the more I didn't want the Army life to draw me in to its clutches.

If I was told to move up I would not have done anything else, but if it were on a 'would you like to move up" basis, I think I would have turned it down. I just had to sit and wait to find out what the battalion wanted to do with me.

****

Letter #38

Tues. 25, August

Dearest Pete,

This will probably be a very short letter as I have to move my stuff out of FOC tonight up to the BOG. The officer of the day is going to sleep down here every night from now on.

Last night I told you I would probably become Battalion Supply Officer. I was wrong!! Today I got a call to report to Division Artillery Headquarters Personnel Section as soon as possible. It's only a twenty minute ride from here to there, but I got completely lost—ended up in Freedom Village, and was 3 hours late in reporting. When I arrived I reported right away to Major Poussard who informed me I was now Divarty (short for Division Artillery) Recruiting Officer. I am to report there on the 27th and as soon as I'm there I'll send you my new address.

Divarty runs all the field artillery battalions attached to the 7th Division and it shouldn't be too tough a deal. I'll just go around to the various units, and try to induce men to re-enlist. My heart won't be in it, however. As much as I hate to leave Charlie this new job has many advantages. Good chow, shower, PX, movies, etc. Still in all I guess it doesn't add up to being an executive officer of a firing battery. The Major up there told me to get new uniforms, new boots, and a soft cap—I guess I'm going to have to stand tall!!

We had a driving rainstorm last night which completely woke me up. I'm glad it did, however, as I like to listen to the rain drum down hard. You'll find out I'm in 7th heaven during a summer thundershower. I just sat up in bed for 15 minutes and listened— It cooled the air off, and made everything seem so nice and comfortable. Even today was cool—Cloudy but hardly any rain. It was real fine!

No mail now for two days! The battalion mail clerk says the planes can't fly over Japan because of the heavy rains. I did however, get one letter from my old outfit, and a package from my Dad (the silver bars) which apparently had been lost somewhere over here. Everyone is going around with long faces and it will be the mail clerk's neck if we don't get anything tomorrow. That guy sure takes a lot of abuse from people like me—

Well, another day gone, and one day nearer to you—I sure hope early release comes through. I've been away from you too long, and I don't think I could last till next Feb. or so—

I've got to run along now, honey, but not until I remind you of a few things. I dream of you all the time, Pete, and miss you more and more as the time goes by—

Please take care of yourself for me, and remember what I've told you—

> Goodnight treasure, and bless you—
> My deepest love to you always,
>
> Ronnie

∞∞

Well, things are moving right along in the 'affairs of the heart" and in the "affairs of a soldier." First, let me tell you about the soldiering part. Apparently, up in Division Artillery HQ they were looking for some junior officers to fill in various positions. Someone saw that I had attended a Public Relations college and my name was put on a possible list to be brought up to Division Artillery HQ.

It was only a short ride to HQ, but my driver and I got lost and we spent the whole day on unmarked roads and trails. We were too embarrassed to stop somewhere and admit that we didn't know what we were doing or where we were going. It took us almost the whole day to find our destination, and at that point I guess all the other invitees turned down the offer, and I was told that I should report the next morning ready to assume my new duties. I did as ordered, but when I reported in to Major Poussard (my new section leader) he told me that the recruiting part of the job was to be postponed, and that my new assignment was to be Decorations and Awards officer for the whole Division Artillery. I knew nothing about the job or what it entailed, but one of the sergeants in the unit gave me a notebook filled with previous awards, and I was able to use them as a guide.

One of the first awards I was to write up was an award for our Commanding General Trudeau. I was told that during the last Pork Chop flap he personally went up and suggested some places for us to fire our artillery. I seized on that and wrote the award commending him for his ability to stabilize a situation, and in the placing of artillery rounds that would be most beneficial. I think they gave him a Silver Star award for that, but I am not positive. I know they gave the Legion of Merit award to our DivArty (Division Artillery) Commander, Brig. General Ralph Cooper, when he was transferred out of our unit, because I wrote that one up. Writing awards only took up a very minor part of my day. Mostly I sat at a desk that sat on an earthen floor of a very hot tent. I would sit there with my hands folded and doze in the heat. Because I had so little to do the Major lent me out for all kinds of jobs and duties.

The good part was our chow accommodations. The Officers Mess was composed of two full-length Quonset Huts strung end to end. In the middle there was a four sided bar with a bartender during our evening meals. The bar was closed until that time as per army regulations. The General and his staff of Field Grade Officers sat at one end of the hall, and we junior officers sat at the end of the other. I was not a liquor drinker, but I was tempted after I tasted somebody's Tom Collins. That became my drink until I realized how much more expensive they were than a can of beer.

At our end of the building there was a patio made of the two-foot-or-so lengths of wooden boards that composed the boxes which contained our artillery shells, and they were placed two-units high to make a privacy fence around the end space. They then took a blowtorch and dappled the inside of the fence to make it feel somewhat homey in design. The chairs out there were Adirondack style, again made out of ammo containers. Bernie Rulong had also been transferred up to DivArty, and we became good friends while sitting out before chow with our drinks, and afterward we always attended the evening movie together.

We had a third party join us. Don Oberdorfer fit in perfectly. He was a stringer for Elmer Davis of the OWI (Office of War Information), and as such he would report on the QT to Davis about morale, and what the troops were doing and thinking. The three of us shared a squad tent, and had a lot of fun together. Don went on to be a reporter for the Washington Post, and I often saw him on "Meet the Press" or programs of that nature on TV.

When the Olympics were held in Seoul in 1988 I was reading a local newspaper when a picture of downtown Seoul came on the TV. I was so amazed to see the highways and big buildings. I had no idea that those people had come that far. I picked up the paper that I had put down, and saw that the lead article was bylined with "Don Oberdorfer—Washington Post". I picked up the phone and called the Post, and was quickly connected to Oberdorfer. I told him who I was and he said "I don't have time to talk to you. I have a deadline to meet." So, I hung up, and that was the end of that. I don't think he even caught my name, but I have read his books on Korea and Vietnam, and found his writing to be first class.

Bernie Rulong was a true character. He really was a fifth wheel up there at DivArty as there were other Warrant Officers in the unit doing what he was trained to do. He was as bored with the whole thing as the rest of us were, and couldn't wait to get home or back to Germany which he loved. Being older he was a much more accomplished drinker than either Don or I were. He would mix his drinks and beer, and it seemed that every night he would get tangled up in his mosquito netting while trying to get out of the sack and get rid of his stomach problems. It kept us awake, but it was amusing. The chow was good up there, and it was a pleasant atmosphere to wait for the news to go home come down.

****

Letter #39

Thursday 27, Aug.

New address
Hg Btry 7th Inf. Div. Artillery
APO 7 etc. etc.

My Darling Pete,

What a wonderful, wonderful, wonderful world—The best day I've had in a long time! Let me tell you why I feel so good—I got up at 7 a.m., and was ready to leave for my new job about a $\frac{1}{2}$ hour later, but I waited to see if there would be any mail from you, and there was, you wonderful you—two nice sweet letters, and I just knew nothing could go wrong from then on. More about the letters in just a few minutes.

I arrived here about 10 a.m., and did nothing all day as I couldn't make the phone connections I needed in order to find out just what was expected of me. At about 5:30 p.m. I wandered up to the "General's mess" (ahem—ahem) where there is a bar, and guess what—TOM COLLINS with real ice cubes—I had three before chow, and then sat down to eat—big thick juicy steaks, vegetable soup, croutons, and apple pie and ice cream—then two more T.C.'s, and here I am—Really, it was just a perfect day—I guess it doesn't sound like much to you, hon—but I don't get two letters from the most wonderful girl in the world every day and I don't eat chow like that every day.

Really Pete—your letters are what did it all—I had no mail from you for a few days, and I was worried sick, and lonesome beyond repair—I never realized you meant so very much to me—Before, you were the only one on my mind, but even though I knew I cared very, very much, it wasn't till a few hours ago I realized just how much you really have done for me. When you write things like you did about this Marine, and how your mind was preoccupied with me although you were with him, I just could walk down to the motor pool, steal a jeep, and drive right home to you—

I know that you want me to be nothing but frank and truthful with you, and so if you don't mind I think I might tell you a thing or two that you might never have realized before.

When we first started writing I was just hungry for mail, I'll be honest—I remembered you as something that would always be out of my reach, and just thought it would be a big morale booster if I could get some mail from you—and so it went, just a girl I would have given anything for, but who always seemed to be just out of reach (I remembered all the times I called you, and especially the last time when our date fell through).

Then things got rough for me—I did something I knew all along I shouldn't have done—Transferred!! I found out I needed someone to lean or depend on other than Mom and Dad (like the Marine told you), and you were the only one I wanted to feel that way about. I was a little bit afraid you might not appreciate my telling you the things were happening, but I decided to plunge in head first and tell you—I had my fingers crossed you wouldn't ask me to stop writing as I did—and like the wonderful person I wanted you to be—you answered me like I dreamed you would.

Still, I had the feeling somehow you were just being nice to me because I was away from home etc., but yet I found every day your name and your face was with me in everything I did. But I still didn't know how you really-really felt, and I'll be frank with you—I still don't.

You give me the impression you're not writing all you feel or think. You seem to hold yourself back from saying the things you want to say—I know sweetheart, at one time your world came to an end, but the sun came up the next day didn't it?? Even you yourself wrote me it all worked out for the best, and I know it did-

I too, have held back, but only because I was afraid I might say something you didn't want me to, and I would lose whatever I might have gained.

I could be wrong or let's say not tactful in writing what I have, but I'm sort of funny that way—I'm the type of person who can't beat around the bush too long—If I feel a certain way about you then I have to tell you—It doesn't seem fair to me to play games with people you want to open your heart to—

I don't know—perhaps you only want me as a friend, and I would rather have you that way than not at all. The workings of the female mind is the 8th wonder of the world to me, and I fear I may have hurt you by writing all this, but damn it Pete—I want only you—and I have to tell you that—you can certainly read behind that statement. The only reason I won't go further on it is because of the way I think you might feel.

If I told you I loved you—you'd tell me in no uncertain terms I was crazy because I'm in no position to feel that way. You'd say I said it only because I've been over here too long—You'd be wrong in feeling that—yet I wouldn't argue because I know how strongly you'd feel on the subject. I'd agree before I said that—we'd need about 24 hours of solid discussion on the subject, but do the heart and mind always work together?

Pete, I'm writing my thoughts as they come to mind, and I'm very much tempted to finish this, and then destroy it, BUT—if I don't send it I'll only be tormenting myself—Nothing ventured is nothing gained!!!!! And so, my dearest one, just think about what I've said, and please don't be too harsh in your judgment. Think for a while before you write. If you want me to wait before I go on this way just write and say so, and our letters will continue in the same vain as they have until this time. I've just had to unlock a bit of my secret heart to you, and I wish you'd do the same for me—

Treasure, I won't for your sake let myself go completely as it won't be fair—We need to be together, and talk this all out—I will tell you I could very, very easily give my heart to you forever by saying I love you now, but I can't. Let it suffice to say once I do get home, and you find me (if you do) to be what you want—than I'll tell you—

I'm afraid mainly I've gone too far. I'm afraid I have hurt your heart - Remember once I told you I would never do anything to hurt you—Well, I hope and pray I haven't now.

To me you're the dearest thing in this world, and if by this letter I've done you any harm or wrong then I'll never forgive myself—But I just couldn't go on without telling you, and you'll have to answer me—one way or another.

I realize how many obstacles and barriers you have to cross before you answer this, but let your heart—whatever it may hold, write—not your mind.

Goodnight you—and remember whatever may happen you've been everything to me, and have taught me a lot about myself and the other people in the world—

I'll be with you always, dearest one—in all you do—

My love is yours, Ronnie

Pete—did I do the right thing in writing this to you?
Should I mail it?

ೞೞ

I guess the new chow accommodations really impressed me as this is the second time I have written about them. It was quite a change from the mess halls I had been eating in to this new experience. We sat on regular chairs, not benches, and we had our meals brought to us by mess personnel. Also, we never had booze of any kind in the other messes, and to be able to have a Tom Collins with our evening meal was quite a change for us. The food was much better prepared and served in very appetizing manner. It was truly a treat to go to chow. When I was contemplating joining the service, my Dad said that it only "costs a nickel more to go first class" meaning I should attempt to become an officer, and he was right. The difference between life as a commissioned officer, and that of an enlisted man is very great. Just this experience in dining makes that point obvious. On our trip overseas to Korea, we officers had three different choices at every meal while our troops down below ate mostly rice and beans while standing up. I hate to sound snobbish, but that was the way it was, and I accepted it as my due.

At this time my thinking was all about going home and being with Pete. I was falling deeper and deeper in love with my almost ghost-like pen pal. It was apparent that I was in love with what I thought would be a perfect fit for my future. I didn't want, however, to say anything along those lines until I could actually see her face to face when I got home. These thoughts made my daily living a little more exasperating, yet the thought of "my girl" was exhilarating. There was no longer any war to occupy my mind, and really no difficult duties to hold me back or preoccupy my life, and at that time, my whole outlook, almost, could not have been any sweeter, but wasting away in that land was still a royal pain in the butt.

DivArty Headquarters area was much like our former battery or battalion areas, except there seemed to be more people, and more things happening all the time. Just down below our hill was an Army airstrip which was part of our unit. Small Army airplanes, like Piper Cubs, were used for aerial spotting missions, and after the cessation of hostilities we used the planes for various and sundry jobs. The strip was hemmed in on three sides by a steep range of small hills, and to a non-pilot like me it was a frightening way to fly. On the fourth side was a road that ran north and south, but could not be seen by the pilot until he reached the east side of the strip; the hills to the north blocked any view of the road that ran parallel to the runway.

I often wondered who picked that spot for an airstrip, and had he had any of our evening libations before he made his decision. Actually, the flat area of the strip was probably the only area near our unit for the runway (singular) to be built. I found it hard to believe that anyone could take off or better yet even land in such a confined space, but there was air activity all day when the weather permitted.

One day, soon after, my arrival in my new position, I was told to report to the "terminal" at the airport to undertake a mission for my boss, Major Pouatre. The terminal was not hard to find as it was a raggedy tent on the east side of the road. I reported in and was told that I was to be a courier, and that my job was to collect monies that had been collected from other units for our lottery to support a local orphanage. I had never flown in such a small airplane as that one, and I was quite nervous about the whole mission. It was a high winged monoplane with a lot of plastic windows (for aerial spotting purposes), and was designated as an L 19, which meant nothing at all to me. I was crammed into the rear seat directly behind the pilot. A set of earphones were jammed on my head as the pilot climbed into his seat in front of me.

The first thing I noticed was that he was wearing glasses, and that the lenses were so thick I truly thought they looked like soda bottle bottoms. Talk about being nervous when I first saw the airstrip. I couldn't believe the Army let this guy walk let alone fly an airplane in such a tight place as that. Over my earphones I heard the terminal radio man say, "Break right at 500", and even as a novice I recognized this meant we should turn right when we got to 500 feet of altitude. We didn't break right, we broke left instead which caused a lot of laughter between the pilot and the radio man. I was so nervous, but it was all a joke them. We flew for about twenty minutes or so before we came to a saner looking airstrip, and soon landed. I collected my money and we headed back to the DivArty strip. The terrain we flew over was so rugged and desolate that I could see why travel in Korea was mostly by air, whenever possible, as that trip by jeep would have taken hours.

I had been given the money in a strongbox, and I placed it between my feet on the way back. The landing was coming up and I didn't know what to expect, and was quite nervous about the whole maneuver. The pilot brought us down to just above the hills at the southern end of the runway. It seemed I could touch the hills on my left as we went by. We bumped down almost immediately, and the pilot leaned so far forward that I could see out the front window that the hills to our north were looming up fast. He grunted as he pulled some lever or other equipment that I rightly or wrongly assumed was a hand brake like in a car. Whatever it was that he did caused us to slow down just enough to turn a very sharp right and cross the road to the terminal.

I have often wondered what would have happened if a vehicle had come down from the north just as a plane was taxiing to its parking place. A driver could not see the plane and a pilot could not see the vehicle until it was at the roadside. My pilot explained that a road guard was normally stationed there to direct traffic, but for some reason he was missing that day.

Eventually I made a number of flights from there, but was never comfortable in taking off or landing on that strip. Flying in a small plane like that is fun, but you can really get bounced around by the wind and air currents. I truly prefer the jumbo jets.

****

Letter #40

Fri. 28, Aug –

Dearest Pete,

Just a *skoshie* line or two tonight as I have some reports to square away. Not too much has happened since last night, but I turned down a chance to go on R&R about an hour ago. Only reason I had was to call you, but as you'll be vacationing when I got to Japan I decided to put the thing off until I knew exactly where you were.

I'm hoping anyway, by the next time the R&R quota comes down I'll have some definite news on my early release. As yet the applications are still in the Division, and won't leave there for a few more days.

My office is in the S-1 section, and so I'm in just the right place to get information firsthand. S-1 is the personnel section—S-2 is Intelligence—S-3 is plans and Operations, and S-4 supply—Squared away now??

The mail didn't go out today until 1 P.M., and for 4 hours I sat looking at that letter I wrote you last night. It just sat there in the outgoing mailbox, and many times I was tempted to go and get it back, but it went out on the 2 P.M. mail truck. I wonder, honey, if that letter will bring me happiness or sorrow. In a way I'm sorry I wrote it because it didn't do true justice to my feelings. To fully understand what I said you're going to have to read between the lines. You'll find I still left quite a bit unsaid—

I certainly hope your Mother's illness wasn't at all serious, and she's better by now. I'm sure the 2 weeks rest will do her a world of good. You're quite forgiven for the "lost" mail darling, and don't you feel bad at all about it. Also tell your Mom she shouldn't have felt bad at all because things like that can and do happen to everyone

By the time this reaches the states you should be relaxing in a fishing boat—Man- how I could see that!! I never was too good a fisherman, but I sure do love to sit in a boat for a couple of hours and relax—We'll have to go fishing together. One hitch, however, you'll bait the hooks.

When will you send me your school address, or will I keep writing you at home? What's the name of this school, and exactly where is it? I've got to know, you see, if I'm going to walk in on one of your classes someday and surprise you—I still can't decide whether to let you know exactly when I'll be home, or if I should just walk in on you—what do you think??

The Marines all around us here are out practicing night patrolling, and every few minutes, flares are going off—TNT is exploding, and these Indian-like screams are piercing the air. Those people are nothing but crazy—Well, as long as we humor

them and let them think they won the war then I guess they
won't bother us—

The weather has finally cooled down, and in fact I'm getting
quite chilly at night. Please, Lord—don't let me spend another
winter over here—Man—that would be nothing but terrible—

How are your premonitions coming along? Still think I might
be coming home soon? I sure hope so—You sure you don't want to
retract that statement about my helping you paint your kitchen—
I'm nothing but terrible with a paintbrush. You'd probably send
me packing after watching me paint for only 5 minutes—

Well, Sweet—I've gotta get a move on so I'll close my letter
once again, but never my heart to you. The things I told you last
night are still what I wanted to fill this letter with tonight, but
even though I didn't write it down tonight, I still feel it the same
way I did last night.

Goodnight Pete darling,

My love always, Ron

CR80

I can see by the previous letter that my emotions were running rampant at
the time. Although Pete's letters to me were very bland, there were times when
I thought she might be trying to tell me something, but as I didn't really know
her mind at all, I guess I was conjuring up things in my own mind.

Earlier in a commentary I said that she never did send me photos, but as I
read my letters again, I find that she did send me a few. They were not very
memorable or else I would have brought them home with me. I want, however,
to set my record right by reporting that she did do as I asked-eventually.

There was a mention of fishing in one of her letters, and after we got to
really know each other, I found out that she had learned to fish with her father,
and that she had received a fishing rod for her high school graduation gift. Her
Dad, Ted, was an ardent fisherman and golfer. He built his own little pram, and
often took it along to use when he fished during his lunch hours. Years later, he
and I went up to Quabbin Reservoir, in Massachusetts, and spent a whole day
fishing. We got skunked, and Ted didn't say anything to me other than "It's
lunchtime" the whole day. When we got back he told the rest of the family that
I had changed rods, lures and positions more than anyone else that he ever
knew. He never invited me to fish again.

Fishing was not an option in Korea. The Special Services, who handled things like that, never came around to our unit, and any activity such as fishing never was offered to us. I don't even think the battery had any softball or baseball items given to us to use in our spare time. Back when I was with the Anti-Aircraft our platoon had a softball team, so I know that sports equipment was available in that part of the world. Up at DivArty I don't recall any breaks in the schedule for PT (Physical Training) which was an inherent part of any other unit. It was a must in all the other parts of the military, except of course for people involved in combat. Even then, when they came down from the hill, and went into blocking, I'm sure that some sort of PT was part of their training.

Speaking of training, we were based just up the road from the Marines. I think they trained 24 hours a day from all the noise that emanated from their area. Explosion, flares and rifle sounds could be heard and seen at almost any time of the day or night. The marines were an elite force to be sure, but most of them looked down on the Army. They thought they were the only ones fighting the enemy. There was never an opportunity to remind them that there were other American and foreign country forces also fighting in Korea.

Before I transferred up to the 7th Division, Bud and I drove our friend John Brosnan up to his new unit. John was a career soldier, and was allowed to transfer after his original tour of duty. He was sent up to the 2nd Infantry Division, and was assigned to the 82nd AAA Aw Battalion as his new duty station. When Bud and I dropped John off we bumped into Tom Bondurant who was an old OCS buddy, and who, at that time, was the Commander of HQ Battery of the 82nd. He offered us a sightseeing trip in his jeep, but first he issued us flak jackets and helmets, and then we took off over the hills heading for the front line area.

We crested a small hill and ran into a group of GI's that were behaving in a very active manner. A sergeant told us that his group had just been subjected to an artillery barrage which was from a friendly unit. Nobody was hurt, but their bivouac area was a mess. Afterwards, Bud and I talked about the plight of the front line infantryman. Not only was he subjected to enemy fire, but he had to contend with friendly fire, as well, although one must admit that was a very rare circumstance indeed. On top of all that, he lived in very difficult circumstances, and had a tour of duty that was supposed to encompass one whole year. Their situation is not completely understood by the public in general, and I feel that they are vastly underpaid for what they do and totally under appreciated by our citizenry. No twenty-five missions and then home for those people. As an FO I lived among them for some time, and can attest to their ability to live under those circumstances.

Fall was upon us, and we really appreciated the cooler temperatures. It made sleeping a lot easier except for the fact that Chief Rulong was still going through his antics every night.

Letter # 41

Sunday Aug. 30

Hi Honey—

    Sunday is a day of rest for personnel of the famous 7th Infantry 'Bayonet' division, but apparently somebody didn't get the word because the division Artillery Recruiting Officer has been on the job all day—(a helicopter just landed about 20 yards away—must be a wheel of some sort).

    As Recruiting Officer I don't do anything as the division hasn't organized a program as yet, but in the meanwhile I've been given a few other jobs. One is Postal Officer, but I don't take over until next week, and the other is Awards and Decorations Officer. Actually, I'm not really the A & D Officer, but I ghost write all the awards. My biggest claim to fame so far is a Silver Star Award I wrote for the General. It doesn't take any great author to write an award as they all follow the same pattern— You know—"with total disregard for his own personal comfort and safety, General Cooper—etc. etc." The funniest of all awards are those written up by foreign units in English for presentation to Americans. One friend of mine received one from the Ethiopians in which they wrote he had "inflicted an inconsiderable great amount of damage to the enemy." Those people have enough trouble speaking the language let alone trying to write up a precise military decoration.

    Things up here at BOSS (code name) are rather slow, but as I told you before they have their advantages. Where else can one have a brand new movie shown to a group of about 25 people sitting on a patio sipping cold beers or Tom Collins?

    The VD rate is getting to be alarming now. The General is blowing his top because nine more cases were reported yesterday. Maybe he'd feel better if I told him about my old outfit where 9 every day was abnormally low. The Army will not allow us to court-martial any man for catching VD nor can we punish him or reduce him in rank—legally. What we do, however, is get him for something else, and he knows he's being punished because of the VD. One method we're trying right now is to have a VD lecture substituted for a movie every day about a man in a battery who catches VD. It's mass punishment in a sense, but might be allowed—I personally feel if a man is stupid enough to expose himself to it—then let him suffer—It's a tremendous problem, and yet there doesn't seem to be any solution. You'd be awfully dismayed if you knew the high percentage of VD cases amongst the troops. It's been said in official bulletins almost 90% of the women in the country are infected. I think they must have meant 90% of the prostitutes not all the women. The only prevention or cure is abstinence, but you try and tell that to an ordinary G.I. Before we came overseas I screened all the records of the men in my platoon—Out of 67 only 1 ever attended college, and the average grade level was only 4 years of grammar school. I had a predominance of mid-westerners, and the majority of them were farmers. Maybe my screenings weren't a true picture, but to me the Army seems to be composed mainly of southerners, and mid-westerners. Education is one of the best means of combating VD, but it's pretty hard to educate people who just don't want to learn.

My mail has once again been fouled up, and naturally my moving has been the cause of it all. Mail doesn't come in here until 7:30 P.M., so maybe tonight, you'll be there. I sure could use some of your letters. The days just don't seem to go right when I don't hear from you. It's funny how one can chase all the clouds away—

I wish this early release will come through real soon, and we won't have to write. I'll be able to sit down and talk with you, and right now that's my biggest dream. Just to be with you—in reality not just in dreams.

The movie last night was preceded by a Pete Smith Specialty, and it seemed funny to see your name on the screen, and I yelled 'hey'. Everything and everybody including the General turned around, and asked me what happened, but all I could do was sit there with a big grin—

Time out—the Major wants me—

Back again, hon—Major wanted to know where I left some papers—The idiot—he could have looked and saved me the trouble—but—

While I was down in the office, the radio was playing one of the prettiest songs I've heard in a long time—Joni James' "Almost Always." I hear it almost every meal on the radio in the mess, and I really like it. Kinda reminds me of you—!

This will probably be one of the letters that will arrive while you're cooling it on that lake. I'd deem it an extreme honor if you'd catch a big bass for me, but I'm afraid even were I with you I wouldn't help you eat the poor creature. I'm just not a big fish eater—Shellfish—yes, but negative on the other kinds—In the word of a famous expression in use around here—I think fish is "nothing but terrible!" However, when you're out their relaxing in the boat I wish you'd think of me 'cause I could see doing that right about now—anything would be good for me if you were there—I'm missing you more and more, sweetheart, and I find it's getting harder to keep my mind on what I'm doing. No complaints, however, Pete as I can't think of a nicer thing or person in the world to preoccupy my mind. It's time to go, treasure, but I won't stop thinking about you. Please make a big wish they'll let me come home real soon, and maybe it will come true—

>So long darling—
>>Always all my love to you, Ronnie

৪৩୯৪

Life was becoming so humdrum at this time that there was very little to report on in my letters. My world at that time was about two acres in size, and was completely devoid of opportunities to create a better atmosphere for myself and the other people I had in my circle of friends. In fact, if I spent a third of my letter to Pete discussing the VD rate in our outfit, then it is apparent that I was down to the bottom of the news barrel.

In an earlier comment I mentioned that I had a theory on where many of the MIAs (Missing in Action) were located. Now, this is a theory, and it is only my considered opinion. It does not necessarily reflect what our government thinks about this subject. At this time, we still have approximately 8,000 men missing in action during the Korean War, and although the North Korean government has let our Graves Registration teams into their country the results of their searchers have been very slow and minimal over these last years. In line with this, I want to go back and finish up an item that I had mentioned earlier.

One of my many duties at DivArty took place one morning when the Major told me to supervise the construction of a squad tent over to one side of our area. Putting up a tent of this size required about 10 men, and was not an easy task. The canvas alone is very heavy, and the two main tent poles are like ships spars. They have to support the whole weight of the tent, and then the sides and ends have to be pegged down using engineer's stakes to hold all the ropes that are required. After the tent is erected, and all parties are satisfied that it will stay in place, and not blow down, a rain ditch has to be dug around the perimeter so that all the water will be drained off the immediate area of the tent to insure that the goods and people inside stay dry.

The tent was put up properly, and then the men started to dig the rain trench around it. After a number of minutes went by I was called to the side of the tent to see what they had discovered in the ground. It was the body of a dead Chinese soldier, and it had been in the ground for some time. The remnants of its uniform were still noticeable and his glasses were still usable. We found tattered shreds of papers in his breast pocket, and were about to examine the whole body when I suggested calling our Grave Registration people, and let them handle the exhumation. Afterwards I thought about this whole experience, and realized that because of the rice paddy construction all over the countryside that there must be many of these bodies, both American and Chinese, lying in the mud. These plots had been worked for so many years previously that the waterlogged soil must be many feet deep, and a body could sink down into it after some time. It would be impossible to find all the missing that might be buried in this manner, and we would never find them all. It is quite sobering to think of all the families that will never find a final answer to their questions about their missing men.

I also want to mention one more thing regarding our daily lifestyle, and that is the AFRS (Armed Forces Radio Station) radio that played constantly in every office tent or billeting facility. The radio played all day, and it was the only up to the minute way of staying on top of the current world situation. The disc jockeys played all the new stateside music, and reported all the latest news for us to devour. Naturally, everything had Army approval, and so no rumors or false information was transmitted to us. Just to hear what it was like to be back home made listening to the broadcasts so enjoyable.

As I write these words, I am reminded how farcical MASH was, and how the real truth differed from what was portrayed in that show. In later life, our friendship with a young priest brought Pete to meet Gary Burghoff (Radar) who was a featured performer on that show and in the movie. He lived in our town and our friend John Ahrens had gone to school with him, and arranged for a get together at a local pub. I should have gone along with them, but I had something else to do instead. Burghoff probably heard a million times about what Korea was really like, and didn't need an old man like me to tell him more about what he didn't want to hear.

Letter #42

Monday, 31, August

Sweetheart,

Coming home! Coming home! Coming home! Oh Pete, how I've waiting and ached to write this letter to you!! I had it all written in my mind for months, and now that it's about to happen I'm so happy I can't write anything—

Let me tell you just what happened. I had been very busy all day ... a Colonel Panke wanted 4 awards into his office by 8 AM tomorrow. I ran my head off trying to get them written up, and at 4:30 I gave up, and went back to my old outfit to get paid. That's when my day started to be lucky—<u>TWO </u>letters from you!! and $315 in pay—I came back about six and picked up a brand new Lord Elgin Watch (lost my old one in Seoul).

While eating a big rare thick steak, and French fries—Lt. Chapman asked me to pass the salt, and be quick about it if I wanted to go home. I told him to stop his kidding around, and then he told me Col. Kimmitt (my old battalion commander) who is now assigned up here told him early tonight he and I had received our releases, and would be on our way soon. After chow Col. Kimmitt called me over, and asked me if I'd like to go home in Sept. Man—did I get excited! He says he saw the list in division, and I'd leave sometime in the last two weeks of September. He also said he'd guarantee my being home or in the states by Oct. 10!!

Now you understand it's all unofficial but I know he wouldn't joke about that. It's not official until I see the paperwork—

I'm so excited I don't know what to write—Gonna see my honey is all I can think—Sweetheart—just a few more days, and I'll be seeing you. It's almost too much to believe.

You know—things really work out funny for us—I mean the way we both seem to get the same ideas and feelings—Like my mentioning a blue Chevy convertible, and you buying one—You're feeling I'd be home sooner than I thought—Things like that give me that wonderfully warm close feeling about you—It sort of

makes me shiver up and down. Sweet—I just can't wait—I sure
will send you a telegram when I hit the states—It'll say "On the
way—wait." That's an air artillery phrase the forward observers
received from the fire direction when the rounds are on the way
to the target—Well, I'll be on the way to my target, and I'm
going to send you that message—I wasn't even going to tell you I
was coming, and was just going to walk in on you, but that
wouldn't be fair. Besides, I just couldn't contain myself and had
to let you know—I'll write my folks and tell them when I finish
this—

Listen hon—about this first day in school—You know as well
as I do even the kids will be nervous, and you should feel that
way or else it wouldn't be normal. The day will pass so fast you'll
hardly believe it. It will be good for you to be nervous, in fact.
Believe me, I'm an expert on nervousness as you'll find out in just
a few short weeks—But darling—if it will be any consolation to
you then remember what I'm going to ask you to do—Just clasp
your hands together, and pretend the other hand you feel is mine
because even though it will be night over here I'll be with you—
right next to you—as I'm always dreaming about—

Just rereading the part in your letter about picking me up,
and I couldn't think of a better idea, but I don't think Mr. & Mrs.
Smith would approve, nor would your school. Wouldn't that be a
wonderful thing to walk down the gangplank, and find you waiting
there for me? That's too much to expect. Just let me walk in on
you—

I'm sure glad you found someplace to live in West Hartford
as I didn't like the idea of you commuting. That's too long a way
to go every morning, and especially during the winter. I like the
idea of you living in West Hartford. Besides—if I come home on a
ship that's going to New York it will be much easier for me to
stop off at West Hartford rather than Longmeadow on my way
to Newton.

I get so damned lonely for you when you write things like
about our date at Storyville. But it's a wonderfully lonesome
feeling—Pretty soon, however, we'll be able to find some
trombone to sit under, and some of my loneliness will go away—
OK—honey—it's too good to be true—I'm sure it's all a dream.
I've dreamed so long about being with you, and now it's actually a

reality I'm afraid I won't believe it when I am with you—

I've missed you so very much, and longed for you for so long everything seems to be all a product of my imagination. Even your letters I'm sure are something I only think I receive—

Hon—I don't know how patient a listener you are, but you'll probably hear me say some things to you over and over – Just about how much I missed you, and how wonderful it is to be home, but I'll tell you other things if you'll want me to—

The time will grow slower and slower as I start to become more and more impatient, but soon darling—soon—the evenings I spend with you will go by too fast—

However, I'll worry about that when the time comes—Right now all I see before me is you—and it's a wonderful sight.

Well Pete darling—time to write home and then to bed— Goodnight sweet, and remember I'm with you always—Take care of yourself for me, and wait, I'll be coming home to you real, real soon—Please keep writing until I tell you to stop—

Love to you and for you always—

Yours—Ronnie
I MISS YOU, TOO—an awful lot—

⁎☃

Finally, I was able to write Pete that I was coming home. I don't know if you can feel about those two words as I did then. At last I had something solid to hang on to. The reason was that Colonel Kimmitt told me he saw my name on a list and that I was slated to leave late the next month. It was like getting out of jail. When Tom Chapman told he had heard that our names were on the roster I listened to him, and truly tried to believe him, but in the back of my mind there was that little old "seeing is be believing" guy, and I did not trust him at all. Later when the Colonel told me was true was when I really believed it was going to happen, and what a weight it took off of my shoulders. It was actually the truth, and I'd be seeing Pete in only a few weeks. Of course, seeing my family and friends was in my thinking as well, but Pete was my primary thought, and really I didn't think much beyond what seeing her would be like.

Even though I was going home, life up there would continue on, and whoever took my place would probably be as bored silly as I was. Don Oberdorfer would still be on duty up there, but I 'm sure Bernie Rulong would either be moved up or sent home shortly. Well, that was the way the ball bounces (a phrase that was used heavily by our troops over there) and they would just have to wait their turn. I didn't feel sorry for those that had to stay on, in the least. It was their turn.

At that time back home Pete was preparing for her first teaching job. She had been accepted into the West Hartford, Connecticut school System, and was going to teach at the Elmwood School in West Hartford. I daydreamed all kinds of scenarios of what it would be like to see her for the first time, and the one that came to mind most often was the thought of walking in on her during a class. I really could picture it in my mind, but that was not what actually happened, and I will tell you all about that in a later comment.

As I read my letters of those days I find names that I have no recollection of whatsoever of Colonel Lemly, or Colonel Panke. I can't even picture them in my mind, but I imagine they couldn't picture me as well. They probably didn't even know my name at that time. People moved in and out of units like trains moving in and out at Grand Central Station. If you had only a few days or weeks to go you were called a "short timer" or "*Skoshi* timer". Either way you would be going home soon, and as many of the men flew over to Korea, I guess they all felt that they would fly home. To tell the truth, almost everyone went home by boat to either Seattle or San Francisco. Our trip over took 38 days by boat, and so going back by boat didn't matter as much to us as anything would be shorter.

Leaving there was still scheduled around two weeks away, but our military life went on as usual, but thinking about home gave us something else to think about as we sat our desks, and that helped to pass the time away. Awards and decorations were beginning to slow down as most of the medals to be awarded had been handed out, and not everyone who left the unit got any kind of an award at all. By the way, a medal is not "earned or won, it is awarded" It is a recognition by a government of an unusual act that is performed by somebody, and often in a valorous manner. There are some medals that are awarded for non-valorous service that is unusual and difficult to perform. The Bronze Star without a "V" device is often awarded by the U.S. Military in this manner.

When I wrote these awards I had to make sure that there were corroborating witnesses. Mostly, an officer's word was a necessity, but there were many cases when a non-coms (a non-commissioned enlisted man such as a sergeant or corporal) version was acceptable.

As we sat there at our desks, many thoughts about our 5 o'clock rendezvous at the bar was uppermost in our minds. We could see the chairs in the patio through our open door, and they were so inviting, and they looked so professionally made. Now that we were guests at the generals Mess the beer was cold. It was still that weak, 3.2 percent alcohol, but it tasted like beer, and although we complained as much as we could it never got any stronger.

I had given up on the Tom Collins drinks as they were too expensive, maybe 50 cents a glass, and above all they were too strong for the beer drinker I was in those days. Our meals were good as well, but didn't stack up to what the Navy served us on the way over to Korea. Actually, it wasn't the U.S. Navy that ran those ships. The men were civilians, merchant mariners, hired by the navy to run the ships. The captain of our ship was a U.S. Navy Captain, and we also had an Athletic and Recreational (A&R) naval officer on board. That guy didn't do much except run Bingo games and remind us of the library on board.

I read *Catcher in the Rye* on the way over. I was often the only one in the library, and I always wondered if I was missing some great going on out on deck, but of course, nothing ever happened out there except we watched the flying fish as they flew alongside. One of the enlisted men found a rope and tied his clothing in a bundle, and threw it over the side. It came up clean as a whistle, but he still had to iron it. We had laundry service on board, and that was quite acceptable to most of us. Lamar Daugherty and I used to go up at night on a small deck, and we often sang old songs. "Aura Lee" was one that comes to mind. One night we watched a green flare shoot up out of the water. When we arrived in Colon, Panama a submarine pulled in next to us, and we talked to the men on board it. They told us that they sent up the green flare to let our ship know that they were with us and on station. On Christmas Eve we heard them standing on deck singing carols, but we couldn't see them. That sure was a lovely experience.

I was a short timer, and boy was I ever happy with that title. Gaynor was also on the list as were most of the men I knew. It wouldn't be too long now, and was I ever ready for that day to come. No matter what the brass threw at us now would be a "negative perspiration" situation (another phrase that emanated from the Korean War that became "no sweat" back in the States) as far as we were concerned. We were going home. That's all that mattered. "That's all she wrote."

****

Letter #43

Sept 1, 1953

Dearest One—

Just finished chow, and want to get this off to you before I shower and go to the show. Our movie won't start until 9:30, and as it would be too late to write afterwards I ate early so I'd make sure this got off to you tonight. The world is so wonderful, and everything is going just right. I'm coming home, and I've got the most wonderful girl in the world to come home to—Darling, do you realize I was fortunate in being sent to Korea? If it didn't then our relationship would never have come about. I'd be going home to nothing—in fact I might have even turned down this chance, as I had nothing to make me want to return other than my family. I had spent 24 years with them, and I don't think a few more months would have made such a great difference.

I received your letter with the pictures, and have shown them to everyone. I have the one of you in graduation dress (don't tell Connie) in front of me. I cut Connie out of it. Every time I look at it I want to put my head down on the desk, and think about you—

You can never imagine what it means to me to know you care. I can see now how lost I'd be if it wasn't for you. You make everything go so right. You do the things to me every guy dreams his girl should do to him. It's been ten months almost since last I saw you, and they've been long, lonesome times. I'm quite proud of myself when I remember I never forgot about you when things started to go the wrong way—In fact I think I thought more about you as I needed something to brighten my mind. Sometimes I wrote you discouraging letters, and darling, from the bottom of my heart I apologize for the discomfort I may have caused you, but they were a necessary thing to me. I needed someone to listen to my troubles—someone whom I could feel near me when things got dark. And like a miracle I found you—Now every thought and action of mine is governed by what I think you might want me to do. I pray whatever I have done to make you be so wonderful to me will not be disappointing to you when we are together—I've tried to write as my mind and heart dictated so you would know me as I really am—I've never really known myself, and I'm sure your opinion of my inner self is quite different than mine. I never really self-reflected, and I don't think I'll ever be able to.

I know myself to be a person that usually seems to be pretty happy-go-lucky, but deep down I know I'm a little too sensitive for my own good. I'm like a little puppy—don't pet me all day, and I'll sulk—Please realize now, when I get home I'll probably be like a long-lost soul—I'll just want to raise the roof and have a good time, but beneath the wildness I'll be living your name, and wanting you with all my heart. No matter what I may do—like seeming to be inattentive to you for short times—please try to understand why—I want to show you how happy I am to be with you—Don't misunderstand, sweet—I don't mean leaving you for long times or being mean when I say inattentive—I'm talking about the times when we might be with some people, and all I'll want to do is just raise hell. Who knows—when I come back I may be the most quiet guy you ever saw, and maybe I'll be over-attentive—that isn't good either, but if you'll tell me what way you want me to be—then that's the way you shall have me—

More than anything else in this whole world I want to be with you always, but I can't force myself to tell you why until I have been home long enough to prove to you this feeling doesn't stem from the fact I've been away for so long.

You wouldn't be normal if you didn't have that fact enter your mind once while writing to me—"Is he writing to me because I'm just a woman or because I'm Pete Smith?" Didn't you ever say that to yourself? If there is any way I can prove to you it was because you <u>were</u> you—then I would write it down now. However, I think the only way I can do this to both our satisfaction is to wait until I can prove it in person. You will see then, my darling, how much you mean to me—So—just wait for a few more weeks, and you shall see!!

If this letter confuses you like the one of a few days ago, I wouldn't be at all surprised, but now the time is drawing so near I'll be able to tell you just what I want to say—Just know to me you're the world's most wonderful person, and will always remember you and think of you as such—You are my life now, sweetest one, and I know I wouldn't ever be happy without you—If I mixed you all up now—please just wait until I get home to tell you—Goodnight—miss you—miss you—miss you. Your

Ron

₧∛

I didn't realize that I was such a mush mouth until I read my latest letter to Pete. I do know that she was truly the only thing on my mind at that time, and the thought that I would actually see and talk to her in person in the near future was what kept me going at that time. Her last few letters finally showed me that she appreciated all I had been writing to her, and now that I have known her for so many years I realize that she wasn't able to truly express herself as fully as she would have wanted to do. I think her upbringing precluded her from allowing her heart to express itself. She came from an English family background, and probably never allowed herself to let her emotions run rampant in her mind. As one can see in my writing, I didn't let anything get in my way when it came to letting it all pour out of me. Ask my family, I say what I think without reservation. Often that gets me into trouble, but I don't know any other way to behave.

The days were warm, dusty and very long for us, especially those of us who were going home. Letter writing was not a chore for me, and I anxiously waited to be able to sit down and write to Pete. When I was young and went away to camp every summer we were expected to write home often. I only penned a few letters home, and had to be reminded constantly. It wasn't that I didn't love my folks, but I was sure that they knew I was having a good time, and as long as they weren't notified that I was sick, then everything must have been all right with me. The camp owners' daughter lived there, and as she was my best friend she would have known if anything were wrong with me, and I'm sure the message would have gone home to my folks.

In Korea, I didn't have that kind of backup, and so I had to take care of all my problems myself. That thinking about camp and Margie must have been on my mind while I was over there because I did write to Bud's parents to tell them that he was doing well, and I think they read between the lines that I truly enjoyed his friendship. We didn't see too much of each other at that time as he was a few miles away, and there was never a military reason for us to get together. In fact, I don't recall seeing him until we met in Pusan when we boarded the ship to go home.

My spare time was spent either writing to Pete or sitting out in our patio drinking beer with Don and Bernie. Don was a little different from the usual beer drinking companions one would normally associate with. He was of a higher intelligence level than most of us, but didn't make that a known to us as constantly as he could have. He fit right in to our conversations, and handled our level of thinking very well. He was a stringer for Elmer Davis, and he sent a lot of information home that let Davis know just what the troops were thinking. Bernie, on the other hand was as pithy as one can get. He was the old soldier, and we heard every complaint that was possible to be heard. He kept us laughing all the time, yet we listened closely to all his complaints as most of them seemed valid to us, and we valued his opinions as they were products of his many years as a soldier. My camera was broken, and I didn't have the money to have it repaired. If it had been in good repair I would have taken pictures of life in DivArty, but instead I have just tried to paint a picture for you. I hope the boredom showed through.

Letter #44

Wed. 2, Sept.

Hi Sweetheart,

    I can't remember whether the letter I wrote you last night was sent to West Hartford or not. In case you didn't get a letter dated 1 September you might try 130 Westmoreland. I wrote you, but have got the funniest feeling I used your home address.

    I'm in rather good spirits tonight, but I'd be sitting on top of the world if I had a letter from you. The division got very little mail last night, and I was one of the unfortunates who didn't receive one. But maybe tomorrow will be a lucky day for me. Sure hope so!!

    I'm a little regretful now I definitely said I'd be coming home soon—I'm still sure we'll be together within a few short weeks, but as I delve into the mystery that surrounds this early release the less I want to be positive when I write to you. The whole thing is a typical military deal. I'm sure your Dad can explain to you how fouled up things can get. The officer that will release me knows only I've applied and that I'll be home by November. However, the higher-ups have told Colonel Kimmitt that Lt. Freedman would be on his way by the last two weeks of this month. Tomorrow they are supposed to publish a list of who is leaving when, and if the Colonel wasn't kidding me my name will be near the top. There are 3 groups going, and I am in about the middle or last part of the first group, I'm trying to sound a little pessimistic so both you and I (those are three wonderful words- you and I) won't be disappointed if the Colonel was wrong. The way I look at it is; I've spent almost 10 months here, and if I don't leave for a few extra days I don't think I'll have a nervous breakdown—as long as I'll be on my way soon is all that counts.

    I've been really living up these last two days because of the wonderful news. Those of us who will be leaving have been walking around with big smiles all day long. Everything that happens seems to be the funniest thing in the world, and at night when we have a few drinks I'm ashamed to admit we get downright silly. Right now we're having a hell of a time kidding this Puerto Rican

Captain about his accent. It's just a lot of fun, and makes the time go by a little faster—

But all through our joking I can only think of seeing you— Honey, words can never express the feelings I hold for you—This separation is good for me as it makes me appreciate you more—I also have reason to think of you more strongly these last few hours as a tragic accident has turned the headquarters into a small turmoil. One of the boys drowned while swimming in the Imjin River, and every time I think of it I can only think of how horrible it must be to his parents after he lived out the war. He was due to leave soon as he had spent quite some time over here. When I think of it, all I can say to myself is "there but for the grace of God—go I". However, accidents happen all the time everywhere, and I'm quite sure I'll be back to you soon without any mishaps.

I flew to Division Headquarters yesterday in a light plane, and although they claim it's safer than riding in a car—I still was a bit nervous—I guess you have had the same sort of feelings at times—

The nights are getting a *skoshie* bit colder. I only throw two blankets over me as I don't like those itchy woolen summer sleeping bags. What a pleasure it will be to use white sheets again. I shouldn't complain, however, 'cause whoever heard of an Army living in the field with canvas cots, sleeping bags, air mattresses, and mosquito nets. Even on the hill I had a cot and mattress—but I never took my clothes off at night. I remember sleeping in flak jacket and helmet a couple of times. I got so tired I'd just stretch out on the sack in the OP, and would fall asleep before I knew it. Another thing, by the way I have to add to my "food at home list" is corn on the cob. I had almost forgotten all about it, until I got the craving for it tonight. Sweetheart—when my wife is pregnant and wants some crazy thing to eat—she'll never have to wait for me to go out and get it. I've learned how it is to want certain items until you can almost imagine what they look and taste like.

By the way, I figure this letter will arrive either on the day school starts or just a bit sooner. In either case I want to wish you the best, honey, on the first day, and want you to remember what I've told you. You're going to be a wonderful teacher I know—'cause if I were a 3rd grade student and had a pretty teacher like you I couldn't think of you being anything but wonderful. Make the best of this year, darling, because I think by the time next September rolls around you'll no longer be a Miss Smith. Most schools don't use married teachers either—do they? You wait, Pete honey—some awfully, awfully, lucky guy will grab you—and those poor 3rd graders will just be put in the cold.

Gotta go as I have to tell Jack and Cele their darling boy is still in Korea, and that all is well—Goodnight wonderful—mind if I tell you that I miss you, want you, and think you're the most wonderful thing that's ever happened to me—

All my love is yours, always—Loveydo, Ron

 C 

It sounds like I was as silly as I said I was at that time. The very thought of going home was all anyone could think of, and it was happening to me, and real soon. In the back of my mind, however, I knew of the Army way of doing things. I had only been a soldier for not quite three years, but as a typical GI, I learned very quickly that the old cliché was quite true. There's the "Right way, the Wrong way, and the Army way. If anything happened on the day it was supposed to you knew that something went wrong, somewhere. I'm sure that all of us who had heard the news about going home must have constantly brought the subject up to the brass like Colonel Kimmitt. Those people were career men, and going home was not as big a deal to them as it was to us. Besides, they knew about the Army way and had learned to live with it.

As I review these letters and comments, I am reminded of situations that arose that I have not mentioned before, but they may give the reader some insight into Army life. I wrote about our arrival in Inchon, but I never completed the story. There was a train waiting there to take us somewhere, but we didn't have any idea where that would be. We should have used our brains and realized that we would not be going anywhere near a combat zone as we were semi-mobile, and couldn't get out of our way if we had to.

The train was, I think, narrow gauge, and was long enough that I couldn't see the engine. The cars had wooden bench seats, and all the windows were broken out. There was no heat nor were there any lights in the cars, and the men's room was a closet up at the right front of the car. I asked a sergeant who worked on the railroad what the temperature was at that time. It was 1600 (4 p.m.) and the thermometer said 17 below zero. There were ice floes out in the Flying Fish channel just to our rear. Each Officer was in charge of a car, and I took my seat next to a window opening with my left leg pressed up against the sidewall of the car. A sergeant in our battalion came to my seat and told me that he had just deposited a foot locker on the rear vestibule of my car, and that I was responsible to see that it was off loaded at our destination.

The train started, and we chugged along at about 5 miles per hour. The train stopped in the Yong Dong Po railroad station where we were told there was an air raid going on. We saw or heard nothing except we were met by the most decrepit group of young people I have ever seen. They were beggars and spent their time around the station. We had not been issued any rations so we had nothing to give them. I remember one man came up to my window area, and said, "Me engine driver. Switchy switchy". I didn't quite understand him until a few days later when I learned that the young people talked like this in their attempt to learn English. As an example, young thieves were called "slicky slicky, boys".

The train took off again, and I was told to bring myself and two men forward to the Battalion Commanders car as they had food and drink for us. By the way, there were no drinks as everything was frozen solid. Walking forward was difficult as we were very cold and stiff. The Commanders car had a potbellied stove in the middle of it, and all the upper level personnel were sitting around in their shirtsleeves enjoying the ride. I was really upset by this, but tried to remember that RHIP (rank has its privileges) was the rule the rest of the world had to live by. The C rations they gave us were almost frozen solid, and most of the men did not even bother to open theirs. They threw the cans out the windows when we saw that there were people around to pick them up.

We rattled along until 0100 (1 a.m.) when we arrived at K55 airbase. I heard someone up forward in the car yell, "We have a man down up here", and so I tried to get forward as quickly as possible. I distinctly remember not feeling my legs from the waist down, but they worked, and I got up to the man to find him having trouble breathing. The medics told me later that he had ice crystals in his lungs. It had taken us nine hours to go forty two miles. I stepped down from the train and saw a jeep with a Red Cross emblem on its side, and beckoned the driver over.

As I attempted to re-board the train, our Executive Officer, a Major Bornscheur, stopped me, and asked, "What in hell are you doing Lieutenant" I told him that I was going to check my car for stragglers, and that there was a foot locker in the rear vestibule that I had to take care of. He told me to forget everything, and that he would check my car. "Get the men up for coffee in that hut over there".

We went in for coffee, and then we marched up to the top of a hill. It was probably the worst night of my life, and I'm sure all the others that were there would say the same thing. Here we were without any cold weather gear, and standing around for 5 or 6 hours until breakfast the next morning. The men burned every piece of lumber our advance party had scrounged for us, and so when it came time for floors and doors for our tents, we were out of luck.

In some future commentary I will relate what happened at breakfast that morning. We eventually were assigned to tents to sleep in and for our orderly rooms. At around midday I was told that the Colonel wanted to see me, and I was taken to his quarters. He had a metal hut with sheetrock lined walls, and a young house girl to straighten the place out. He informed me that because I hadn't taken care of that footlocker on my car, he was going to put me up on a Statement of Charges (a precursor to a Court Martial) as there were many important things in that foot locker.

There was supposed to be the battalion Medical supply of drugs, etc. Also the Colonel's personal camera and field glasses were in there along with the Secret Anti-Aircraft defense plans for Limestone Air Force Base in Maine. I went back to my battery area in such a foul mood that Captain Doherty told me that he would write a letter for me that would absolve me of all my charges. That sounded good, but here I was, in Korea for only one half a day, and I was already up for Court Martial.

A few days passed, and no letter was written. A day or two later I had to be at some place down the road at 1100 to appear before the board. I asked the Captain about the letter, and he went into the tent to write it out. He reappeared quickly with an envelope. He said to read the letter, which I did. It was only two words long, and of course, I couldn't use that at all. Then he took me by the shoulders and said, "Anytime, they mention footlocker you say. 'Do you mean the one that the Major said he would take care of?'"

I was sent back to the battery area with all charges dropped. The Major, the battalion adjutant, and a lieutenant were held responsible. That was quite an experience, and quite an introduction to Korea.

Figure 66 - In basic training I won the Guard Mount Award. Got 3-day pass. This was taken at Camp Brunonia in Maine

Letter #45

Thursday 3, Sept.

My Dearest Pete,

   The Commanding General of the 7ᵗʰ Division today endorsed my application for release, and approved my leaving in September. Now, that isn't the final okay, but the general consensus is the Army Department will go along with it, and we should have definite word in about two weeks. I'm sure I'll be ready to leave whenever the call comes. I'm so happy I would almost swim home.

   Got another wonderful note from you today, and had reason to be amazed. Only 2 bags of mail came in for the whole division (18,000 men), and I got one from you, and one from Mom. I tell you, darling, nothing can be wrong when I know you're with me. I'm really living!! By the way, in case you know anyone else in the service who is trying to go out you might tell him you want his general to let him go. That's the secret of my success. I wrote a letter to Gen. Trudeau, and told him my Pete wants him to let me go—and here I am, almost on my way—It's very simple—all he needs is to have a girl named Pete Smith. However, if I ever do find a guy that has a girl named Pete Smith, there'll be no sense in his asking to be let go as I'll see he won't live long enough to get on the boat—

   Honey—even though you don't need to be writing me much longer—you just keep writing no matter if you've got nothing at all to say—Like you say, writing to you also is like talking to you, and it also gives me a different feeling. It's a warm, cozy type feeling, and it's wonderful—I, too have all your letters with only a few exceptions. One of my many superstitions is keeping your last letter with me until I get a new one. Then I carry that around until another one comes. After a few days of being out in the rain, or crawling around a hoochie—the letter is nothing but crumbles. I keep them all in a steel fuse box, and will bring them back with me. Some night we'll get them out, and trade them—to me it would almost be living the best parts of these past few months.

I think I could remember all that happened on most of the days I wrote—Especially 1 and 11 July. Those days weren't part of the pleasanter moments, but when it was all over I sure felt good. Sometimes I felt real gloomy when I wrote you, and other times I was sitting on top of the world. Some nights when I went into the cave in the O.P. to write you—I'd sit there writing by either candlelight or flashlight. I'd write a few lines, and think for a while, but all the time I kept wishing you were there—I guess I was a bit selfish in wishing you there in place, but damn I was lonesome for you. Some nights up there the valley and the mountains were just beautiful. The moon would light everything up, and occasionally a flare would go off in the distance. It's quite hard to believe one can find beauty in war. Maybe if I didn't have you to think about everything wouldn't have seemed so calm and peaceful. I use to imagine so hard you were with me I could almost feel your hand in mine. I'd talk out loud to myself as if I were talking to you. If anybody could have heard me they would have thought I had cracked up. Well, soon I won't be imaging that you'll be next to me.

Our minds <u>must</u> work the same way, hon. You wrote a couple of days ago that you thought it might have been me the other night when your phone rang—I often get feelings like that—especially about you—A door opens, and I expect you to walk in saying the government sent you over—or else I'm sure the sealed envelope on somebody's desk is a note from you telling them not to tell me, but that you'll be over in Korea in a few days, and want to surprise me—Silly—yes—but fun!!

Hey—I just remembered something!! You claim I used to come over to take you to the movies after our first date—I may be wrong, but I think you've got <u>me</u> mistaken with somebody else. I remember taking you to the ice cream place near Sears and Roebucks now, but as I recall it was in place of a date—man, you had me going in circles there for a while—but honey—whatever happened then I'm glad that it did—'cause look what's happened now—I've not a complaint in the world—How about you??

I suppose I could go into one of my deep and confusing descriptions on my thoughts about "knowing" things will happen, not "wishing" that they would. I think I always "knew" that I'd get home alright, but just the same I prayed and wished all the time. Sweetheart, I know that when I get back, and have some time to talk to you that you will know almost every feeling and thought I've had since last February or so—almost all of them, had some direct or indirect bearing on you—I have many, many things to tell you, that won't sound right unless I can say them to you. I'd like to write them to you, but let them wait; it will be best.

There's a private in here by the name of Rocco Scacutto who is telling me how his marriage is all washed up, while I'm trying to write you. He's really got his troubles, but I can't let them bother me now. That boy needs to go home, and the more I let him talk about his wife the more he torments himself—

Well, Pete, another day—another dollar, and real soon I'll be with you. Just keep waiting, darling—it's only a few more weeks— Please take care of yourself for me and when I tell you to stop writing then you can start waiting for the phone to ring or listening for a knock on the door.

Goodnight you—miss you terribly, and really long to be with you—think of me that first day at school for I'll be thinking of you—

All my love to you always, darling, Ronnie

CB♥O

To finally get something official on our "rotating" home (that was the term used by the Army at that time) policy was all we needed to make us know that we were actually going to go home. We didn't know exactly when, but knew that it would be in the very near future. I don't think I ever thought about my three years of service except maybe in a non-pleasant way, but now, sixty years later, I look back on that time as one of the best learning experiences of my life. Irving Berlin said it best when he wrote, "The Army's Made a Man Out of Me." Although I had been away from home for extended periods of time during the summers, this was really being away from home. When I was younger I could call or write my folks as often as I wanted to, but in the Army the telephone seemed always to be just out of reach, and letter writing time was not always available unless you had a girl like Pete to write to. Actually, I didn't write, I spoke to her out loud, but put it down on paper just as I thought the words.

I saw things that I never would have seen during that period in my life. I saw the wounded, the dead, the frightened, the bold. I saw everything I wanted to see, and things I hoped never to see. When I came home I had more self-confidence than ever before, and I could feel it in my actions and thoughts. Even now, things just pop up into my head that I never thought I would remember or even think about again.

Korea was a poverty stricken land when our army arrived in 1945. It was almost like stepping back into the dark ages. No electricity, no roads, no running water and even less to be had if you were a native of that land. The people lived in mud and stick houses (I hesitated to use that word), and ate a very limited menu in their daily lives. Rice, rice, and more rice is all they ever seemed to eat.

Our rations also included rice, but ours came from Louisiana as we weren't allowed to eat any local foodstuffs. They varied things by adding garlic and peppers to their rice, but never had enough where-with-all to buy spices or other condiments. Although I didn't get there until 1953, there apparently had been no improvement in the people's way of living, except for the fact that they weren't being oppressed or shot at by the North Koreans. Our presence there allowed them to restart their lives, and I am sure gave them the reassurance of prosperity in their future. But while we were living amongst them I saw some strange things.

One memory that comes back to me at times is the day I saw the garbage pick-up truck come into our area back at K55. The truck was large by Korean standards, but not quite as large as our 2½ ton Army trucks. This one had two front tires filled with sand and had metal bolts holding the tires to the rims. They were like cleats that baseball players wear. The truck was piled high with their collection of the day, and on top sitting on all that refuse were two or three men eating whatever they could find. I couldn't believe that there was this type of poverty in the world, and it has left a lasting impression on me.

I went back to visit Korea in 2006, and one cannot imagine the change in that country. The inherent abilities of the South Korean people have come shining through, and with our country's help South Korea now enjoys the tenth or eleventh highest standard of living in the whole world. The road network is marvelous with highways and roadways all throughout the populated areas. There are skyscrapers, and cable cars, and hotels that are equal to the best in the world. I tell people that walking through the streets of Seoul today, is like walking through the streets of New York. Every Korean has a cell phone or a boom box, and they all seem to be using them. The streets are clean, and all the food is now edible.

I tried Kimchi, their national dish, but didn't care for the method the preparers used. I thought it could have more peppers or garlic or maybe the chefs were afraid of our delicate palates, and toned things down for us. They weren't bashful about their pricing, however, as I found out when I ordered a draft beer in the bar. The bill was $8.00 American dollars per glass which surprised us all. All our meals, transportation, room and tickets to events were paid for by the Korean government. It is their way of thanking the U.S. military personnel for all they did there. I paid the full fare to fly from Florida to Seoul, but now the government will pay 50 percent of the veterans fare from Los Angeles to Seoul and one third of a spouse or guests fare.

Financially, it would have been better if I had waited to visit, but it was too good to pass up earlier, and I truly enjoyed my visit. We were there during the anniversary week of the start of the war, and the Korean government wanted us to attend all their ceremonies. I went with Bud, and we both had hopes of re visiting some of the forward areas that we had been stationed in, but they kept us hopping around Seoul and all its venues instead. We did get up to Panmunjom to see the Demilitarized Zone. That was a very interesting excursion, and a pleasant way to end our trip.

Figure 67 - As opposed to the main highway, Route 1, through Suwon's South Gate in 1953. This was as good as it got back then!

Figure 68 - Truce signed on this table, 27 July 1953

Letter #46

Fri. 4 Sept –

Pete Honey –

Sure is a beautiful night tonight. Maybe not what you or someone else might call beautiful, but my own kind of beautiful night. Fairly warm with big dark rain clouds jumping from hill to hill. The rocky peaks make the picture complete, and add to my feeling of warm loneliness. No honey—I'm not trying to sound like some author, but at times the ruggedness and beauty of the elements gets me to thinking. I'm not sad nor do I feel moody—I'm just in the quiet blue happy mood that sometimes gets me. I'm alone with thoughts of you and the future, and can't think of any way more pleasant to spend an evening except being with you.

You know something, darling—I like being lonely—I can't explain it—It just makes everything turn a beautiful blue-grey, and any image I picture in my mind seems to be that soft, fuzzy kind you see in a movie when the actor is dreaming. I can actually make myself see your face right now even though there are noises and people that tend to distract me. I wonder what you did today. Did you think of me as much as I thought of you? If you did, hon—then you were a busy girl. I wonder what you will do today as it's only about 6:15 A.M. on the morning of September 4th back in Longmeadow or on that lakeside. Darling, I want so much to come home to you!!

I hope you don't get into a blue mood after reading this letter. If my letter can make you feel that warm blue feeling, then okay—but just a blue depressed feeling is no good. I wish there were some way you could get into the same mood I feel as I write you when you read my letters. I'm sure I'd get you to understand me better.

It's really quite difficult for me to believe that only 9 or 10 months ago I hardly even knew a girl named Pete Smith—Now the day doesn't seem right without a letter to or from you. It seems that I've known you for so long that writing you is only natural. It's almost like you've been my girl since grammar school. You will forgive me, won't you for taking the liberty of feeling that way? I'm a dreamer, sweet one—can't you see?

I'm no accomplished woman's man—believe me—far from it—but something's I have learned from my limited experience and from other people. Maybe the reason I'm not an accomplished lady's man is that I never paid any attention to what I've learned or heard. One of the most important maxims that males try to follow is one that I've always disagreed with. The rule is—"Never let a girl know you care for her, and above all, never give her an even break." You being a woman would certainly know if that rule works when a guy is trying to catch a woman or not, but for some reason I could never go along with it. I have had girls tell me that they'd much rather have a man that had a little mystery or something to him, and I go along with that I guess. But, I could never see it. Maybe it's because I lack the confidence to give a girl a hard time.

My own idea on the subject boils down to one definite thing. If the girl is worth paying attention to then there's no sense in giving her any reason to doubt your sincerity. I'm telling secrets out of school. These things should be discussed with a sister or some ordinary girl—never with the object or subject of the whole thing, but I can't help not keeping things from you—that's the whole point—I can't play games with you as I can't afford to lose you. Wrong to feel that way? Maybe so—but I'll never be that aloof, don't-give-a-damn mystery man. I can't feel close to you unless I open my mind to you—

For some reason I picture you as being the same way—The only thing is that you're smart—you don't let on!! I'm an open book for you to read—if you want to take time to search each page carefully—

I have a lot more to say, hon, but these are some of the things that don't come out right on paper—I've said too much as it is.

Things still haven't changed in regards to the early release deal, but from the talk I hear around the higher-ups it may not be until the end of the month before I leave. But—I am leaving, and will be home with you soon, and that's all that really matters to me.

I've been writing almost every night now, and I love it—No

kidding!! And if a letter every day pleases you, hon—then there's hardly anything that could make me feel better. If you don't get home or to Hartford for a few days then the mail will pile up. I enjoy getting mail like that –

Well, a few more days and Sept. 9ᵗʰ will be with us. As you read this you should feel practically at home with those kids, and I'll bet now you can see how unfounded all those first-day jitters were. It was easy as all hell wasn't it?? Take it from a man who has had more cases of the jitters then a bowl full of Jell-O. I know what they're like, and I know how hard it is to rid yourself of them no matter how much somebody tells you not to worry. How hard it is to take advice, and how easy it is to give it!! I was with you on the 9th, treasure—right there the whole day—Sure, I'm writing it in advance, but I know that I'll be there that day.

Well, Pete, time to get along. I had no mail today from you, but I'm sure it's because of the cancellation of flights from Japan due to heavy rains. It better be!! Goodnight, darling—I miss you very much, and will always hold you in my heart.

I'll be with you in dreams tonight to tell you that, and also to tell you that my love is yours-always-Bless you-Ron

I forgot—take care of that car!!

I'll have a name for it real soon—

And I hope your whole family has a wonderful vacation—It will probably be almost all over by the time you get this, but still—have a wonderful time—

Good nite again, honey
Sleep tight

ଓଞଠ

As can be seen from my letters to Pete, there was very little to write about. The days seemed to blend in with each other, and I never knew if it was a Sunday or a Thursday. I had to consult a calendar every time I wrote a letter. Of course, that made time go even more slowly when I thought the date was actually more advanced than it really was. A lot of the odd jobs were handed down to me, and I made them all seem to be more involved than they really were. It reminds me now of people who work on an hourly basis. When they are out driving around they are never in any kind of a hurry, and it seems like they want the whole world to slow down to accommodate their pace. I was guilty of that syndrome at DivArty, but there was no other way to make the days go by at an acceptable speed.

I mentioned in a previous note that a certain incident took place on the first morning that we were in Korea. Our encampment was on the top of a hill that looked down on the almost completed airbase. The tents our advance party had set up were in parallel rows, and my battery, Baker, at that time was at the highest point on the hill. We had been standing around in that terribly cold atmosphere for a number of hours, and I know that frostbite was working its deadly deeds all that time.

An announcement was made that the battalion would be fed breakfast if they would only go downhill away from the airstrip where a pit about 6 by 8 feet and a foot deep had been previously dug out. In Army parlance, this was called a sump and would be the place where our refuse from this meal would be dumped. There were two big barrels of water being boiled by "Doughnut heaters" next to the sump. We moved along in a line and had a breakfast of powdered eggs, powdered milk, and soggy toast with some type of margarine on it. After we ate we scraped the leftovers into the empty sump and dropped our mess kits into the soapy boiling water where we used brushes to clean our utensils. We then dunked our mess kits into a clean barrel of boiling water, and then let them air dry until the next meal.

Most of the troops finished their breakfast and meandered back up the hill to their battery areas to await further orders. As Baker battery was about the last to be fed, because we were the furthest away from the mess area, I stayed around and saw the cooks dump the barrels of water into the sump on top of all the garbage. There had been two or three stations where the men could use the barrels of water, and their contents seemed to fill the sump up full. Through the rising steam a colony of little people appeared, and most of them waded right into the water. It didn't bother them if it was hot or wet or whatever. Here was a breakfast for them to gobble down.

We had never seen anything like that, and it caused us all to stand around and gape at their actions. Some of my men pulled a small child out, and immediately took him to our tent area where they could dry him off and dress him in whatever they could find. I went over to see the youngster, and found all my men jabbering about like a bunch of nursemaids. The child looked about five years old, but we knew, from our guidebooks that most Koreans were a little older than they looked. The boy didn't speak any English, and we certainly didn't know anything in Korean beyond what the Army guide books phonetically told us to say. At that time the phrase for "hello" in Korean was "*Ahn-yung-hashem nika*" which was all we could say. And all he had to say in return was the same phrase. Later in the day the men determined that his name was what I thought to be Bak Il Bong. The Koreans, as most Asian people do, say their last name first so in our method of speech he was Bong Il Bak. Many years later I found his real name to be Pak Y Bong.

One of my men, T.J. Bingley called the boy "Kettleboom", and that became his Americanized name. That night all the cots in the tent were being used by my platoon members, and the only thing Kettleboom could lie down on was a stretcher. When this was presented to him he started to cry, and folded his arms to the side of his head, and repeated "*Sayonara*" or Japanese for good bye. It took time, but it was deduced that dead or wounded people were the only ones to lie on stretchers, and he wouldn't do it. One of the men changed places with him, and that solved the problem at that time.

These little people were mostly all abandoned by folks unable to care for them or were orphans and they lived out in the field huddled over large No. 10 cans filled with dirt and saturated with diesel fuel that they had stolen. They were all blacker than tar from the smoke, and it took quite a while using yellow soap to clean them up. It was our real first example of how poor and debilitated these people were. We just could not believe what we had seen. Later when Kettleboom became more language efficient, he told us that his parents had been killed in a U.N. air raid, and that the orphanage he was sent to was worse than living alone out in the fields.

We had a lot of fun with this youngster, and one of my favorite memories is seeing him dressed in his cut down army fatigues with his own personal mess kit hanging from his belt as he ran down the front side of our hill to chow down.

When I returned to the States I tried to locate him, and bring him over, but had no success at all. In later years I answered an email from an American living over near the airbase, and when I told him about our little houseboy he said that he had found him, and although he remembered "Tenant Ron" he was too embarrassed to talk to me as I would be terribly disappointed in the fact that he now owned and ran a house of ill repute in the village of Osan-ni. I'm glad that he made it through, and is on his own now.

****

Letter #47

Sat. 5, August

Hi You Darling,

I'm writing this early tonite as I may have to help move our office from one side of the hoochie to the other. It's only about

3 P.M. now, and unless they wait until 8 or so I just won't be available.

Got a sweet, wonderful letter form you today, but was surprised to read that you hadn't heard from me all week. I've written almost every day now for quite a while, and can't imagine what the holdup might be. Maybe it's because you've been over at Cal's, and haven't been able to pick up the mail. I sure hope that's the reason—

Well, one more day gone in my "great adventure." This is one sightseeing trip I could have done without. Maybe 8 or 9 months ago I wouldn't want to have missed it, but now, honey—things are different. My ideas and thoughts on some subjects were completely wrong as I now can see. Some I still believe. I used to think that only by forceful methods could we win this war, and I'm still of that opinion, but yet I don't think we should have done it. After I saw what things could really be like I didn't want to see anybody expose themselves to anything. One never can understand anything truly until he has seen it or felt it.

My other thoughts have changed some too. I left home without any real feeling of depression. It was a good way to leave—clear conscience and all that, but now I suddenly realize how much I took for granted. I was never appreciative of the little things I had, but now I know enough to "count my blessings". Maybe I'm getting a little too philosophical tonight, but it all boils down to one thought, and I think it might be unfair to you to mention it. Not only that, but I'm sure you'll never really know how deeply I feel on the subject. I've mentioned it before, but as it is part and parcel of your wonderfulness to me; it only seems natural to tell you over and over again. Maybe this time I make you see what I'm driving at a little more clearly.

If it hadn't been for you, my darling, this past year would have been a completely empty, useless void in my life. I saw nothing good in the world, but you. I must qualify that by including my family and close friends in your category, but outside of that—I lived in greed, filth, perversion, hatred, unfairness, and other depressing things.

You, and this time only you, brought me any ray of hope or remembrance that there were people like you still alive. The folks were always there behind me, but I took them for granted, and when things were looking black I found my only consolation in thoughts of you. You're probably wondering how I can say that, as our only real contact has been through letters. But like a blind man, I don't have to see the sun—I can feel it, and you've been just that to me—Everything seems to revolve around you. Maybe you feel that I am saying things beyond my reasoning, and should wait until I was with you—that's why I said in the beginning that I thought that mentioning all this might be unfair to you. You see now, don't you Pete why I've written that I have to tell you some things? I could never sit here and write you of the things I thought for I could never make you see the situation that surrounded me in a letter. I want you to know how I felt, but I'll have to tell you not write you—

But—let it all wait—it will only be a few weeks more.

Well, your vacation should be ending now that school is about to start. I hope you had a wonderful time, and I thank you honey for wishing me there. The lake and the country wouldn't have mattered so much—just the thought of being with you— But—we'll make up for it.

In regard to your question if I like argyles or not—Honey— you asked the wrong thing—'cause I will be pestering you from here to kingdom come to knit argyles for me—Any colors, any style—anything but olive drab khaki—but if it won't trouble you can start knitting now—You've let yourself in for it—I won't let you stop! Size $10\frac{1}{2}$ to 11 will be fine. Man—you're a sweetheart! Remind me someday to kiss you and tell you that I love you!! I'd much rather have them than a sweater.

I almost had a present for Donald, not you—I went down to Charlie Battery the other night, and got talking to some of the boys, and just casually mentioned that I was taking little Skoshie home with me, but they raised such a howl that I just couldn't do it. He'd love the little thing. She's almost like an animated Teddy Bear. No kidding, hon—it was the perfect present—Maybe Cal and Hutch wouldn't have thought so, but it always seemed to me that a little boy just isn't a little boy without a puppy tagging after him. Well, maybe we'll do something about it when I get back—I'm awfully jealous of him you know—he's got a certain "doting Aunt." I'll have to talk to him, IN PRIVATE, when I get back—maybe we can consolidate forces or something. Would you please tell him to read up on tactics as I aim to have some long discussions with him real soon. And I repeat <u>IN</u> <u>PRIVATE</u>!!

Still nothing more on early release, but will hear soon! I've been writing to you in Hartford, and hope that all my mail is catching up to you—Especially the first one in which I said I'd be coming home—It gave me a real thrill to write that to you. I don't know why, but being a sentimentalist at heart anything good like that affects me—Someday, sweet one, I will ring a doorbell on you, and then both our daydreams for once will come true. I keep wondering just where I'd find you that day—I wonder if it will be someplace that I've pictured. Probably will as I've day dreamed almost every possibility—I'll probably forget everything that I planned to say to you—I'll just stand there and stutter—but at least I'll be home with <u>you.</u> Damn it, but I'm lonesome for you right now.

Well, treasure—it's about time to run along, but I'll be back with you again tomorrow night. So, till then, Pete, remember that I miss you more now than all the other times I've told you put together, and will always be thinking of you. Goodnight you! Always all my love,

Yours, Ronnie

CБ80

I don't know how Pete felt about it at that time, but pouring out my thoughts to her just seemed so normal to me. I do distinctly remember how superstitious I was about writing either to her or to home. I was absolutely positive that that would be enough to keep me safe from any kind of harm.

In the heat and dust of the day I often thought about summer camp in Maine, and how cool and clear the lake water was. Believe it or not I had visions on the ice cold water bubbler that sat in front of the mess hall steps. If we could have had anything like that in Korea It would have been worth millions of dollars. The nightly movies were our primary form of entertainment. They were generally older flicks, and quite often "B" level, but we were avid fans, and almost everybody attended them after the sun went down. Only the intelligentsia in our group ever seemed to think about why we were where we were, and what we had accomplished. I am not of that group, and probably never really gave any thought to those subjects unless I was talking to Don Oberdorfer or some one of his caliber.

The Korean War was the first time the west had ever physically faced Communism in a battle and once we were able to comport ourselves properly were we able to face them down. It seems that they were only better than us when it came to numbers of bodies they could employ.

They didn't have any air support at all for their troops, and certainly no naval force of any kind. They used mortars, and fairly small caliber artillery along with their rifles, and their fabulous "burp guns". They were excellent mortar men, and the saying went that they could drop a "round in your hip pocket", if they wanted to do that. They had no vehicular traffic anywhere within the range of our artillery, which was close to 18 miles, and all their supplies had to be hand carried or on the backs of mules, and almost always at night.

I have read that the U.S. fired more artillery in the Korean War than we did in all the WWII. That sounds hard to believe, but when one saw the piles of used brass then it did seem possible. We used to fire what we called H&I's at night without even seeing if there was anything there to shoot at. H&I stood for 'harassing and interdictory". If we saw an unused trail junction, as an example, in the daylight then we could send the coordinates down to the FDC, and then would program H&I fire that night. Right between the two Horseshoes I used to see a junction of two small pathways that stood out because of a light colored sand base. I never saw any traffic or even footprints, but I just knew that that was an important travel way for the enemy.

Also, we had contact with the enemy on our radios. They must have had men who did nothing but listen to our channels, and try to disrupt our conversations. I don't believe they spoke any Asian language when they did this. It all sounded like garbled voice exercises to me. If they did try to interrupt my conversations I would get so frustrated, which was probably their intention. I would swear at them at the top of my lungs, and if they spoke any English they probably heard words that they never knew existed. That didn't stop them, and when I learned a couple of hard words in Chinese they probably just laughed off my pronunciation.

They were poorly prepared for combat with reference to equipment, etc. (except for that burp gun), but they adhered to the political aspect of their leaders, and were tough in a close combat situation. Read Gen. S.L.A. Marshal's book *Pork Chop Hill* or his *River and the Gauntlet*, and you will get firsthand knowledge of the capabilities of the Chinese fighting man.

I didn't have much to do with the South Korean Army as we only had individual ROK's attached to our division. They were all learning how to fire artillery pieces, and never acted as a self-contained unit when I was involved with them. Just prior to the last Pork Chop flap the Chinese attacked Arrowhead which was directly to my right front. It was a South Korean held outpost and was actually within the Xth Corps region, which was off limits to me. The two Horseshoes stood just west of Arrowhead, and that was fair ground for us to fire into. That battle raged for a few days, and I had a grandstand seat for the whole thing.

One afternoon, a South Korean lieutenant appeared in my OP with an outsized radio that was probably a U.S. hand me down from some ancient war. It was so big and bulky that I thought there should have been two handlers to work with him. He went right up to my window, and said to me in Korean "*Nam Jin*" meaning "to the north". I replied "*Nay, Puk Jin*". I only meant that to say "Let's go home", but he didn't take it that way, and so he picked up his radio and stormed out. Just as well, there wasn't room for the two of us anyway.

I lived and ate among the Ethiopian "Kagnew" battalion. I believe "Kagnew" meant victor or victory in their language. They were not required to use code words in their radio transmission as there apparently weren't any Chinese who spoke Ethiopian. I learned only three words in their language. One was "*imatalika*" (sp) which was Lieutenant. The second was "*Chambelli*" which meant captain, and the last word was "woot" which I was told meant "soup". It didn't matter anyway, as all my conversations were in whatever broken French I remembered from High School.

****

Letter #48

Sunday 6, Sep.

Dearest Pete,

Well, honey time for the daily sugar report, and if there's one report I don't mind submitting this is it. It's funny how G.I.'s can think up names for different things. I think that this one is one of their best. A daily sugar report in case you don't understand is any letter to or from your girl. I get a kick out of that name—

Tonight the General is throwing a farewell party for Colonel Kimmitt. He's leaving around the 11th or so, and all the other wheels in Divarty are coming over. Should be quite a good party. Plenty of booze and filet mignons. We peons had filets for chow tonight, but I guess they weren't the same thickness and size that the General will have tonight. Rank has its privileges you know—Can't complain, however, as I really enjoyed my supper. French fries, chocolate ice cream and a couple of bottles of

Japanese beer really added to the steak.

Although today was Sunday, and we were supposed to have the day off, I still worked right up to 5 p.m. At 1:30 this afternoon I was notified that I was to be on a board to determine whether a private in this outfit should be listed as dead rather than missing after he drowned. It was quite a tragedy from what I could learn from the witnesses. He was bathing in the Imjin, and must have been carried away by the terrific undercurrent. They've never found his body. This Imjin is quite treacherous as it has sandbars, quicksand, and a terrific current. It sure is a terrible thing—

I got a letter from Steve today, and he's going to be in Tokyo on the 10th of Sept. He wants me to meet him, but I can't make it. He says he thinks Zeke is over there, but I haven't the slightest idea where to locate him.

Hon—I just placed a call to Steve, but as they have to make connections and all—I'll have to wait for them to call me back. Sure would be great to hear his voice—I'm going to write him anyway after I finish this.

The days are really dragging by for me, but each one is one day closer to the boat. The new rumor is that we'll leave the division in about 2 weeks—That would be wonderful. Just think, darling—I'd be home in mid-October-I really feel lucky!

My kid brother Steve wrote the other day, and said his address is 104 Baker House, U-MASS—so if you should ever be just driving through in that blue bomber why don't you stop in; it would give him a big thrill—You'll love him—He's really terrific. But don't ever tell him I said so....

We have a teletype machine in the other half of this tent— (I'm writing from the Public Information Officer's Office), and earlier I tried to type out a letter to you—I had to give up, however, as I couldn't make the machine work right. Instead of D's I got $-signs, and every time I pushed the spacer it printed an "N". Hell, it's easier writing to you. Besides you'd never get the message as it only goes as far as division.

There's very little news to tell you tonight, and maybe you can read that by my little uninteresting items. But, if you can listen to me prattle on—ok, 'cause half the fun is just the fact that I am writing to you.

I didn't hear from you today, but I guess you're busy moving or something. Today would have brought me a letter written from you on August 31st, and I imagine that was the day you left for the lake—Your mail has been terrific lately—I do know a letter almost every day sure can do a lot for a guy—It makes me feel a lot closer to you, honey. In that respect I'm almost sorry that going home will mean fewer letters. I hope there'll be no occasion for us to do more writing once I get home, however—Letters are nice, but nothing at all like the real thing—You just keep writing until I tell you to stop.

Honey, I'm going to cut this short tonight as I have to answer Steve, Jim Gillen, my brother, and a quick letter to the family might be appropriate—You'll forgive me, won't you?

Take care, darling, and think of me for I'm thinking of you all the time—I really do miss you terribly Pete, but maybe in a few days that feeling will be alleviated when I'm with you.

Goodnight, sweetheart. I send you all my love as always—

Yours forever,
Ronnie

Figure 69 - Spoonbill Bridge on Imjin River at the front

CRBO

My memories of those days are all beginning to run together. As much as I remember about Colonel Kimmitt I can't seem to conjure up his farewell party in my mind. Perhaps because he was surrounded by all the higher ups all night long that we lower ranks did not get to spend much time with him. Our goodbyes had started when he left the 48th, which was just before I did, but we did not want to see him leave without our final and personal farewells. His replacement was a Colonel Lockwood, and really all I remember of that man was his eagle beak nose, and that he replaced what most of us felt was an un-replaceable leader. To me, the new commander should not have been out in front of us as only Kimmitt should have been there. Thank goodness, we weren't in combat with this unknown quantity. Perhaps he would have done well, but I would have been much more at ease if that situation ever came to pass, and our Colonel Kimmitt was there as he should have been.

A lot of spare time was becoming available to us, and you can see that I spent a lot of mine in writing to Pete. Being a "pen pal" was not as difficult as I imagined it would be when I thought of the effort that had to be put into the project. My words just seemed to put themselves down on paper, and I had no thought of changing any of the words I had written. I just took Pete for granted, and perhaps that was too much on my part, but I wrote as I thought, and that was that.

Working on the death of that soldier in the Imjin River brought me to Graves Registration, a place where I could scrounge ice. I took my share of it, but I am still not sure it hadn't been used before it was given to me. Ice water that was tasteless and fresh milk were two things I used to think about. Those thoughts did not help as they only made me thirstier, and more frustrated.

Thinking about that cold milk reminds me of the time when I went on R&R in April. I ate a frozen breakfast of powdered eggs on the tailgate of a truck at around midnight before we left on our ride up to Kimpo Airport, outside of Seoul, to catch our plane to Japan. They didn't feed us anything again until around 5 p.m. the next evening, when we arrived in Nara, Japan after a train ride with a bunch of school children. We had landed in Osaka and I guess the children lived far enough away from their school that they had to take a train to get home. They all had on their sailor-suit uniforms we'd seen school kids wearing all over Japan during our visits.

In the Otsu camp in Nara we were brought into a building that had a stage and on the main floor was a group of tables all set up with linen and utensils. There were about seventy-five of us, and we were ravenous and very anxious to get to our hotel in Kyoto. An officer came out on the stage, and we roared our approval when he asked us if we were hungry. When the noise settled down he clapped his hands, and from behind the side curtains a group of young girls brought to each table pitchers of ice cold real milk. It was Japanese milk, but a cow is a cow wherever you find one. What a treat that was! This was followed up with steak, salad, and French fries. We finished with Apple pie a la mode and hot coffee. It was, at that time, the best meal I had ever eaten. The officer re-appeared on the stage and asked if we could to do it again. You bet we could, and after he clapped his hands once more, the girls appeared with the pitchers of milk, and we ate the same meal all over again.

I mention that incident as the ice cold real milk was so badly missed in Korea that the rest of the meal there in the Otsu camp was almost anticlimactic. Notice, I said "almost". Japanese food was not restricted from us by the Army, and I enjoyed my meals there. John Christopher and I stayed in a *ryokan*, Japanese for a bed and breakfast or transient inn. We ate with the chefs, and many of our meals were just noodles with peanuts mixed in.

John and I took the ladies we had met at the cabaret to the *Miyako Odori*, which was part of the ongoing Cherry Blossom festival. That took place while we were there. The theater had a stage, and on the left hand wall there was a cutout with a solitary Japanese woman and her guitar like instrument sitting inside. The instrument, we learned later, was called a *Sami-sen*, and was basically a one stringed guitar. The songs she sang and the music she played did not sit well on our western ears, but we dutifully applauded when the cacophony ended.

Next, we were treated to a Kabuki play or perhaps it was a *Noh* play. It didn't matter. It was all in Japanese with their appropriate over acting sounds and accompanying noises along with the heavy physical moves that one sees in some Japanese shows. It was long and drawn out, but the backdrops and costumes were fabulous to see. I needed to use the bathroom, and I only knew that word, but I didn't know how to ask where it was in Japanese. So, I applied my high school Spanish and asked the lady "*Donde esta el banjo?*" She apparently understood and with hand signals from her, I found the place.

It was typically oriental in that it was only a hole in the floor with two cut out footprints, one on each side of the whole. The ladies' room was the other half of the men's room. A 10-inch high picket fence separated the two places, which taught us a lot about the difference in culture. We had to learn to look for the *banjoes* wherever we were as we drank a lot of Asahi beer. That was the only brand of beer offered to us during our stay, and was very different from what we were used to. It came in liter bottles and each bottle was wrapped in straw. There were four bottles to a case. It was almost black in color, and had a bitter pine or woody taste to it. That may have been my imagination, but John agreed that it was very different from our 3.2 Army beer, and definitely tasted like the woods.

It was difficult to return to Korea after that break, but go back we did. I had taken quite a few pictures while there, but after all these years have not been able to locate them. My memories of that stay are quite vivid and will have to replace them for now, at least.

Letter #49

Tuesday, 8 Sept.

Dear Pete,

This letter just might be a bit short as I'm not feeling too well. I had some inoculations today, and they hit me in the stomach. I had cholera, typhus, typhoid, and those three always give me a fever. But maybe it won't be too bad. The reason I got them today is so I won't have to take them the day before I leave. I don't want anything to mar my spirits the day I get on that ocean-going bus. While I was in the Acid Station they brought in the body of a little Korean boy who had been accidentally shot and killed by a guard this morning. It sure is a pity, but you have to look at it as one of those unfortunate things.

I was presented my Purple Heart today, but not in the usual fashion. Normally, they present them during parades etc., but mine was just handed to me by the Personnel Officer. Just as well—I couldn't have made any parades today—not the way I feel.

I didn't write last night as I had to work on that drowning case. They found the boy, but are unable to identify him. They're sending him to Japan to check fingerprints. Then they'll let us know—Man, this has been a morbid letter so far—hasn't it?!

I got your letter of the 31st today, and needless to say was thrilled. You're spoiling me too, by all your letters—but don't you dare stop—I love to be spoiled—especially by you!!

You sounded like you were having a wonderful time, but I'll bet you're sort of happy to be teaching school. From what I've learned about you through your letters I think you're going to be a wonderful teacher—You're like me I think—You won't ever really get mad at one of those kids. I don't think you'll ever want to either. You know something—I've never chewed out a soldier in my life, and one of the prime requisites of a good officer is the ability to take a bite out of a soldier every so often. It makes them afraid of you. But—I don't want anyone to be afraid of me—They'd only be kidding themselves if they were!

Sweetheart—I wish you'd remember one thing I told you a few months back. Please Pete, do everything you can to make those little people appreciate what they have—their homes, their school, their parents and their country—I really feel that sentiment very deeply, and I just know that you'll be yourself with the kids; then they can't help but learning something good. Will you do all that for me honey? I sure would appreciate it.

I read in the papers about a week back that you people were suffering a heat spell. I guess that really made the cottage and the lake look good. Did you catch me the bass? If you did—don't plan on saving any for me!! If you do save any fish for me, make it a steamed clam or lobster—even salmon or tuna—but not bass, mackerel, flounder or cod—Thumbs down on those.

I'm sure glad you found three letters that Friday—I was sure that something had happened to my mail when you wrote you hadn't heard all week—All I think was that we'd be off on one of those merry-go-rounds—You know—"I can't write 'cause I didn't get a letter." I'm sure glad it didn't work out that way, and really appreciate the fact that you kept writing. I want you to feel the same way about me that I feel about you, if something happens and you don't hear from me. I'll never let you down, honey—I promise that ...

Nothing more on early release today, but Tom Chapman got a letter from a buddy who has already been released—He was in an 8th Army Headquarters Unit—so naturally his came through quite fast. Another rumor I heard is that our boat will leave on the 20th. That's one rumor I put very little faith in. I really shouldn't tell you these rumors, as it's not fair, but I like to tell you all that's going on, and that's part of the daily happenings. I tried to call Steve the other night, but couldn't hear him. He's in Tokyo with a ball team now, and I'll try him again there. I planned to write you tonight so I wrote to him at noon today—

Well sweet one—I've gotta get along—Please, hon—take care of yourself for me. I'll be with you real soon, but tomorrow night about 10 p.m. I'll be standing right there with you in class. It will be about 8 a.m. in Hartford—Here's wishing you luck and lots of it, Pete.

And here's sending you love, honey. And lots of that too—

Goodnight—you—You know how much I miss you don't you. If you don't then I guess I'll just have to come home and tell you—

All my love always to you—Ronnie

 CR&O

I can't remember getting those shots, but maybe they were in preparation for our going home. When we left the U.S. back in November of 1952 we had to immunize everyone to the most common diseases we expected to find over in the Far East. I was assigned as Battalion Immunization Officer, and as such I had to make sure that everybody got their shots. I had a list and checked the people off as they came to our Aid station. Sergeant Anger was our Surgeon's assistant, and he had a group of medics trained to give the shots.

On the last day it turned out that the only person who had not received their due was the Battalion Immunization Officer. I took off my shirt, and proceeded to allow Anger to give me nine different immunizations. The shots didn't bother me, but I think it was the diphtheria one, where they scratch your forearm with the medicine, that caused me to come down with an overnight fever and headaches.

I survived, and returned the next day to my job as Battery Packing and Crating Officer. We had to box up our major weapons and equipment preparatory for their shipment to Korea. Bob Huntley was Battalion Packing and Crating Officer, and he had the only manual that told us what to do. Fortunately for me, I had a Corporal Shadlebauer in my unit, and he was a carpenter in civilian life. He made all the crates and boxes for us, and did great job. I supervised the action, but really left everything up to the Corporal.

I've written about my planned date with Pete, and how I arrived at 4 pm to find that she had gone home, in an earlier missive. The reason I was late that day was because one of my men was sick, and didn't show up to drive his fork lift. These machines picked up the large and heavy crates, and delivered them to one of many railroad box cars that were standing at the side of our packing and crating area. I took the place of my missing driver, and was able to learn the functions of a fork lift, and managed to load a number of the smaller boxes to the car. It looked like we would finish the job in time for me to make my 1 p.m. date with Pete.

I wasn't as accomplished as I thought because I managed to tip over my fork lift and that delayed me by about two or three hours. I tried to pick up a very large crate, but somehow I didn't get it on the forks squarely enough for proper balance. It leaned slightly to the left, but that was enough to allow the whole unit to lay down slowly on its side. Returning the fork lift to its upright position wasn't the major problem. We had to separate the box from the lift machine, and that was what took all the time. We finally solved the problem and put the crate in the box car, and called it a day. I went back to the BOQ, showered, and put on a fresh uniform. I had missed lunch, and so on the way I stopped at our favorite Clam shop, and had an order of fried clams to take along on the ride. That may be why I missed Pete that afternoon. At that time, I think the clams were more important than a date with someone I truly did not know.

To conclude the story of the loading of box cars would be incomplete if I didn't relate what happened the next time we saw these big and bulky boxes. We had arrived at Staten Island, New York, and were all watching from the starboard railing of "C" deck on board the Hersey when the local longshoremen removed the crates from the box cars. Some of the smaller crates could be manhandled by two men as they contained our directors, and didn't need to be transported by lift or truck. The director was the machine that contained our optical pieces for tracking airplanes, and were the primary way in which we were able to train our 40 mm. cannons on a target. They were fairly delicate instruments, and we were appalled at the way they were rolled end over end to be stacked out on the pier. We yelled at the workers, but they thought we were only cheering them on, and they paid no attention to us at all. Months later, in Korea, when we uncrated these units we found them to be useless, and we never saw them again.

****

Letter #50

Wed. 9, Sept.

Hi Darling,

Well, here it is the 9th of September—7:16 p.m., and back East it's only about 5 a.m. In just a few short hours you'll be in school. I'll bet you're just a bit nervous, and that's good. Being that way sharpens you up, and makes you more attentive to details. You'll do alright, honey—I know you will—There's no worry—Seems sort of funny to be writing this knowing that this letter won't reach you for another week or so, yet I'd feel awfully strange writing to you in the past tense. I'm talking to you now, not a week from today—

I just had to leave for a minute. Major DeWees is being transferred to Japan tomorrow, and General Cooper wanted to present him with the Bronze Star Medal. I wrote the award up a week ago, but as it hasn't come out on orders as yet I had to call Colonel Lemley, get permission to give it to the Major, then had to have some interim orders typed up. I get mighty teed off at the Army when they pull stunts like this. The General knew all day that he wanted to do this, yet he waited until 10 minutes ago.

He should have known not to interrupt me when I'm writing you.

Today was beautiful, but it was hotter than all Hell—I drove down to Camp Casey (Division Headquarters), and came back looking like I was made of white dust. The shower really felt good when I got back.

No mail from you today, but Mom dropped me a line, and complained that I wasn't telling her all that had happened during the war. I got a feeling someone told her I was wounded. Damn those things she shouldn't know until I can get home and prove to her that it didn't harm me—But from the sound of her letters I don't think she thinks that I was badly hurt—If she did I would have heard a long time ago—I would have heard her yelp all the way over here!

My arms still hurt from the shots yesterday, but hardly as much. The hot shower really loosened up the sore muscles—I love good hot showers. I'll probably live in one for about a month when I get back. They're really relaxing.

I'm glad I got those shots, however, as I could just see me trying to carry my duffle bag up the gang plank—I probably would have dropped it right in the water.

Capt. Sullivan just came in, and asked if I was going to the show—I said that I was, but only after I finished this to you—He was really funny—gave me a long lecture on what awful roads to ruin I would walk down after writing a letter to a girl. I don't know what the hell he's talking about—He's got 4 kids himself!! He's a great guy.

We're supposed to have a double feature tonight—"Angel Face" and "That's all I desire." I hear they're two good ones, but I doubt if I'll last through them—The movies don't start till the Gen. is finished eating, and sometimes he dawdles over his food until 8:30 or 9. We saw a terrific one a couple of nights ago— "Sombrero"—If you didn't see it I want to take you to see it when I get home. It's really a good show—

There's quite a few places I want to take you honey, but first and foremost I just want to get home to be with you—The days really have been dragging by, and it seems that 5 o'clock will never come. Pete, it's strange for me to write and tell you that I miss you when one normally doesn't miss anything unless he's accustomed to it, but the heart sometimes works in strange ways—doesn't it. I feel that I've known you, thought about you, and missed you for centuries. Do you understand the way I feel? I hope so because I want you to know what I'm really like down deep. If I don't seem to act like my letters make you think I will when I come home—you will just have to realize that It's going to be quite a drastic change for me for the first few days—But if you'll go along with me, and sort of close your eyes to whatever I may do that might not seem like a thing I would normally do— then I know that everything will turn out just right. My biggest fear right now is that I may not be the Ronnie you know when I get home. I don't want to lose what I have of you now—My heart and mind are in too deep. String along with me darling—I won't ever let you down—that's a promise.

Goodnight you—I miss you very, very much tonight, and want you to know that I'm constantly with you—You've been wondrously sweet and nice to me Pete, honey, and I'm coming to the sweetest and nicest girl in the world—I don't think you could be anything else—

All my love to you, darling—always, Ronnie

****

Letter #51

Fri. 11 Sept.

Dearest One,

Maybe you don't realize it, but because of you I'm apt to come home a starving scarecrow. That's right—a veritable, starving, scarecrow. Tonight I only ate part of my supper, and completely forsaken devil's food cake and ice cream for dessert. When I sat down to eat, I all of a sudden got a bug that I had to write you right away. So I jumped up and walked out of the mess hall, and came down here to the office. I guess I just felt that I had to be near you. I missed writing you last night because Colonel Kimmitt threw a party, and I was a little too tipsy to even try and write.

I haunted the mail room all day in hopes that I might find a green envelope awaiting me, but no such luck. It sure hurts to see all that mail come in, and think that there might be a letter for me, and not be able to get at it. You see, you're still writing to me at Charlie Battery, and when the mail arrives here at headquarters it's already packed and tied according to battalion. So, I have to wait until the following day so that the mail clerk down at Charlie Battery can readdress my mail up here. And when something as important to me as your letters just go by me like that—I get quite a bit irritated to say the least—I haven't heard from you in a few days now, but I'm keeping in mind that you're getting ready for school and all that—Well, maybe tonight's mail will bring me something tomorrow—I sure do hope so—Days without letters from you are pretty long and lonesome ones for me—

You know honey, that through our letters I've come to feel awfully close to you, and it makes me feel strange when I write to you about coming home, and know that I won't be able to read your reaction to it until about 2 weeks later—It's then that I realize there is 10,000 miles between us right now. Here I've know about it for almost 2 weeks now, and yet I can't feel that you know about it until I read it in your letters. I know that you know now, but it won't seem real until you mention it.

The days just drag by Pete, more so than any other time in my life. I can't wait until that first minute I see you—It's almost a dream to me that I'm going to be on the way soon. Like my mother, you had it in the back of your mind that I'd be home soon—never even thought about it. I figured that if I left by February I'd be lucky—but maybe there is such a thing as a woman's intuition!! We've had a lot of rumors on the early release, and all are good. However, nobody seems to have any definite word. They did call today to find out if I had any baggage stored in Japan. That's one of the preliminary steps in rotation home. I feel quite confident that I'll be on the way soon, but until the day comes I'll probably die a thousand deaths—It means that much to me—

As I write to you know I'm trying to call Jim Gillen in Seoul to see if he can find out anything. I sure am an impatient son of a gun, aren't I?? Lines are busy!!

Aw, honey, this Korea's getting me down. I just can't take the place anymore. I shouldn't complain, I guess—Those poor guys who got stuck in the Pacific Islands for three years in the last war had it real tough, but they had a different purpose in mind I think—Without fear of being called a flag-waiver by use of some trite phrases, I'd say they knew their goal, and had a reason and a desire to stay to the end. But this war is different—We all live to go home—Some poor unfortunates will never make it, either. I guess I'm pretty much the same guy that I was last year at this time, but even so I know I've changed, and I think it's all pretty much to the good—There are certain people that will see that in me—Mother and Dad, and Margie, I grew up with them.

If you had really known me before I left I'm sure you'd notice the slight changes. But now that Margie is married and lives in Philly, and you've only known me since I have changed—I guess only Mom and Dad will see it. Never before have I opened my heart and mind to anyone—All of a sudden one day I just had to write you and tell you everything—My folks never knew my real troubles 'cause as a kid I kept them pretty much to myself. However, without my mentioning anything to them they'd be able to see some of the deeper things I'm thinking—I've written you before of these things, but still I want to sit down with you sometime, and just talk them all out again. You've shared an awful lot of my troubles, darling, and you'll never know how much I thank you for it. I'll try to tell you when I get home.

Goodnight, Pete honey, I miss you so very much. Please wait for me, I'll be with you soon.

All my love always,

Ronnie

⌘

At this time I was really at a loss to find anything concrete to write to anyone. It was just a case of waiting for something to happen either there in Korea or back in Washington where they pulled the strings that made us jerk convulsively whenever an order was issued that personally affected us. The brass hats back home were trying to figure out how to reduce their expenditures without affecting the economy or defensive posture of our country. We were still at swords points with Russia and its ally Red China, and Washington had to protect us from these antagonists and at the same time they had to figure out a way to keep the people back home fat, dumb and happy, as the saying went.

Those of us in Korea didn't spend any time on those problems. All we were interested in was what was tonight's movie, what was for chow, is there any mail, and when do I leave this place? We had other problems—Can I get my laundry done today? Do I really need a haircut? Do I really have to sit at that desk all day? They didn't tell us anything about this kind of living when we were taking our classes in OCS. If they had talked about that subject, I don't think any of us would have paid much attention to it once we left the classrooms. We were on our way to fight a war, and there was no time to get bored while that was happening. Beside all that, no one had ever been involved with a truce before. It was always complete victory and or an armistice, but a permanent truce never occurred before, and I'm not sure anyone knew how to handle it.

We were fortunate in one respect; handling a truce was for the higher ups, and all we had to do was follow the leaders. Back at battery and battalion level I'm sure the FDC's were open although they weren't firing any actual missions, I am also sure they practiced their parts day after day. I remember something else that went through my mind at that time. I didn't care what happened to anyone else and their release date. I became quite selfish and thought only about my personal plight. Getting home to see Pete, and then my folks was my problem, and no one else's. I did wonder about my friends, but knew they were thinking in the same vein that I was, and they were big boys, and could take care of their own problems, and didn't need me to help them. I couldn't have helped anyone at that time as I was sure all my troubles about early release were bigger than any on else's, in my mind. The big day was coming, but when?

****

Letter #52

Sat. 12, Sept.

Hi Honey—

I'm duty officer tonight, and had visions of writing a couple long, long letters as I have to stay put in one place most of the evening. A few distractions have come up, however, so I'm writing this to you real early. There's going to be a USO show tonight, and following that a double feature movie. From where I sit right now I'm less than a hundred yards from the stage, and I guess they'll put the movie screen there after the show. All I have to do is check the guard every so often, and be handy in case anything comes up. The troops are starting to come in now—I expect we'll have about 1,800 or 2,000 here tonight—

Pete, I still didn't hear from you today, and it's got me worried sick. I can't help thinking something might have happened to you—That hurricane and all that you had plus the fact that you're doing all that driving around. Please darling, take it slow will you? I worry enough about you all day as it is.

There's really very, very little news to tell you about—This place is the most boring place in the world. I sit in the office all day long, and do absolutely nothing. I write those damned awards for about an hour every morning. That's all I can spend on them as I just can't think up enough to put down. Then I read a magazine for a while—then go up to coffee call—Come back and read—Eat chow—Read again—answer the phone, etc—Then go to the club at 5:30 and have a few drinks—Write you—go to the movie, and then to bed. Or else go to the movie then write you and off to bed!! Exciting huh—Man, it ain't nothing but terrible!! Mail call—the club, and writing to you are the only enjoyable times of the day.

The Army sure is trying, however, to keep morale up with all the movies, shows, and sports, but they have a tough job on their hands.

Ok—today I saw the August 20th issue of Life—Did you see it? It has some pictures in it that were quite interesting to me. The first one where they mention Hill 347 was especially interesting as that is the hill where my OP was blown up that day. Also the picture of Pork Chop there—That's the view I had, another picture is the one of the 32nd Hg-Co. moving out. Our Battalion Headquarters sat right next to them as we supported their regiment. I saw the Time & Life Photographer when he took some of those shots—As a matter of fact he took some shots of our boys while they were tearing down our forward gun positions.

The show has started, and I don't think it's going to be too good—It's just a bunch of G. I.'s and one girl—Oh—is she ever ugly—Man my faith in American womanhood almost dropped to the bottom when I saw her at chow tonight—But awful as she is, she's still a queen compared to the Korean queens.

Well, the daily news on the early release is still nil. I call everyone I can think of to see what rumors I can find out, but everyone else knows as little as I do. The other day we got a call from Division, they told us that every officer who was supposed to leave in September would go on the 13th after all those officers were notified—Division called back to say that they weren't going—That was a real blow—Let me tell you—Some guys I know have been told 3 and 4 times now that they were on the next shipment, and each time they've been cancelled. They're a—hurting—

I can't complain about whenever I leave—I'm supposed to be here until February or so, and any day I leave early will be a blessing—My folks are in Maine, or they were, and didn't get my letter about coming home until just the other day—As I mentioned last night, Mom has said that she expected me home early, so I guess she'll be extra glad to get that letter—Dad was the realist. He expected me in early spring sometime. My letters must get pretty monotonous to you. I write practically the same thing all the time, but hon—that's all there is to say—Home is about all that anyone thinks about—can you blame us?

Well, Pete, I realize this letter isn't my finest effort, but the noise of the show, and the people in here are quite distracting—I'll do better tomorrow—promise, and I'll do one hell of a lot better if I get some mail from you.

One of the Majors just now told me that there's a lot of mail held up in Japan because of the rains. That's probably the reason why mail is so scarce. They better put an end to this Japanese rainy season real soon, or old Ron is gonna put in an official complaint.

Well, darling, time to end this. I still miss you very much, Pete—don't ever forget that—please—

All my love forever—

Ron

****

Letter #53

Tues. 15, Sept.

Dearest Pete,

It's 10:45 A.M., and certainly no time to be writing a letter—especially in office, but I just got a letter from you, and want this answer to make the outgoing shipment at noon.

Believe me, darling; when I come home I want you to give me a good swift kick. I certainly deserve it. I went crazy with worry all last week because I didn't hear from you. I had all sorts of visions conjured up in my mind, and the result of it all is that I only tortured myself half to death. I <u>knew</u> all along that it was the fault of the mail, but still being the worrier that I am I couldn't drive the other ideas form my mind. One thing, sweetheart, and I'm sure you'll want to know this, is that I never forgot what you once told me about thinking if I didn't hear from you. I guess I'm just so crazy about you that I worry about you all the time. Am I ever relieved now, and what a wonderful letter it was. All week long I tried not to show you how worried I was, and I'm afraid it ruined my letters. Now that I got one from you today I'll easily be able to fill three pages or more. By the way, the letter I got was written by you on the 2nd, and wasn't postmarked until the 8th and Pete, honey—you can write in pencil, chalk, blood, ink or orange juice—anyway you write me is wonderful—So don't worry about the pencil writing!

You still hadn't heard anything about my coming home in that letter, but I'm sure you know by now—The latest rumors have us leaving here on the 27th. I really don't care what day we leave as long as it's soon. This being apart from you is just a little bit more than I can take—as you say—if I'm not doing anything why don't they let me go home to take up some of your time. That's the best idea I've heard of in a long, long time. I had thought about it quite a bit, but didn't know just what your thoughts were on the subject. But I'll tell you what—that's just what I'll do!! Believe me, you'll probably see too much of me. As a matter of fact, hon, all my plans sort of hinge on you—Are you interested??

This subject of calling you on the phone from Japan is just a

thought of the past now that I'm not going there, but it's still
something I'd like to mention. Pete, I would have called you first
no matter what you think is best. My parents certainly do know
you exist, and would understand completely if I called you first.
As a matter of fact I think they'd sort of expect me to. After
all these years now they know that when I've got somebody or
something on my mind that they have to take sort of a sideline
seat for a while. That's one of the things that make them
wonderful. I would have called them too, but not until I spoke to
you—I wish you'd get it through your pretty little head that you
mean an awful, awful lot to me. I guess you're just going to have
to sit down with them some day–then you'll see!!

You're right about one thing, however, that it would be
rather hard to say anything on the phone—I, too, would be
speechless, I know, I'd probably just say your name a few times,
ask how you're feeling, and what the weather is like—Maybe it's
best that I didn't go to Japan and call—After I hung up I'd
probably go find a corner to go sit in, and sulk for a few years. It
really could hurt to talk to you, hear your voice, and then not be
able to see you-

But now, the next time you hear my voice on the phone I
promise that it will be from someplace where I can say that I'm
on my way to see you. Even if its form California—I'll still call,
and if I don't have time to put a call through I'll send you a wire.
I understand that some people only spend a few hours in
California after docking there. I had to leave my little Korean
sweetheart back at Charlie Battery, but I think I told you about
that—However, her little sister is up here. Her name is Betty,
and she belongs to the cooks—She's almost as cute as my
Skoshie, but no dog would ever take her place—

Honey—I feel wonderful now that I heard form you – God,
was I ever worried that something had happened to you.

The letter I wrote you last night was still in the mail box
here, so I just pulled it out and re read it. I don't think I'll send
it to you as it's a bit down-hearted in places—

Sweetheart, I guess I've told you a million or more times
how much I miss you and want you, but I don't think I ever meant
it more than I do now. We will have a lot to talk about in just a
few weeks, and most of it will be about how much I did miss you

while I was over here—I've got an awful lot of love saved up, honey, and I'd like to spend it all on you!!

My time over here is growing shorter every day Pete, and one of these nights I'll be writing you not to write me anymore as I'll be leaving shortly—That will be a big day for me darling—But until that time, please remember all the times I've told you that I missed you, and add them up and multiply them by a million times, and you might get a small idea of how much it really is. I can't say goodnight like I usually do as its only morning, but you know—good morning darling, sounds awful good to me also.

So long for now, you—

Keep those telephone lines clear, honey—

All my love always, Pete.
                              Yours—Ronnie

P.S. <u>You're wonderful!</u>

CR&O

Although the letter to Pete is almost 60 years old, I don't think I have changed very much regarding my foolish worrying over small items that occurred in my life over all those years. If someone is not where they said they would be at the time they said they would be there, I worry. If anything does not happen as it is supposed to, then I worry. It turned out that Pete is just the opposite. Things are almost always exactly as they are supposed to be in her thinking. She doesn't let worrying run her down. She is as upbeat and optimistic as it is possible for a human to be. I, on the other hand, am a realist, and I always want things to be as they are supposed to be. Such varied thinking makes the world go round, in my estimation.

At that point in my life, time moved so frustratingly slow when I was waiting for stupendous events to happen, and there was nothing more stupendous then "the Word" that we were all supposed to leave, was ready to be sent down to us. Our daily activities were of a fairly minor inconvenience, and we yawned our way through each day at work.

The DivArty commander was Brigadier General Ralph Cooper. He left us before I left, but I never found out anything more about the man. He had a "dog robber" (Aide de Camp) named Bill Freeman as his aide, and we saw much more of Bill than we did the general. Bill was the only guy who seemed to be busy every day. Years later when I attended an Artillery reunion at Fort Sill I saw Bill's name on the Wall of Honor out there. I think almost all OCS graduates from the Artillery school who made it to a full Colonel's rank were on that wall. I saw Bill DeWitt's picture, and also Lamar Daugherty's when I was out there and they had made it to that rank.

I tried to locate Bill DeWitt a few months ago, but got a nice note from his widow that he had recently passed on due to a rare form of cancer. I also tried to call Lamar, but found that he was also gone.

In my OCS contingent, I have found quite a number who are no longer with us, but our little group—Gaynor, Huntley, Kalil, and me—is still around, and we email each other quite often. Ray Kalil, who started out as a schoolteacher in New Jersey, found his future with Weight Watchers. He and RoseMary own and operate a Weight Watchers' franchise covering middle and eastern Tennessee. Ray is very active in the local Nashville chapter of the Korean War Veterans Association, and I know that he donated more than just time and effort to that particular group. Ray owns his own airplane, and has flown down to see us on occasion. I have a nice photo of Pete (she was Nancy at that time) sitting up in the co-pilots seat flying the plane.

Figure 70 - Nancy in co-pilot seat ... enjoying her flight!

That was quite a thrill for her, and just having Ray and Bud visiting us was quite a treat as well. Many other acquaintances are now gone, and I particularly dislike looking at that photo of six of us taken just after chow down in Ft. Bliss. I miss the others who are no longer around.

That war isn't over yet, and there were 58,000 casualties sustained by us along with 8,000 still missing. I can't imagine what it is like to be a relative or close friend of one of those non-returnees, and as I am writing these comments for my decedents, I wish that they could all understand how our Army grieves for those people.

Figure 71 - Ft. Bliss after Noon Chow - L-R: Andy Creamer, Ron Freedman, Marshall Climan, Bob Fulton, Harrison French

ॐ৪০

Letters #54—67: A Commentary

When I read the letters numbered 54 to 67 I realize that they are all of the same tenor as many of the previous ones in which I tried to explain that our daily lives were so dull that there was practically nothing to offer as far as something new and interesting was concerned. Even my professions of love to Pete are repetitious and now seem to be overdone. I imagine that I truly felt the thoughts I was writing about, but I just kept on saying the same thing over and over again. The truth is that the girl was on my mind during all my waking hours, and thinking about her was all I was able to do. I didn't have anything else to really wonder about, and so I spent my time with her on my mind. I never realized what a "mush mouth" I was until I saw what I had put down on paper, and apparently Pete accepted my words because she never said not to write as I had been doing.

In one of my later letters to her I mentioned that Bud had taken a trip back to our old Anti-Aircraft unit, and caught up with them at the firing range in Inchon. Although I would have liked to have seen my old friends I was just as happy that I didn't make the trip. The officers in that unit made a shambles of the organization, and many of them were a disappointment to the rest of the people that tried to do their duty properly. The colonel was in charge of the outfit because of political reasons, and some of the older officers were World War II veterans, and not only were they resentful of being called back up for this Korean thing, I think that they were just tired of the war, the army and being away from home and family.

The fact that my assistant platoon leader, Frank Jerome Tone, went home before I did really bent me out of shape. He arrived in Korea long after I did, and I thought he should have been selected after me. Frank was a good guy, but about all that I knew of him was that his uncle was a movie actor by the name of Franchot Tone, and that Frank's family owned some well-known corporation in upstate New York.

I also mentioned in a letter that I had been involved with the Division lottery that supported a local orphanage. One afternoon we had a formation of many of the units in the division, and were treated to a gifting ceremony put on by the children of the orphanage. A little girl presented me with a piece of linen like fabric on which someone had sewn the words "Chun hyun P.S.K." on it. I think P.S.K. stands for Primary School Korea, and there is also a small flower in pink with green leaves sewn in. I wrote to Pete, and said that I was going to give her the little memento, but I think it has stayed in my top drawer for these past sixty years. I spoke to her tonight, and told her that I would be fulfilling my promise to her, and that I would see to it that it was properly presented when we meet next weekend. I also reminded her that I never did get the beer and lobster dinner that she had said she would buy for me after I got home. She promised that that would be on her list for the very near future.

****

Letter #54

Wednesday, 16 September

Dearest One,

I hope you won't mind my typing this letter as I realize that it's a very impersonal way to write. However, I'm in the office now, and the temptation to use the typewriter was too much for my willpower. It's after working hours, but I'm down here because the light is much better than the one in the tent.

I didn't do very much today but sit around hoping that some news about going home would come in. As yet there's nothing to report except that two groups will leave around the 20th and 25th, however, we don't know if they'll be early releases or just regular rotatees. This sitting and waiting can get to be very monotonous, and especially when you don't know whether the thing you're waiting on will come through or not. I feel pretty certain, as does everyone else, that it will come through so it's mostly a case of sweating out just when.

It might sound funny to you, hon, but when I think of you it just seems to me that I have more reason than anyone else for wanting to go home early. It seems that we've been apart for years and years. What a jolt, I just go. The phone rang and a clerk in here answered it. I kept on typing as the phone continually is ringing. I all of a sudden heard him say, "Well, I can tell him now 'cause he's right here." Then he said to me, "There's a letter in a green envelope over in the mail room for you." Like a whiz I was out the door. When I got there it was only a letter from Zeke. Needless to say I was quite disappointed, but there still will be more mail later on, so maybe I still have a chance.

Zeke didn't go to Japan with the 3rd Marines as I thought, but is still cooling it out at Camp Pendleton, California. How his Mother found out I don't know, but she wrote and told him that I was getting out of the Army on a disability because of being wounded. It's not as funny as it sounds 'cause that might get back to my folks, and they'd get really worried. They still don't know I was even on the hill after I went to Exec School in early June. I hope nobody says anything to them as minor as it all is.

Zeke hopes to stay out there for a while, and wants me to look him up when I come through California, but I'm going to have to tell him that when I come through there I ain't going to stop for anybody. I'm going to be on my way to see you, and nothing is going to slow me up ... old friend or not. He says that he can even fix me up with Jack Benny's daughter, but even that won't make me stop. Honey, I really do miss you so much....

You know, as I look on that last statement I realize that I'm going to have to finish this by pen. The typewriter doesn't give half the feeling that a pen does, so wait a minute until I find my pen.

There, that's much better, isn't it? Now I can tell you

again, and this time I'm sure it will look and sound much better to you when you read it now. Honey, I really do miss you so much. I've come to depend on you these past months so much that it seems we've been together all my life. Somehow I don't feel complete, and won't until I can be with you. Did you ever feel that way about something or someone? To me it's a very helpless feeling. Sometimes when I have something on my mind, and want to tell it to you I get so wrapped up in my thoughts that I actually think that you're there beside me. Then when I came back down to earth, and find it's only my imagination working overtime I feel quite disappointed. Some things seem to have been lost because I know that I'll never have that one particular thought and feeling again. You're a big thing in my life, darling, and any moment that I can share with you just makes me feel that much closer to you.

You know, Pete, it's pretty hard for me to write something when I don't know your feelings on the subject, but yet I try not to hold too much back. Some things I won't say, naturally, because I'll want to be with you for a while first. Ours is a strange situation, isn't it? Getting to know someone through the mail. It's a hard thing to do, but you know I don't think I would have wanted it any other way—considering the situation. Your letters kept me going. Well, pretty soon this letter writing will come to a screeching halt, and I'll be happy in one way, and yet sad in another. I'll be with you, but I'll miss reading and rereading your letters.

By now, hon, you're first couple of weeks of school are over (today is only a week, but by the time you get this it will be two), and I'll bet that first day wasn't half as bad as you thought it was going to be. Just don't wrap yourself up in it so much that you won't have time to write or think about me!! If you do I might just come home and burn the place down.

Well, honey—it's getting late, and I have to write to the folks, and answer Zeke—I'll write again tomorrow. Maybe I'll have some news for you by then—Goodnight, sweetheart—let me tell you that I miss you more than anything in the world—'cause I do—God Bless you, Pete darling, and take care of yourself—

My love is yours forever and always,

Ronnie

Letter #55

Thursday, 17 Sep.

Hi Love,

Guess what?? Two letters from you last night! They arrived about an hour after I finished writing you. I was tempted to write you another letter, but it was late, and I was quite tired. There's no need to tell you just how much that meant, and still do mean, to me If you don't know now, then I'm just going to have to come home and teach you.

It seems that you <u>are</u> quite tired from your teaching class, and I wish you'd take it slower. Of course, it makes me happy to find that you enjoy it so much, but being the jealous character that I am—I don't want you to get too interested. Seriously hon, don't let this job wear you down. Working that hard can knock you for a loop!

I hate to admit this, sweet, but you mentioned something (mail just came in, but nothing but a newspaper for me) about a letter I wrote that you'd rather not answer, but wanted to wait until I came home. If it's one that I said that I was a little afraid to send along then I know which one it is, but otherwise I'm afraid I don't remember what was in it. Another thing, Miss Smith, is that you want me to wait until I get there before I make any decisions about you. Well it's you that will have to make the decisions about me as I've just about made up my mind—So put on your thinking cap, and get to work.

Pete honey, I'll do what you ask, but I'd still like to walk in on you. I'd get such a kick out of it, but I guess you'd be caught unaware - wouldn't you. So just wait, and pretty soon, I hope, you'll get a telegram or a phone call from me.

Tom Chapman is sitting here reading the latest edition of Newsweek—Sept 14, and he just read me an article about the POW's. The article says that almost 2/3's of them got "Dear Johns'" while they were prisoners. The reason being that their women said they couldn't wait any longer. That is one of the damndest things I ever heard. I don't see how anybody could be that cruel. It just isn't right. Pete, how can people be that way?

Today was the usual—nothing doing, and tomorrow will undoubtedly be the same. This inactivity sure gets everyone down. If I could take off for the day instead of just sitting around here then I wouldn't mind it so much. However, I usually spend the time thinking of you, and that certainly doesn't make the day go by any faster.

After 5 O'clock things aren't so bad, 'cause we all get together up at the mess, and have a few laughs over a beer or two. Tonight we had free booze from 5:30 to 6:30, and a "goodly crowd was there." We had some real American beer—not that G.I. 3.2 stuff. I'll bet that the first few times I come home, and have me a few of those real beers that I'll probably get drunk. If you see me getting that way—how about stopping me? I'm still counting on that beer and lobster dinner—so don't forget! From the sound of your last letter you might be too busy to bother with me—This getting home at 6 p.m., and not getting to bed until 12 isn't good for you. You'll probably want to sleep each weekend through, and that won't be good for me—

The only solution I can see is for me to enroll in the 2nd grade at Elmwood. Then I could see you every day. I'd call you Miss Smith and I'd stay after school every day to sharpen pencils and clean erasers if you'll let me be the teacher's pet. And I wouldn't put girls pigtails in ink wells or bring dead frogs to school if you'd let me sit in front, and who knows—I might bring you an apple every day if you'd come in the cloakroom so I could kiss you. That last idea sounds so good I might even bring you two apples!! How about that??

Well, sweetheart—time to be running along once again, but I'll be back with you tomorrow. Take care of yourself now, and I mean that. I don't want to come home to find you worn to a frazzle and hollow-eyed.

Goodnight you, I miss you terribly, and really can't wait to be with you—Got lots to tell you, want to listen??

My love is yours darling—always—

Ronnie

****

Letter #56

Sat. 19, Sept.

Hi Sweetheart,

Just knocked off for the day and seeing as the club won't open for half an hour or so I thought I might get started on this letter to you. It's been a hot sticky day, and a long one to boot. The Division Commander was prowling around in his helicopter so we had to stay on our toes pretty much. He likes to swoop down low over an outfit, and land before anyone can get ready for him. He had dinner with us today, and kept us waiting 45 minutes. Naturally, that's his privilege, but that didn't make us any less hungry—

Bud Gaynor came over today with news of our old outfit. He just returned from the Inchon Firing Range, and while there he was able to go down, and see our buddies. Lots has happened since I left, and I'm sure glad I did. That outfit was no good. The Colonel was married to a General's daughter, and that was why he was a Colonel. He was relieved for inefficiency last June. The Adjutant was transferred to Japan because he tried to take the Assistant S-3's girl from him. However, the S-3 and Assistant S-3 are very good friends with the Battalion Executive Office and they ganged up on the Adjutant and got rid of him. The communications officer went batty when his plane got lost in a fog while returning from R&R. The Motor Officer wants the Labor Officer's girl, but the Labor Officer won't tell him her name. The Labor Officer is going home next month, and thinks his girl deserves something better than the Motor Officer. One Battery Commander was relieved because he spent all his time making model airplanes instead of commanding his battery.

But the biggest news of all is the fact that Jerry Tone (he arrived in Korea last April, and was my assistant) went home the day before yesterday on early release. They are starting to come through now. I'd be on my way home now if I stayed down there, but that's one thing I would never do, and because of the things I told you at the beginning of the letter—I have no sympathy for those guys—if they want to come home bugged up they can, but I wasn't going to stay around there to watch them.

That outfit ruined more good soldiers than it produced. It was, and still is s blight on the Army. They worried more about the state of their Officer's Clubs, and where they could find another woman than they did about their job and their men. That outfit had one of the highest V.D. rates in Korea!! And as far as I'm concerned that just shows a lack of leadership and command responsibility. V.D., and I've told you all this before, represents one of our biggest problems over here. We ran a sample the other week on just men in the Divarty. One sixth of all the cases handled by out medics in a 4 day period were V.D. cases and that included everything from headaches to a drowning. That's appalling of course, but not too bad for Korea when you realize that 97% of the women have some form of V.D. or leprosy, or T.B. But—look at it this way—There aren't supposed to be any civilian women in the area either. So—all these prostitutes are living in the hills around us. They're fed and cared for by ROK soldiers—

Why I got wound up on this subject, I don't know—It shouldn't be anything to write home about, but sometimes I get a little teed off at things around here, and I can't help but write about them—You'd think some of these dumb soldiers would realize what they're doing, but apparently they have no consideration for themselves or their families—

Let's see if I can't find something more pleasant to write about—Oh—got a tremendous package from home yesterday that had just about everything in it. That was the first one I've got in months—and it was real good—I'll have to write the folks tonight and thank them—My cousin Missy sent some jam she made along, and that was number one—You'll have to meet Missy—She's about 34, but looks only 21 or so. She's having her third child sometime this month. Her other two are my favorites. I wrote you about Johnnie and Nan before didn't I? That little Nancy is a living dream, when I have kids, I want them just like that. She's really something.

Sweet, I've been lonesome for you all day today—I just wished and wished that you were here so I could hold your hand. I spent the whole morning writing your name and day dreaming about you. I wonder what the first thing we'll both say that first time we see each other. I'll probably utter something historical like—"Hi"—If I am a little dumbstruck how 'bout you taking over, and snapping me out of it? I'm afraid that's just what I'll do. Stand there, and not be able to say a word. By-the-way, honey, I think I'll probably come home via New York, and not through Frisco—I'll call you the minute I get off the ship, and wire you at the same time so I can be sure you know that I'm home—and I just might call you at school!!

Whatever way it happens honey will be the best way possible to me—'cause you'll be there, and that's all that really matters to me—Wait for me, darling—I don't think it will be too much longer—so long you—

I miss you, want you, and send you all my love—

Ronnie

****

Letter #57

Sunday 20, Sep.

My Darling,

Remember once when I told you about a superstition I had about carrying one of your letters (preferably the last one) with me as I had a superstition that it would bring me another one— Well, tonight I proved to myself that superstitions are silly things. I changed clothes, and forgot to empty my pockets, but still I got a letter—You've got me sitting on a star, honey-

I'm in a funny ole mood tonight—Your letter was short, but still it just said the right things, and made me feel just the way I want to feel—I still feel bad because of all those letters I've written you at different times about the lack of mail—even when it wasn't your fault—I know I shouldn't have done it, but as you say my letters mean so much to you—you'll have to imagine how much yours have come to mean to me. Never, darling—will you know how much good it does me just to see you write my name and tell me that you miss me—The length of your letters is really minor just as long as you write—Oh Pete, darling—I have so very much to tell you, I'm just about ready to burst! If "xs" and "os" could bring me home sooner I'd have been home to you 10 years ago!! Honey, I miss you so. I wonder if you've ever had a heartache like the one I have now—It's enough to make me put my head down and cry—and it's like this all the time with me—It makes me feel wonderful to know that you're waiting for me.

Hon—please slow down in this schoolwork!! You'll knock yourself out before your first vacation. You're happy in your work, and that's most important to me, but darling—remember that this is going to go on until next June, and you've got to save your interest and energy for some of those days when you just won't feel like going to school.

Don't listen to me, honey—I'm just in love, and don't know what I'm saying—You go right ahead, and put everything you have into it—'cause everything always works out right in the end—People like you sweetheart, never lose.

Goodnight, love—I miss you and want you terribly.

I'm yours, as is my love always and forever—

Ronnie

P.S. If we're going to send kisses by mail—let's not be stingy—How's this for a start—X 1,000,000 times....

****

Letter #58

Tues. 22, Sept.

Dearest One,

Well, another day has passed and still no word. The waiting is awful. We still have two officers in the Battery here who were supposed to go home at the beginning of the month on regular rotation, but they haven't been called as yet. Division called them today, and said they'd let them go on the 26th if they were willing to travel in the hold with the regular troops. They turned it down in the hopes that they might be flown home—Nobody seems to know why they can't get regular officer's compartments—maybe it's because there are so many officers going home on this early release from the rear areas. It doesn't make things look up for us, but my desire to see you so much makes me feel quite confident that I'll be with you soon.

I'm not feeling too well tonight, darling—I've got this bug that seems to be hitting everyone around here. The doc doesn't know what it is exactly, but he's sure it's some form of the grippe. It's a combination of chills, slight fever, and nausea. Usually clears up in a day or two.

Finally got a letter from the folks yesterday acknowledging my letter to them about coming home. They're playing it cool, however, by not expecting me until I show up—I hope you've taken that attitude—I think it's the best way!

The weather has been beautiful, hon—just warm enough to make the day pleasant, and cool enough at night to make sleeping just right. We have those winter sleeping bags, and they're wonderful. Right now they're a little bit too warm, but when I remember how cold it can get over here then I'm glad I have it. They're filled with eider down, and zip all the way up to your neck. They're shaped like mummy cases, and during combat are dangerous to use. You can't get out in time if Joe sneaks up on you. That's what happened to the Columbian Soldiers on Old Baldy last March. The Chinks sneaked up on the out guards, killed them, and shot many troops before they could get out of their sleeping bags.

We don't have stoves as yet, and probably won't have them over here for another month. I certainly don't expect to be here to see them, however. You know—I haven't slept between sheets since last January with the exception of a couple of times on R&R. I've almost forgotten what it's like—

Gee, doll—I wish I could be home with you tonight—just to be able to ring that doorbell, and see you standing there. I think I'd probably take you and hold you for a good 10 or 15 hours, and then sit there, and look at you for a few months—

Shouldn't give away secrets like this, but I told Jim Gillen in a letter today that if you were only a 1/1000th part as nice and sweet as your letters; then you'll be much, much more than a guy like me will ever deserve—that was one of the things that I wanted to wait to tell you when I got home, but I had to tell you tonight—

Remember always darling, that no matter what happens that I will always—always hold you in my most secret heart, and will never forget all that you've done for me—

I think of you constantly, Pete, and your name is on my lips all during the day—at night I fall asleep thinking of you—You'll be with me tonight in dreams as always—Goodnight—you—I miss you something terrible, sweetheart—

All my love to you Pete –
Your Ronnie

****

Letter #59

Thursday 23, Sept.

My Dearest One,

Just a short note at 8:30 A.M. to tell you that I miss you!! I should be writing an award for Capt. Sullivan, but the place is in turmoil this morning, and nobody is here to oversee us. Division just called a surprise practice attack, and caught everyone with their pants down. The General is tearing his hair out—what's left of it, and the Colonel is running around behind him saying—"Yes, Sir"—"No, Sir"—But old Ron is just sitting here cooling it—No sense in pushing the panic button—I have nothing to do now when it comes to tactical operations.

I felt rotten all day yesterday, but woke up this morning feeling great. I spent all day yesterday trying to sleep, but I had chills and nausea, and couldn't keep my eyes closed. I guess a good night's sleep was what I needed.

I'm supposed to go down to division this afternoon to a meeting of all the Recruiting Officers, but because of this practice attack, all unnecessary road travel is prohibited. I'll wait awhile and see what develops before I call them and tell them I can't make it. The General wants to see us so maybe I'll get authorization to travel. I'd just as soon not go as it will be a hot, dusty ride.

Yes, darling—your letters have been short, but I don't mind too terribly much as long as I just hear from you. One thing you said, however, you miss me just as much, and <u>maybe</u> a little bit more—It better be a lot more than just a little bit, and no "<u>maybes</u>" about it. You keep talking like that, and I might just have to come home and personally stop you from saying naughty words like that –

Well, honey—this is a *skoshie* letter I realize, but I'll try and write again during the day—Just wanted to let you know that I do miss you, and am thinking about you. Take care of yourself—please—you sound like you're working too hard— Remember what I said—you've got a whole year of this in front of you—and I want you to be alive when I get home— <u>Understand</u>??

Well, Pete—that's about all for right now—
Until I'm with you—I'll just have to keep on dreaming—

Bye now, sweetheart,

All my love to you always, Ronnie

****

Letter #60

You know something!

You're the prettiest teacher in the whole world—

Have a good day, darling—
            See you soon,
               Ron

Letter #61

Friday, 25 Sep.

Dearest One,

These days without mail from you never seem to come to a fast ending. The time just drags and drags until one day seems like a whole month. However, something did happen today that gave me a little push, and it's sort of driven the clouds away. The releases are starting to come into the division now, and it looks like the program might get under way—I was quite foolish at the start to tell you that I was coming home—I should have waited a few weeks until I knew more about it, but you know how those things are. It meant quite a bit to me to be able to write that letter to you, and rather than using common sense I just went ahead and wrote it. I always was impetuous. Well, as it stands now, I won't be home by the end of September. I'll now set my sights on October 31st. However, I can't complain as anything will be better than February or March as I originally expected. At first we expected all releases to go home on special shipments, but now we find that they'll have to go on regular rotation quotas. We'll sneak around that by requesting extra shipping spaces! Transportation at present in the Far East is tied up as the POWs took all the ships over, and we can't ever begrudge them that—

I wish, darling, that all the people back home could be G.I.'s over here for one day just to see and know how much going home means to someone like me. We have nothing to distract our minds from it, and I for one won't let anything take my mind off of you. Hours really seem like eternities to me, and I'm sure everyone else feels the same. Pete—words can't tell you how much I miss you!

Got a wonderful letter tonight from an old buddy of mine. He got married just awhile back, and already they're going to have a baby. It seems funny to have your old buddies get married and go away—I sure hope we can all get together again soon. These two kids are wonderful people, and news like that really thrills me. I just wrote them, and told them all about you—I tell everyone—Don't mind, do you?

I'd give a million dollars for your thoughts just as you read this—or any letter of mine for that matter! You've probably just come in from school—kicked off your shoes, and are so tired that you're not even sure who wrote this—Or maybe it will be Saturday morning, and you'll be able to take your time reading it. No—let's see—Saturday—you won't be in Elmwood Sunday night then. Well, whenever it is—I'd still like to know what you're thinking.

I'm sorry that I really don't have too much to write about, but you know that there is absolutely nothing going on here.

I saw a shooting star the other night while watching the movie, and I remembered the first one I wrote and told you about. Well, I can't tell you what I wished on this one or else it won't come true, but as soon as it does you'll be the first to know about it—Strangely enough, it has something to do with you.

Hey—you know you never sent me pictures of your car—On second thought—hold on to them, and I'll get them in person. Every time I look at that picture you sent me of yourself by the tree (Massachusetts) I get a big kick out of it. All I can see is the sign and nothing of you—Maybe all my writing to you hasn't made it clear, but I'm more interested in you not the sign. But—no complaints—it's you, and honey that's all I care about.

I cleaned out my wallet tonight, and found two bank notes I've been carrying for months as souvenirs. Thought maybe one of your kids would like them. The older one is the old currency and the newer one is the present type. They revalued the currency in the hopes of combating inflation, but you still can get a terrific price for only 1 G.I. dollar.

Hey you that's about all for tonight. I'd sure like to be able to have enough news to fill 10 pages, but things just aren't happening.

I can tell you over and over again how much I think of you, but I'd rather wait and save that to tell you later.

Let's just hope that this will be one of my last letters from over here, and that soon I'll be writing these things that are in my heart to you with a pen.

But until then, sweetheart—just stay as sweet and as wonderful as you have been, and remember I miss you, want you, need you, and that I think of you all the time—

Please darling, believe in me, I want so very much to tell you more, but that must wait. I think you understand—

Goodnight, you—sleep tight tonight, and dream of me—huh?

Bless you, Pete, and love

Always and forever

Yours,

Ronnie

****

Letter #62

Saturday 26, Sept.

Pete, Darling—

Slow down now—relax—that's it. Stop rushing around—I just got your letter of the 17th, and it seems that you are trying to be a perpetual motion machine. I really wish you wouldn't chase yourself around like that. I mean it now! Instead of saving up all your spare time for me you'll be saving it for the nuthouse at the rate you're going. How about sitting down some night, and writing me a nice long letter, about anything that comes into mind. Not only will I appreciate it, but it might make you slow down for a couple of hours. Your letters are short, but I really don't mind, hon—as long as you keep writing the things you do. However, don't stop writing altogether now!!

It certainly makes me feel pretty good to read what you have been writing, but I'm still kicking myself for even telling you that I was on the way. I know that I for one feel quite disappointed that I haven't left here as yet, and I'm also quite irritated. Please don't be mad if it takes me a little longer than expected. This damned Army hasn't been showing me much lately.

I turned down a chance today to become a General's Aide. It meant that I'd have to stay over here until April, but it would have had its compensation. I said no, however, and I don't think anything could make me change my mind about coming home to you.

I'm duty officer tonight, and that's one job I hate in the Army. I just went out and inspected the guard. It's a pitch black night, the moon hasn't come up yet, but still I found one Korean guard wearing dark glasses. They just issued ammunition to the guards, and believe me I think that was a dumb move on somebody's part. It's hard enough trying just to talk to them in daylight let alone approaching them in darkness while they have a loaded gun.

Honey, what a mixed up, topsy-turvy world this is! I just wish I could go to sleep for about a month, and wake up and find myself home. And yet, I'm a little afraid of going home. I don't know just what I'm going to do once I get there. I'll probably wish I had stayed in the Army. I've got to start from scratch all over again. It's going to be difficult, but other guys have gone through it all, and I guess I'll survive.

It's quite hard for me to write you, and make you understand <u>completely</u> what is in my mind. I keep saying to myself that it will only be a few weeks more until I can actually say these things to her, but yet the days bring nothing more on release. We've both hit a rut in our writing, but it's no one's fault. We have nothing else to write about but "coming home", and our letters contain nothing else. If this release doesn't come through as soon as I expect it then we'll really have troubles.

Pete, I want nothing more in this world than to come to you and I expect to hear you say that you're waiting for me, but it would be better for both of us not to expect me until you get that telegram. I should have known better than to have said anything about it.

This letter isn't too good, is it, hon? I'm a little mixed up tonight. Thinking too much about you, I guess. Damn it, Smith, but the thought of you does things, things to me! Darling, I love you for telling me that you're lonesome, miss me, and are waiting. No greater feeling in the world to know that someone cares about you and wants you. Don't stop writing like that, will you?

I'm going to bug out for tonight, honey—If you pray hard enough maybe I'll hear something soon.

Good night, darling—

You know I'll be home as soon as I can. Till then, however, remember that I'm thinking of you all the time, and that I miss you terribly.

All my love, always, Ronnie

****

Letter #63

Monday Night

My Dearest,

You don't know the thrill you gave me tonight when I picked up three letters from you! Pete, you've got me walking on air! Hon, if they let me out of here tonight—I'd walk the whole way home to you –

I went to the movie, and as it got over late I thought it might be best for me to hit the sack, and try and write you an extra-long letter tomorrow night. But, following my usual routine I went down to the mail room to see if I was lucky or not. Corporal Schiraldi saw me come in, and said, "Sir, you'll be happy tonight"—and was I ever! I went back up to the tent—read your letters, and came down here to the office to answer you. It is late, but I don't care—Right now I'm the happiest guy in the world, and it's all because of you—Darling. There may be 10,000 miles between us, but I feel so very near you as I write this. I'm really beginning to feel miserable about the release business. I honestly have no idea when I'll be leaving, but am waiting on the word momentarily. All I want is a date to set my mind on. I'm thankful enough that it's not February as I planned. Will you mind if it takes a little longer than I planned on? In a way, I'm a little happy that it's being delayed as it makes homecoming seem all the more desirable to me. Please, my angel, sit tight and try to keep patient.

I have the pictures you sent, and they are propped up against the in and out basket on the desk in front of me. That car is beautiful, but not as much as the owner. The picture I like the most is the one of you and Donald. It's the best picture I've seen in a long, long time. But what do you mean—use my imagination? I read quite a few connotations in that, and I just want to make sure it's the right one.

Sweetheart, all I do is think about the time I get home. It's on my mind every single minute of the day, and I turn it over and over in my mind. The very, very first thing I shall do after I walk off that gangplank is look for you in the crowd. You won't be there I know, but still I'll look. Then I'll send you a wire which will say, "On the way, wait." Then I'll send one home—As soon as I find out just when I can actually leave I'll wire you again, and let you know. Now, if I come in at New York I will stop off at Hartford according to the time. Naturally, if they let me go at midnight, for example, then it will be too late to bother you, but if I can make it early enough I'll stop there. I'll continue on home to Jack and Cele after I've seen you. If I come in at Frisco then my plane or train will probably go on through to Boston. If so, then I will drive down the next day—Weekday or not!! Naturally, I'll call you before I leave either, New York, Boston, or Frisco— That will be as soon as the Army tells me what they're going to do with me-

Now don't worry about the folks. Like I've told you before— they know me—Sure, I'm crazy to see them, but I'm crazier to see you first!! To them an extra few hours won't make too much difference, but those hours with you will be the world to me.

As I sit here trying to think of how to work my next sentence, I get completely lost in thought of being with you soon. My mind just fills up with things I want to say, and I get confused that I don't know what to write. I'm completely dumbfounded about the way this whole thing has turned out between us.

I can remember way back in the early part of last winter when we first started to write. A letter from you at that time was a wonderful thing, but nothing like it is today. I remember too, when I saw that purse in the hotel in Kyoto. I just knew that I had to send it to you, and I remember that I thought you'd think I was crazy or something. Then I remember writing two letters in particular to you. One was either written on the night of the 11th or 12th.

The one I wrote on the 10th must really be something. I was so scared, honey, I didn't know what to do. I had all sorts of visions that night that I'd never see you again. I wanted to run away—play sick—anything. Every time that phone rang I died a million deaths. Everyone, however, now admits they felt the same way. Then the next one I wrote. I can't recall whether or not it was Sat. the 11th—I was pretty confused by then. Every time someone sneezed or made a loud noise I jumped like a scared cat.

I remember writing the letter. The table sat in the middle of the hoochie with the only light shining right down overhead. My fatigue jacket had no left arm and the left leg of my pants was slit from the calf to the belt line where the medic tried to help me. I needed a shave, and about 10 straight shots of whisky—I also needed you that night. You know, I think I sort of grew up in those two days. I learned more about myself and other people in that time than I ever did in my whole life. I saw a man die violently only 3 feet from me—I saw a man crack up mentally (he's still in the hospital), and I saw myself as frightened as could be. I'll tell you more about it some night.

But all through those times, Pete, from last winter up to now, I was prodded on by your letters. I don't think you knew at the time what your mail was making me think, because I was a little too shy to tell you. I still am, but like I've said before—I've got so much to tell you. You have been everything to me that I have ever desired a girl to be. You were there when I wanted you—I'm not being corny, sweet, I'm just trying to thank you with words—The actions will come when I see you—You know I've got a kiss saved up for you for every second since last winter!!

That's about all for tonight, darling, maybe tomorrow will be the day. If it isn't—will you wait another one? Take care of yourself, and tell Ellen that I'm placing her in charge of you. She'll be held responsible if you run yourself down—Please, honey—take it easy, will you? Goodnight—you—I miss you—you know that—wait for me now—

All my love tonight is yours, Pete—

Ronnie

Letter #64

Tuesday 29, Sep.

Dearest One,

I was going to wait for the mail to come in, but I'm too impatient for that—maybe before I finish this it will be in.

I have some news—whether it's good or not, I don't know, but it's got me a little bit down in the dumps. Quite a few of the releases came into the office today, and mine wasn't among them. I expect mine will be in soon, but an idea dawned on me tonight that might not be good. When I received my commission from OCS I applied for a 2-year hitch. Why I did, I don't know now. I guess that at that time in Army career looked good. I didn't know you then, darling! Now I'm afraid that the army may say—well Freedman signed for two—so we'll hold his release up for a few months.

Deep down, honey, I don't feel that way. I sincerely believe that I'll get the word in only a few hours—maybe tomorrow. They want me out as much as I want out. I really wouldn't mind if they held me longer if they would only give me a specific date to send you.

As I write to you I can hear a Victrola across the area playing "Say You'll Wait for me." That sort of expresses just what I feel. Darling, I'm lonely and blue tonight—and quite a bit down in the mouth. I want to be with you soon so much that I ache all over. Honey—if you could only know just how I feel! Without you I really feel like I'm not quite whole—Did you ever feel that way about something or someone? Your every action and thought is directed to one goal, and if you can't reach them you almost feel like there's no sense in going on. They have to send me home soon—I'll be no good to them if they don't—that's all there is to it.

I stayed up rather late last night writing to you, and tonight after the mail comes in I will sack out right away—Each night that I close my eyes I think that it's one day nearer to you. I only pray that you won't be disappointed with me when I see you. I may not be the guy you think you know. I already know now what my feelings will be towards you as I've been dwelling on that thought for months now, but you know how it is with a guy that's never sure of himself.

I'm really sorry that I wrote that, as it shows my greatest weakness ... lack of confidence, but it also shows another weakness of mine. The inability to withhold my most innermost thoughts from someone I hold dear. I guess I'm not the kind of a guy most girls want. I should be aloof, cold, and uninterested at times with just enough secrecy to make girls wonder why. I could never be that kind of a guy – when I feel something it's either all the way or else nothing at all. A good example of that is my writing about it. I just can't hold those things back from you.

Yet, honey, here is a contradiction!! I'm holding back some things, but my better sense tells me that I should—I need the answers before I ask the questions—

G'wan ... try and figure me out!! Darling, no matter what day or what month I return, I'll still want you and my only you— Maybe if I didn't wish so hard about the release being soon then I might be luckier.

Sorry that this is short, but the days are long, angel, and dreams of you at night are my only pleasures.

—Pete—You're everything to me—Don't ever diverge—

Goodnight, you—

Always, I'll be yours—Ron

****

Letter #65

Thursday, 1 Oct.

Hello Darling,

Sort of hurt to write that date in the upper right hand corner. At one time I never thought I'd still be here! Well, the only thing that I can do is sit back, and stop bitching. That certainly isn't going to get me any place.

Tonight was a night I'll long remember. The General is being transferred, and we had a big party. I had <u>3</u> steaks, quite a few drinks, and one hell of a good time. It's still going on, but I sneaked out to write to you. I started a letter to you last night, but it was so cold that I had to stop, and climb into that warm sack. Sorry, I didn't mean to let it happen. I got some new jobs today—I'm now Divarty Public Information Officer, and Special Services Officer. I also run the Athletic and Recreation section. Those 3 are all full time jobs, and my first day was a lulu. Right now is the first time I have relaxed since 7 a.m. this morning, and it's now 10:30 p.m. Tomorrow promises to be worse with 2 parades, and a dedication. Also I have to fly to Division to deliver the money that our battalions have collected for this big lottery the Division is running. I'm going to have to find someone to do that job for me, as I won't be able to get back in time.

I got 2 letters from my folks tonight, and one from Henry Hacker. They both want to know more about this "Pete". As far as I'm concerned, sweet, words won't do the job. They'll just have to wait and see you.

I may sound in fairly good spirits tonight, honey, but actually I'm pretty much down in the dumps still. I want to be with you so much that I'd do <u>anything</u> to get out of here. I've heard so many encouraging and discouraging rumors that I no longer believe anything. I'll just sit back and wait.

I dreamed last night, for the first time in a long, long time, and it was a very frustrating thing. The boat was pulling into the dock but I never saw myself walking down the gangplank. I couldn't find you in the crowd, but I saw a Chevy Convertible parked behind everyone. Darling, I'll go crazy if I can't be with you soon! Gawd, how I miss you.

Kid brother Steve wrote the folks, and says he really likes school. I'm glad as I think someday he might go places. It all depends how the breaks fall for him. I'll be a nervous wreck if and when they draft him. Oh, my cousin Missy—remember … she has the two little redheads—well, she had another little boy on the 24th. I'll have to write her first thing in the morning. Oh, honey you've gotta meet that family. They are tops! What people they are—I'd use that family for a model any day. But I don't have red hair!

I've never mentioned this before, I don't think, but I have a little pin that was given to me that I've worn since Jun 5th. An Ethiopian Lt. gave it to me one night, and I've only taken it off once. It's their battalion crest, and it's quite an honor to own one. The Commanding General of our Division wears it, and that is the only ornament other than his insignia of rank that he wears. I've been saving it for you, and am very much tempted to send it on to you, but being superstitious I want to keep it until the day I see you.

I am enclosing something that I found one morning near my O.P. It's not a pretty thing, and I shouldn't send it on, but somehow I feel that you can understand what is going on in the back of my mind when I reread it. Some things have been deeply engraved in my thoughts, and feeling the way I do about you, Pete. I don't think that I really understand unless you do too. I found this leaflet while cleaning out an old letter box, and after reading it I wanted to burn it. But I held onto it, and tonight I'm mailing it to you. Please keep it for me—I have reasons.

I hope you don't think I'm too weird. I'm really not—I just happened to be one of those lucky guys who has found himself somebody to talk to. I wish I could be with you tonight, right next to you now so I could just open the gates, and let my heart pour out. I wish you'd get into that car of yours and go find someplace where we can drive to and park so we can be alone where nobody will bother us. Somewhere where we can go on a Sunday afternoon or on a dark stormy night where we can talk. Have I ever told you about my affinity for thunder and lightning or a good heavy downpour? Rain on the roof affects a lot of people, but not like it does me. However, it has to be a certain kind of a rain. The big heavy drops that seem to blind you—not the drizzling kind.

If you didn't think I was crazy before, I'll bet you do now—

Well, angel, it' getting late, and rather chilly. I've go to run along, and wait for tomorrow.

Goodnight, my darling—My every dream and thought is yours—I miss you tonight more than ever.

Thinking of you constantly, sweetheart I send you

all my love and devotion always—Ronnie

Figure 72 - Example of Chinese propaganda.

Letter #66

Sat. night—3 Oct.

Dearest,

The generator has broken down, and writing by candlelight never was the easiest thing in the world to do. But then again, writing to you by candlelight is nice—It has a certain quality about it—

I heard from you today, and needless to say it brought the day to a proper close. I don't quite know what I'd do, darling, if I lost you. I'm living in a world of my own now, and I don't want it to ever come to an end!! That's something I know for sure, hon—My heart hasn't jumped into this—it's fallen slowly, smoothly, and surely. That's because I've had time to think during these long, long months. I've always wanted it to happen that way when the time came, and now that it has—I wouldn't trade my feelings for you, for anything else in the world.

I know that I told you'd I'd write soon telling you to stop writing, but the Army has come across with another of their usual deals—they make statements and promises and then never live up to them. I can't however, blame them too much. I've only myself to blame—I never should've said anything to anyone until I actually left for the boat. The Army is tremendously big, and sometimes it takes much longer than they originally expect for the machinery to start rolling. I have complete faith and confidence that I'll be home soon, but as to just when—I don't know—I only wish I did.

You know by now how much it means to me to be coming home to you, and how much it will mean if you'll only say that you will keep waiting. Pete darling—<u>read between the lines</u>!! Every word that is in my heart is there for only your eyes to see. I won't write them because I want to say them to you first so that you'll know that I do mean them. Soon, darling, I'll be with you, and the words and thoughts I think constantly will be yours.

My new job is quite a big one, and it's running me ragged. Today I had to go over to the 48th to cover a carnival they ran.

They're trying to raise enough money to rebuild a school over here. It was a hot, hot day, and between all the beer and noise I've picked up a headache that just won't quit. About 3 p.m. the little kids from the school came in, and put on a show. They were dressed in their best school clothes and were the cutes things you ever saw. They sang and danced, and made quite a hit. A couple of the songs were American tunes but with Korean words. The G.I.'s got quite a kick out of that. Some songs showed the terror that they've lived in these past 3 years. One was called "Fighter Planes", and another told how we should all march to the north and destroy every living enemy of free Korea … that from the lips of 5 year olds. At the end they were presented with toys, and I think everyone's heart broke when a little girl let a big alligator tear roll down her cheek when Chaplain Boyce put a Raggedy Ann doll in her arms.

After that the kids all passed out presents, and one little kid about 6 years old came up to me, bowed, and put a little paper package in my hand. It was a napkin or a handkerchief with a little design and the name of her school embroidered on it. "Chunhyang P.S.K." (Primary School Korea). It's yours, naturally, and I'll send it along as soon as I can find a suitable envelope. It's not very hard to realize how very little the actual size, shape, color, or price of a gift means when you receive something like that. Darling, I think you know by now that I'm a real softie. I always feel things a little too strongly for my own good. I know that some things I've written you must have impressed you with that thought. That leaflet I sent you the other night—for example, really gets my mind to working because I remember vividly the day I found it. I want to keep it so that I'll never forget that one time. I sent it to you because I want you to feel these things with me. Silly, but it makes me feel a lot closer to you, now that you know and understand about some of the seemingly foolish things I do.

Darling, don't ever—ever doubt my feelings for you—I'm so strong in them now that I'd be lost forever if you did. Just believe in me, and keep praying that they'll let me come home to you real soon. I'm sure that between the both of us we can work out something. If you're willing to listen to any suggestion I might make on the subject of you and I—then I'm surer than hell going to make them. You'll see you!

If you say you're taking it easier in school now—I believe you—but how 'bout slowing up some more—I know you love it, but I want to make <u>sure</u> that you're rested up—Glad to hear that it isn't a life-time position, 'cause I don't plan on letting you spend your life time in school!! So there!

Gotta close tonight—Promise to write tomorrow night! Goodnight you—I miss you darling, and want you only and always.

All my love is yours—forever -

Ron

****

Letter #67

Sunday, 4 Oct.

Sweetheart,

This will be real short tonight as I have to paint all my furniture. They took my sergeant away for a few days to be the Colonel's stenographer, so I'll have no help painting.

There was no news today on releases, and I'm really downhearted now. How I want to get home!! The days are so long, and the weeks never seem to pass. It's not good for me to let this all get me down.

The day was beautiful, and I tried to relax as much as possible. I wrote all my reports early this morning, and played a little football during the afternoon. That was the first real exercise I've had since the day I had to climb the hill. It nearly killed me. Being out of shape, and with the heat was just too much for all of us and we quit early.

Oh Pete, why do I ramble on about panting and football, and other such nonsense when all I can really think about is you—you—you!! Gawd, how lonely I am for you—They say, and now I know they're wrong, that you never miss what you've never known.

But, I think that we've gotten to know as much or more about one another through writing as we could have if we had been together. I miss you more than you'll ever know, darling, and long for you both day and night.

I hope you haven't forgotten that lobster and beer dinner! That's one thing I'm going to make sure happens. There's a corporal in here typing, and I guess he asked me a question a minute ago, and I didn't hear him. Finally, I came out of my trance, and he said that I really looked down in the dumps tonight. I don't feel that way at all—I was just thinking about being with you.

Hey honey, I've got to get those chairs and tables painted before Captain Bane comes in and chews me out. I don't know if he wants me to stay and fan them all night, but he says that they will be dry by morning. He's a happy soul—ain't he?

Goodnight you. Take care of yourself for me now—all my love is yours, Pete darling, if you want it.

Thinking of you always,

Your Ron

****

Letter #68

Monday, 5 Oct

Darling, Darling, Darling!

Mark this day, and mark it well, 'cause 1st Lt. R.K. Freedman, 01889813, Artillery, United States Army, a member of Headquarters, and Headquarters Battery, 7th Division Artillery is writing to tell you to …

S—T—O—P!!!

I'm leaving the division on the 9th, and expect to be on the boat the 12th. I was down at Division today, and when I got back, I was notified that my release had come in from Division approved for the 30th of Sept. I was happy enough to just get the date, and was celebrating it over a can of beer about 5 p.m. when Al Kohn came running into the tent screaming, "We're going ... we're going ... the ninth ... the ninth—"

We all started yelling, and ran over to my office. It was true— We're on the drop for the ninth—and the General Pope is leaving Inchon on the 12th.

Now, honey, anything can happen—Army or division can cancel it all, but let's plan on my leaving. It makes me so much happier.

Pete, I'm a *skoshie* bit under the weather, but I'm the happiest guy in the world. I love everything and everyone. What a wonderful, wonderful day ....

Lawdy—Miss Claudy—I'm going to see my Pete!

I hope this is the only time I ever have to tell you to stop—

Love—Love, love, love you—Ron

****

Letter #69

Tuesday, 6 Oct.

Hi Honey,

I've got so much news that I'm about to bubble over. I'm happy 'cause of the good news, and yet I got some bad news today that affects me indirectly.

I might as well tell you the bad stuff first so this can end on a happy note for me. Zeke wrote me today and told me that his uncle had died. Zeke and I have been very, very close since we were kids, and his mother is like an aunt to me. Zeke's dad died in a crash a few years ago, and left his family in turmoil and now that his uncle has died it has caused real deep grief. The uncle was the head of a big shoe concern, and everyone in the family owned a part of it. Now Zeke's mother is completely lost, and without Zeke being home, I can imagine the state she's in. It hit me pretty hard as I was always pretty much a member of the whole family—

Well, now for the good news and I hope you'll forgive me if I don't sound quite as exuberant as I should. You know by now that I'm coming home, but what you don't know is that I leave tomorrow! I have to be at the Division Rotation Center by noon tomorrow, and then I'll leave for Pusan very shortly thereafter. We originally weren't leaving until Friday, but a call came in this noon to get us going. I hope honey, that you are as happy as I am! I'm completely thrilled. It means so much to be with you soon. I heard that our boat will dock in Seattle, and if it's true I hope to be able to send you that telegram in just about 3 weeks from today. I'll grab a flight to New York, and then a train to Hartford—I'll call you, and the way I feel right now I'll call if it's 4:30 in the morning .

We had supper with the Colonel tonight, and as we are leaving, we had to buy the drinks all night—I was clobbered tonight, but knew that I had a few letters to write so I tried to hold it down—But, as you can probably tell—I didn't succeed to well.

The hardest part about going home is that I won't be hearing from you for quite a while. I'll try and write you every chance I get until I get on the boat, and if we stop any place I'll write from there—

I'm a little sad to be leaving here also. You make some close friends in the Army, especially under conditions like these, and it's tough to break the ties. I've promised this Warrant Officer that I would send him a picture of you and me together, so you'll have to remind me to do that.

I have to write to Zeke, Steve, Jim Gillen, and the folks tonight so I'd better close this now—

Listen—you—if for some reason you don't hear from me for a few days then don't get mad or worried 'cause I'll be there myself to take the place of this damned airmail system— Meanwhile, just remember how much I miss you and want you— Honey, keep those telephone lines clear, and break all your dates 'cause this boy ain't gonna listen to you say no!

Goodnight, sweetheart—It's for always, Pete—always

Yours, Ronnie

Letter #70

10 Oct. '53

Darling,

Well—here I am in Pusan—waiting for the boat! We left Divarty at 9 Tuesday morning and arrived at Division at 11:30. They told us there that we were going to Pusan and would leave for there at 4 a.m. the next day. Then they changed it from 4 to 8, and then 8 to 4 p.m., then 4 p.m. to 11 p.m. We left finally at 2:30 a.m. on Thursday morning. We were lucky and made Pusan in only 12 hours. Sometimes it takes 19 or 24 hours. Was it ever awful! The trains have <u>no</u> lights, no heat, and wooden seats. The only reason we didn't bitch too much is because we're coming home.

Now that we've arrived at the Replacement Depot here in Pusan we feel pretty good that we've got the first part of the trip under our belts. Rumors are real hot and heavy down here. We are supposed to leave in a few days, but it seems that there are more officers than there is cabin space. Some of us might have to take troop accommodations—I think I mentioned that to you before—I'd even swim to get home! Another rumor is that we'll have to go by troop train across the states. They are no longer discharging you in California, but are sending you to the nearest separation center to your home. That would be Fort Devens or Camp Kilmer for me. I hope that last rumor is false. I want out in Frisco or Seattle so I can fly home.

Well, hon—no matter what happens at least I'm on the way— God—what a wonderful feeling. I'm either too excited about it all or else I won't believe until I see you because right now I feel like I'm in a daze. It just doesn't seem possible that I'm actually sitting her in Pusan waiting for that boat—

I heard from you the night before I left. Did I tell you? They gave me a letter from Zeke, and after a while I heard a terrific racket from the APO. I called them to tell them to quiet down, and then they told me that I had a letter from you. They were holding it so I would come over and join them in a drink. Which I did quite willingly—by the way, I also had a letter from the folks—my mother does all the writing, and sometimes her letters are as funny as hell.

She tries to tell me all about the goings on at home so that I'll be well briefed on what's doing. However, she sometimes tells me the results before she writes about the proceedings. They are quite excited about Steve. They both think Amherst is a beautiful town, and Mom is always saying something about it, and asking if I've ever been there or passed through it. I used to go with a girl that went to school in Northampton, and she knows that almost every Sunday or so I used to drive to Northampton. But still she wants to know if I've ever been through Amherst—I'll have to drive up there and see him one of the first weekends after I get home.

Damn, I'm tired—that train ride knocked me for a loop. Gaynor stretched out on the floor, and I tried to curl up on the seat—Now I'm stiff as a board—Now, tonight, for the first time since I went on R&R, I'm sleeping on a real cot with a real mattress. I shall take full advantage of it, too—!

I'll leave for now, sweet—I'd like to get a line off to the folks, and then sack out—

Just think, darling—in a few days it will be real words not writing. I hope it goes by fast—I've waited quite a few months now as it, and shouldn't mind a few more weeks, but I'm too damned impatient—

Goodnight you—I miss you with all my heart—keep those phone lines clear, and keep watching for that telegram—Till then, darling—

All my love will be yours, always, Ronnie

****

Letter #71

Sat. 10, Oct.

Hi Darling,

Last letter from Korea ... thank God!! We sail very shortly, and I expect to be with you by the end of the month or the first week in November!!

WAIT FOR ME

All my love always, honey—Ronnie

 number symbol

As I wrote Letter #68, I received the news that we would be leaving for home shortly, and that was a real red letter day. We celebrated that evening and within a few hours we were told to report to the Rotation Center. We turned in all our equipment and bade farewell to the people staying on. The train ride from just south of our area to Pusan was an all-day affair, and was basically the same type of train that we rode when we arrived that first night except that the car I was in had a fresh coat of paint, and wasn't as crowded. We stopped after a few hours and took on a flatcar of wounded South Korean soldiers.

We arrived in Pusan late in the day and went immediately to our billets. I don't believe anyone took off to see what was happening downtown as we were all afraid we would miss the boat. We stayed there for a day or two, and finally boarded the MSTS (Military Sea Transport Service) Marine Serpent for our voyage home. I was assigned to a compartment that held twelve officers in very cramped quarters. Poor Bud was assigned to sleep in the forward hold with a group of Second Lieutenants (he had not yet been promoted), but somehow managed to find quarters with other officers in a compartment.

The trip to Seattle took sixteen days, and I don't remember very much about it except the last day at sea, which was a Sunday. We entered Puget Sound and were off the shoreline at Port Angeles when the ship stopped and we had a "man overboard" drill. We all groused about the drill especially as we were so close to Seattle. We did get down near that city late in the afternoon, and were apprised of the fact that the longshoremen didn't work on Sunday, and that we wouldn't debark until Monday morning. That was hard to take, but being so close to the waterfront where we could hear music and noise from the nearby bars, was even more disheartening.

The morning arrived, however, and we walked down the gangplank without any ceremony at all. There was no band playing and the dock was very sparsely populated with greeters, only a very large sign on a low building that said, "Welcome Home, Clem".

We were bussed up to Fort Lewis and given one free phone call home. I didn't have Pete's number, so I couldn't call her. I did get my mother on the phone, and she told me that some lady in the Midwest saw my name and home address in a paper, and she called to tell my family that I was in the United States. It was then that I realized that I never brought a souvenir home for my mother, and so I went into the Post Exchange and bought her a very nice bracelet that had faces of the Japanese Gods of Contentment and Happiness on it.

We flew out of Seattle that night and had a beautiful view of Mount Rainier in the moonlight. We stopped in Minneapolis, and then went on to Idlewild (now JFK International) in New York City. I said goodbye to Bud as he was boarding a bus for Brooklyn, and then headed over to Grand Central to get a train for Boston. I sat with a fellow lieutenant by the name of Joe LaLiberte, and arrived at Back Bay Station at three in the morning.

Mom and Dad were there to meet me, and we drove home. They took me to the front door and when I walked up I found a group of family friends and relatives who were waiting there to greet me. They stayed up all that time just for me, and I thought that was great. The very first thing I did after all the greetings was head for the kitchen and a bottle of ice cold milk. The thing about coming home that I remember most is the walk up the front stairs to our living room, which told me that I was really and truly home, and then the comfort of my old bed and soft mattress. I was home, but not completely.

The next day I put on my dress uniform (I didn't have any civilian clothes at all) and took the train to Hartford to see my girl. We met in the middle of the station and she gave me the biggest and best kiss that I can ever remember. I knew right then and there I had picked the right girl and that everything I had ever written to her was the truth. I still think so.

Author's Note

Upon my arrival in Hartford I knew I could not call this delightful woman "Pete" any longer as she was as feminine as I ever imagined her to be.

We spent as much time together as we could, but my uncle had called me with the proposition that he would retire and leave his very large and wealthy poultry business to me, my brother and my older cousin Bill. He asked me to move to New Hampshire which I did soon after my discharge. My dad and mom also moved up there as Dad was to become the foreman of our business.

This move up to Concord meant a longer time to get to Hartford, and an equally long ride back to Concord usually very late on a Sunday night. I often took a bus which afforded me few hours' sleep, but I had to be ready to go to work at 5 a.m., which didn't allow me to get the proper amount of rest. My breakfasts usually comprised of a sweet roll and a cup of tea laced with Grand Metaxa brandy—not a very healthy meal for someone who returned from the army weighing only 118 pounds. I went into the service at 135, and could ill afford to lose 17 pounds.

My love affair was proceeding at a fine rate and Nancy and I decided to marry after asking her parents for permission. My folks were all for the idea as they had met Nancy and loved her right from the start. But when we approached Nancy's folks, they rejected the idea on religious grounds. We felt quite dismayed, to say the least.

We decided to 'elope' immediately, and on the March 12, 1954 we did. We held the ceremony at my aunt and uncle's home in New Hampshire, and had a small number of guests in attendance. My brother Steve was the best man, and my aunt sang and played the piano. The judge who married us was sure that holding the ceremony on Friday night was not right because of our religious beliefs. He was stunned when my uncle called to remind him that he was to perform a marriage ceremony right then, and he was late in arriving.

The evening was captured on film, and I have put it on a CD for our children's benefit. After a weekend honeymoon in New York City, we both returned to our jobs in our separate cities. I went down to Hartford every weekend that I could, and then ran back to work—sometimes driving, but mostly by bus as there were no trains at that hour.

One day I went down to Boston and saw my old family doctor as I didn't feel quite right. He diagnosed me with mononucleosis, and put me into Hahneman Hospital as he felt my problem might be contagious. Nancy took time off from teaching to be with me, and after a short hospital stay we both went up to Concord where I was supposed to recuperate. I was put to bed upon arrival, but that night I started to hemorrhage internally, and was taken to the hospital for treatment. They never did find out what was wrong with me, and after a few weeks they sent me home with the diagnosis of "unknown gastric problem".

Nancy's mother and father finally gave in and I was eventually invited to live with Nancy in their home in Longmeadow, Massachusetts. During my long convalescence, my uncle decided to declare bankruptcy, which he did with some speed, as he had an opportunity to go to Canada, and become a wealthy businessman which he also did with some speed.

While I was recuperating in Longmeadow, I decided to take a day and visit Hartford to see what possibilities for a job might be down there. I had majored in public relations with the thought of TV production as a future field. In Hartford, however, I discovered that the only TV station at that time had hired enough future TV people, and if I would wait a year or two something might open up. I couldn't wait a year or two, and so I went into a large department store and applied for management training. I was soon accepted, and my life in retailing began. I stayed in that area of business until 1968 when I opened a ski shop with two business partners. The store is in Connecticut, and today is still in business, 43 years later. My son Bruce has taken over, and developed it into a nice money making operation. Not an easy task when you realize how seasonal and weather-dependent that business is.

Our first child, our daughter Lynn, was born in December of 1955, and our son came along in January of 1957. Eventually Nancy returned to teaching, and we lived an idyllic life for the next 46 years.

I wrote those letters many years ago. The memories wash over me, and many times my eyes are clouded over as I think of those hours and days. My service time made me a stronger more confident man, and I believe that those factors entered into my desire to marry and father my children. I truly loved my wife and still do, and am adding these few words so that my family knows how I feel now. They can read how I felt then.

Nancy's idea of making my letters into a book for my family to enjoy was one of the best ideas she could possibly conceive, and although it was labor to write all this down I want you to know that it was a labor of love.

We spent the next forty-six years together without one major disagreement and lived in perfect harmony. I spent what may have been too many hours at my work which kept me from all the family time I would have liked to have done, and Nancy was very involved in her position as a special education teacher at Avon, Connecticut High School. We enjoyed skiing as a family, and particularly relished our trips out west for that purpose. We also became quite enamored of ice hockey, becoming season ticket holders for the Hartford Whalers.

Our home in Connecticut was on a high hill and nestled into a corner of a Girl Scout forest that afforded us complete privacy along with peace and quiet. We bred Old English Sheep dogs, (I should say Nancy bred them), and at one point even owned two Maine Coon cats. I mention that because that was an almost complete miracle for me as I was not a cat lover previously.

In 1989 I retired, and as we had purchased a home on the west coast of Florida, and I had turned my business over to my son, we decided that I should move down there to prepare the home to our wishes. Nancy had two more years to teach in order to fulfill her retirement contract, and lived alternately with our children until she was able to move down to Florida. In 1991 she finished her work and came down to be with me on a permanent basis.

We became deeply involved in boating, and enjoyed many hours on our vessels as we learned all about Florida waters, and their intricacies. Our home was situated in a nice small town, and we made many friends while living there.

In May of 1999, something unexplainable (Nancy says she has no rational answer to give me) entered into her thinking and she left me and filed for divorce. Her actions stunned me, and I have not yet recovered from it. She has found a home in The Villages, about 200 miles northeast of our home on the Gulf Coast, where she has taken up golfing, Mahjong, swimming, study groups, etc., and is completely immersed in her new life.

We have become great friends and spend quite some time together. I had bought a puppy, and found that I physically could not handle the raising of it, and so she took over its care, and they are constant companions. I miss her terribly, but I think she is much happier there than she ever would be here with me, and I am happy that she has found whatever it is she was looking for.

I, too, am happier in that my time is my own, and I can do anything and everything that I may want to do. I watch all the sports I can on TV, and I don't even have to make my bed up every day. I am able to care for myself, and have found that being a volunteer at our local Military Museum fulfills all my wishes regarding spare time. I am the liaison between the Board of Directors and the volunteer staff. I sit on the Board, and am also involved as Vice Commander of the local chapter of the Military Order of the Purple Heart. These activities are dear to my heart, and I truly enjoy the involvement.

In rereading my commentary, I realize there are many disjointed paragraphs, but these are thoughts that came into my mind at the time that I wrote these pages.

All in all, my life has been blessed with a great wife and two marvelous children along with our five beautiful grandchildren.

Punta Gorda, Florida
September 2011

Update—August 16, 2013

On December 28, 2011, Nancy and I remarried. The ceremony took place in Punta Gorda with my brother Steve as best man, and his wife Mary Ann as Nancy's bridesmaid. Our dog Moxie was the ring bearer.

I have since moved to Oxford, Florida where we live in a charming villa. Nancy continues all her activities, and I've been busy gathering photos and writing the comments about each letter in this book. We have a very happy and active lifestyle, and are blessed with a close relationship with our children and grandchildren.

Figure 73 - Second Wedding Portrait, 28 December 2011.

Figure 74 - Family Gathering

Figure 75 - My Favorite photo of Nancy.

Appendix A – Enlistment and Training

➤ May 1951 - graduated from Boston University with a BA degree.

➤ Enlisted May 23, 1951. Sent to Ft. Dix in New Jersey for basic training (6 weeks).

Figure 76 - "Sojer" Boy

Figure 77 - Thrust, Parry, Lunge

➤ Had been "contracted" for OCS, and therefore attended a 10-week Leadership School program afterwards.

➤ Attended OCS in Fort Bliss, El Paso, Texas in November 1951. Commissioned 2nd Lieutenant. in Anti-Aircraft May 23, 1952 (exactly one year to the date of my enlistment).

➤ Sent to Camp Edwards in Cape Cod, Mass. for my first duty station. Left for Korea in November, 1952.

➤ After a thirty-eight-day boat trip from Staten Island, New York (via the Panama Canal), arrived in Inchon, Korea very early in January 1953. It was so cold that there were ice floes in the Flying Fish channel which lies just west of Inchon (now spelled Incheon).

➤ Attended a Battery Executive Officers course.

➤ May 1953 – transferred to 7th Division as a Forward Observer, Division Artillery.

Appendix B - Porkchop Hill Timeline[4]

Background: In June 1952, the 45th Infantry Division successfully attacked enemy forces in the area south of the Yokkok-ch'on River and secured outposts named Alligator Jaws, Erie, Arsenal, Porkchop, and Old Baldy. Defensively, organizing them meant building bunkers, digging trenches, and providing overhead protection while fighting off enemy efforts to retake these outposts. The 7th Infantry Division assumed responsibility of the area in January 1953.

March 23-25, 1953: Enemy (Chinese) troops captured Old Baldy Outpost from the Columbian Battalion which was attached to the 31st Infantry Regiment. This gave enemy direct line of sight on the exposed rear and west defensive positions of Porkchop Outpost and their observers could direct Arty/Mortar as well as direct-fire weapons onto friendly positions. Their interdicting fire against troop and APC service supply movement on the access road from the MLR to the base of the outpost made it necessary to re-route the supplies to the front of Hill 200, which masked the road from enemy observation.

April 16-18, 1953: Following the success at Old Baldy, the enemy attempted to seize Porkchop Outpost, bolstered by their new capability of directing fire from their observers on Old Baldy. Although initially successful, the enemy could not hold onto their positions on the hill and were finally effected by early April 18 by a combination of friendly Arty/Mortar/Tank/Direct Fire Barrages and soldiers of the 31st Infantry Regiment, assisted by those of Company A 17th Infantry Regiment. This is described in detail in S.L.A. Marshall's book.

Early June 1953: It was discovered that the enemy had moved into an area 400 yards north of friendly positions on Pork Chop Hill. Terrain prevented observation of these activities from the outpost, but aerial recons, revealed unknown number of enemy were occupying caves and building fortifications. It was also suspected that the enemy was tunneling underground in an attempt to reach US defenses on the outpost. With aggressive action needed to eject the enemy, 1st and 2nd Bns 17th Inf. Regt. given mission to plan and execute combat

---

[4] McWilliams, Bill. *On Hallowed Ground, The Last Battle for Pork Chop Hill.* Berkley Caliber Books, Division of Penguin-Putnam (New York, NY; 2004).

patrols to probe for enemy strength in the "Rat's Nest" and to try to capture a prisoner for interrogation purposes. During a period of 7-10 days most of our combat patrols were ambushed by the enemy before reaching the objective and higher headquarters finally halted combat patrols against enemy as of June 18.

June 18-29, 1953: During this period numerous attempts were made to neutralize "Rat's Nest" with air strikes and artillery fire but the enemy's excellent defense of their position made it impossible to place destructive artillery fire successfully on the site and three air strikes conducted did not hit the area.

July 1, 1953: Higher Hqs. lifts restrictions concerning aggressive ground action against the enemy in the "Rat's Nest"; 1st Battalion, 17th Inf. Regt., prepares plans and assigns Company C the combat mission. Plan had one Rifle Platoon sweeping the enemy area, one Rifle Platoon with Engineer Squads attached to place demolition charges on enemy (vents to underground tunnels) fortifications, with one Rifle Squad to prevent enemy help from the North. The 3rd Rifle Platoon was broken into 4-man blanket units to police up US raid casualties.

Note: The above plan was executed successfully on Saturday, July 4, 1953, (reference Letter 1). During the actions of June/July 1953, all Weapon Companies of Infantry Battalions involved in ground action and Artillery/Mortar units of 7th Division, provided suppler, notably during the battle for Outpost Porkchop. Tank units and Direct Fire Weapons provided much needed support. All APC drivers and Service units moving infantry and supplies under intense fire to the hill/evacuating casualties to medical units saved many lives. Medics, radiomen, signal/engineer support, arty/mortar observers attached or in direct support all had their place in making the infantry soldiers' mission a success. We must not forget ground-recon personnel as well as headquarters directing the combat effort. Aerial surveillance/directing arty fire, and helicopter resupply of ammo/evacuation of critically wounded from the battle area, were all part of the Porkchop defense effort.

Appendix C - Places to look for on the map of Old Baldy[5]

1. Old Baldy sits south and west of Pork Chop in the lower left hand corner.

2. Hill 347 is where Barry, Fritts and I had our OP 13.

3. Hill 327 is where I was given instructions on how to be an FO. It was called the Generals' OP. OP29.

4. Erie and Arsenal were outposts manned by us that were in No Man's Land.

5. T-bone was owned by the enemy, and is where I saw the big banner that they posted for us to see.

6. Alligator Jaws was not owned by either side, and was constantly patrolled.

7. My permanent OP was #38 and was just to the right of G Company's HQ. My favorite targets were the Upper and Lower Horseshoes.

8. Just below Lower Horseshoe was the Yokkok-ch'on River where I wasted the three enemy soldiers who were going to take a bath.

9. Just under the Arrowhead tag is where Bud and I got the four Chinese wearing Red Cross bands and AK 47s.

10. The dotted line between the two Horseshoes was a dirt path or very narrow road that I watched constantly. The enemy used it at night, and so we fired H & Is in there all the time.

11. My Op 38 was the easternmost point in the I-Corps area. The 10th Corps was just to my right. My main job was to watch the Chorwon Valley which was off to my right as that was the only way the enemy could ever hope to come through if he mounted a full scale attack.

---

[5] See Map, Page 70.